INSTITUTE OF MANAGEMENT AND LABOR RELATIONS
SERIES—RUTGERS, THE STATE UNIVERSITY OF NEW
JERSEY

Editor: James Chelius

REFLECTIONS ON THE TRANSFORMATION OF INDUSTRIAL RELATIONS

edited by

James Chelius and James Dworkin

Institute of Management and Labor Relations

Series, No. 1

IMLR Press / Rutgers University
and
The Scarecrow Press, Inc.
Metuchen, N. J., & London
1990

British Library Cataloguing-in-Publication data available

Library of Congress Cataloging-in-Publication Data

Reflections on the transformation of industrial relations / edited by James
     Chelius and James Dworkin
          p.   cm. — (Institute of Management and Labor Relations series; no.
     1)
     Includes bibliographical references.
     ISBN 0-8108-2259-8 (alk. paper)
     1. Industrial relations—United States.   I. Chelius, James Robert.
II. Dworkin, James B.   III. Series.
HD8072.5.R44   1990
331'.0973—dc20   89-48376

CONTENTS

EDITOR'S NOTE

THE INSTITUTE OF MANAGEMENT AND LABOR RELATIONS of Rutgers University, The State University of New Jersey, was founded by the state legislature with a mandate to educate labor, management, and the public on matters concerning the employment relationship. With this series, it is our intention to further this goal by publishing books that will make a significant contribution to communicating the results of research on various aspects of industrial relations, human resource management, and employment policy.

JAMES CHELIUS
Series Editor
Institute of Management
  and Labor Relations
Rutgers University

PREFACE

AN INFORMAL GROUP OF INDUSTRIAL relations scholars, referred to as the "Bargaining Group," has been in existence for some time. Created by Professor Richard Peterson of the University of Washington, the group had communicated over a number of years through the *Bargaining Group Newsletter*. The exclusively informal nature of the group's interactions became a subject of some discussion, with the idea generated that perhaps a biannual conference would be a good way for members to get together in a structured setting to discuss research topics of mutual interest. Group members responded very positively to the idea of such a focused conference.

A committee composed of Richard Peterson, Richard Block of Michigan State University, James Dworkin of Purdue University, and David Lewin of Columbia University was established to plan the first Bargaining Group Conference. The meeting was held at the Krannert Graduate School of Management at Purdue University in May of 1988. *The Transformation of American Industrial Relations* by Thomas Kochan, Harry Katz, and Robert McKersie, with its discussion and analysis of the most significant industrial relations developments of our time, quickly emerged as a natural candidate for the conference theme. Special thanks are due to those responsible for making this conference a reality. The papers presented in this volume are the results of that effort.

CONFERENCE PARTICIPANTS

James Begin	Rutgers University
William Bigoness	University of North Carolina
Richard Block	Michigan State University
James Chelius	Rutgers University
Joel Cutcher-Gershenfeld	Michigan State University
John Delaney	Columbia University
James Dworkin	Purdue University
Peter Feuille	University of Illinois
Jack Fiorito	University of Iowa
John Fossum	University of Minnesota
Herbert Heneman	University of Wisconsin
Paul Jarley	University of Iowa
Harry Katz	Cornell University
Morris Kleiner	University of Minnesota
Thomas Kochan	Massachusetts Institute of Technology
David Lewin	Columbia University
John Megenau	Pennsylvania State University
Cheryl Maranto	University of Iowa
James Martin	Wayne State University
Robert McKersie	Massachusetts Institute of Technology
Craig Olson	University of Wisconsin
Richard Peterson	University of Washington
Jacques Rojot	INSEAD and University of LeMans (France
Myron Roomkin	Northwestern University
Peter Sherer	University of Illinois
Jack Stieber	Michigan State University
George Strauss	University of California-Berkeley
Lane Tacy	Ohio University
Anil Verma	University of British Columbia

1. AN OVERVIEW OF THE TRANSFORMATION OF INDUSTRIAL RELATIONS

James Chelius and James Dworkin

Introduction

In the 1980s, many aspects of the relationship between employers and employees have changed substantially. In numerous settings there has been an increase in the level of employee participation, with the focus ranging from limited workplace issues to broad strategic aspects of business operations. The extent of unionization has continued to decline and the character of many on-going relationships has been greatly altered. Wage restraint, concession bargaining over both wages and work rules, as well as cooperation are now routine aspects of union-management relations. The publication of *The Transformation of American Industrial Relations* (Kochan, Katz, and McKersie; hereafter KKM, 1986) and the rapidly changing institutions it describes and analyzes mark an appropriate time to consider some of the fundamental issues of industrial relations.

It is not just of academic interest that the turmoil of contemporary industrial relations be better understood. With a broader understanding of events and their context, practitioners can work more effectively within the system and those who desire to encourage fundamental change can develop appropriate policies. An accurate and complete statement of the facts, however, is only one step in achieving this end. More difficult, and ultimately more profound, is the establishment of a theoretical framework within which to place these facts. With such a framework, we can determine causal relationships (so as to know what to manipulate for change) and anticipate developments that have not yet been observed. If the academic field of industrial relations is to be more than a journalistic reporting of facts, the quest for some sort of paradigm is important.

Our efforts in search of a broader understanding will not be a failure if the result is not a completely general theory. The scientific process of deriving hypotheses, testing them with empirical evidence, and adapting theories in light of such efforts is necessary to help us structure our understanding of the environment and its impact on institutions. Similarly, some sort of a general framework is required if we are to discern whether events, which at the moment appear so profound, are simply predictable reactions to changing circumstances or a fundamental shift in the relationship between the industrial relations system and the environment. The essays in this volume, in their analysis of contemporary events and *The Transformation of American Industrial Relations*, address some of the basic questions of the employment relationship. There are certainly no easy answers but this volume will have been successful if it gives the reader a better understanding of where the academic subject of industrial relations is today. It is hoped that the essays will inspire others to build on our field's strengths and to reduce its weaknesses.

In this chapter the basic thesis and evidence of *The Transformation of American Industrial Relations* are briefly summarized. The essays commenting on KKM's work contained in this volume are then highlighted. In order to put the debate, and in particular the role of industrial relations theory, in a broader perspective, the history of such controversies is reviewed and examples of past debates examined. We finish with a discussion of the question of whether the ideas embodied in the *Transformation* represent the basis for an industrial relations paradigm.

The Transformation of Industrial Relations

The Kochan, Katz, and McKersie analysis puts forth a model of industrial relations that relies heavily on the strategic choices made by the system's participants. Although the external environment of the labor market, labor force characteristics and values, product markets, technology, and public policies are explicit in the model, future patterns of industrial relations are not "unalterably predetermined" (p. 4). Practices and outcomes are the result of " . . . the interactions of environmental forces *along with* the strategic choices and values of American managers, union leaders, workers, and public policy decision makers" (p. 5). This interplay of the environment and choice is heavily conditioned by the institutional structure that has built up over time as a result of custom and law. KKM assert that the central role of collective bargaining in the post-New Deal period has led to an inappropriately narrow view of the institutional influences on industrial relations activity. As a remedy for this restricted focus, they propose a three tier institutional framework that explicitly recognizes the importance of activities above and below the traditionally emphasized level of organizational collective bargaining and personnel policy. Their model gives separate attention to the institutional influence of the strategic level of policy formulation as well as the workplace level of policy implementation.

In tracing the development of the post-New Deal collective bargaining system and the emergence of non-union industrial relations after 1960, the authors describe a complex interaction of environmental and institutional forces that derive from their model. Until the 1970s, the long term growth in the economy made the continuity and stability of the New Deal industrial relations system an attractive model for human resource management even in non-union firms. After 1960, and particularly in the 1970s and 80s, increasingly competitive product markets, shifting labor force characteristics, more rapid technological change, and an increased role of government combined with anti-union managerial values to produce a steady decline in the role of unions and the emergence of sophisticated nonunion industrial relations management systems. This "transformation" of industrial relations is then documented and explained by an extensive review of empirical studies.

The book ends with a consideration of four scenarios about the future of American industrial relations. Certainly one possibility is that private sector unionization will continue to decline because of competitive pressures and technological change. This could be altered to some degree by labor law reform but changes in the legal environment would have only a modest impact. Diffusion of the innovations in union-management collaboration that result in increased economic performance and improved relationships is another possibility—one that the authors feel could stabilize unionization. To reverse the downward trend will take all of these changes plus " . . . the emergence of new strategies for organizing and representing individuals found in the growing occupations and industries" (p. 253).

Reflections on the Transformation Hypothesis

In the essays that follow, certainly none of the authors disagree with the fundamental notion that there have been substantial changes in industrial relations practices over the past several decades and that these changes have accelerated in the 1980s. However, in the first essay, Richard Block argues that these changes are "simply" predictable evolutionary reactions to increasingly competitive product markets; and to label these changes a transformation misrepresents their character. The contribution made by KKM in documenting and analyzing the profound industrial relations changes of the past decade is substantial, particularly in their emphasis on the role of business strategy, but in Block's view, the practices identified do not constitute " . . . a fundamental alteration in the way industrial relations is conducted." Block states that if unions are to reestablish themselves as major actors in the industrial relations system, there must be a fundamental change in our labor law that gives unions a status comparable to that enjoyed by corporations.

In commenting on this chapter, James Martin agrees with Block that what KKM observe constitutes evolution rather than transformation. He also notes that while both KKM and Block see management as dominant, they emphasize different reasons. KKM point to the shift in management responsibility from industrial relations staff people to those in line positions, whereas Block feels that employers were always able to seize the initiative but were passive in the past because of the sheltered product markets in which they operated.

James Begin also takes a broad critical perspective on the KKM analysis and other industrial relations theories. In his view, these frameworks ignore organizational level variables that are important for understanding employment relations systems. He presents an alternative model in which the key factor is the need for congruency between organizational and environmental characteristics. Begin asserts that the KKM analysis is " . . . a contingency model that describes how employers, operating through their peculiar value systems, adjust technology, organizational structure and policies, and market policies to ensure survival under changing market conditions." His organizational theory based model attempts to *predict* patterns of behavior based on characteristics of the environment and the organization—something he feels the descriptive models of Dunlop and KKM do not even attempt to do. If the Begin analysis really does take us from a descriptive to a predictive theory, it is a genuine scientific advance. Of course, it is the role of empirical testing to ascertain whether this is the case.

George Strauss next analyzes the KKM book within the context of a far-ranging discussion of the whole academic field of industrial relations. A key point of his essay is that the field needs to broaden its perspective to more systematically include consideration of nonunion as well as unionized employment relationships. Strauss considers the potential contribution to the understanding of industrial relations phenomena by new developments in a variety of disciplines including organizational behavior, human resource management, economics, history, as well as traditional industrial relations. As a step toward a more general perspective on the issues, he categorizes employment systems into four prototypes: unstructured simple competitive labor market situations, craft or occupation based markets, traditional systems that emphasize internal labor markets, and high commitment systems based on employment security. Whether such a descriptive structure contains the elements necessary to provide a theory of industrial relations remains to be determined.

In his comments on Strauss' paper, Jack Fiorito agrees that the field of industrial relations needs to go beyond the examination of union-management relations. In contrast to many of the other authors, however, he feels that the field already has an integrating framework—the industrial relations systems work of John Dunlop (1958). Fiorito asserts that criticisms of the Dunlop framework are based on a popularized and overly simplified version. The Dunlop model is much more subtle and powerful than is currently acknowledged, and certainly, it does not equate industrial relations and collective bargaining. Fiorito acknowledges the contribution of the KKM framework with its explicit recognition of multiple levels of activity and its emphasis on management's role. He points out, however, that the Dunlop model did not encourage neglect of management's role in industrial relations research but that, nevertheless, this neglect occurred.

Myron Roomkin and Hervey Juris then consider the issue of business strategy, particularly in the context of the steel industry. They feel that the three highlights of KKM are their stress on management as an active partner in the industrial relations system, their description of events from the 1930s through the 1980s within a cogent framework that gives proper significance to the nonunion sector, and their demonstration that industrial relations professionals have, over time, played a diminished role in making management policy. Roomkin and Juris view KKM as more than a descriptive framework; they see a theory that seeks to explain changes in longstanding patterns of behavior and identifies those behaviors that are ripe for change. Whereas the prevailing paradigm is one of adaptive institutional response to environmental change, KKM focus on the role of managers as decision-makers and initiators. Using concepts developed by academics in the policy field, they discuss business strategy in the steel industry. They conclude that the interaction between business strategy and industrial relations in the steel industry is consistent with the traditional adaptive model of behavior and that industrial relations have long been influenced by business decisions.

In their separate comments on the Roomkin-Juris chapter, John Fossum and Joel Cutcher-Gershenfeld provide their assessments of the KKM contribution. Fossum emphasizes their synthesis of a great deal of disparate information into a cogent model and the stimulation of research that results from such an effort. Cutcher-Gershenfeld feels that KKM redefine the basic questions that will be asked rather than providing answers to the old questions. In his view the key concept of the transformation is a shift in the underlying framework or assumptions that guide labor-management relations.

Using the current debate over the transformation hypothesis as a basis, Richard Peterson discusses weaknesses in the American system of industrial relations. Peterson argues that the Swedish system has many desirable aspects that should be more closely examined by American scholars. The Swedes have produced an arrangement that is both internationally competitive and, in the view of many, more supportive of individual rights in the employment setting. In his comments on this paper, William Bigoness criticizes Peterson's negative view of many current American industrial relations practices, stating that Peterson sees employer-employee relations as a fixed sum game when, in fact, many aspects of this relationship are mutually enhancing.

In an enlightening discussion of the current situation in European industrial relations, Jacques Rojot then describes the usefulness of the KKM analysis in understanding these events. While KKM use a strategic choice perspective in interpreting events, Rojot asserts that "all" this really means is that responses to the environment are not deterministic. In his view much of what KKM say is easily fit into a model that emphasizes adaptive responses to a dominant environment. Rojot finds the KKM model helpful in understanding European events although he proposes two modifications. First, it is helpful to distinguish geographic levels and the nature of the interactions that take place at these levels. In European industry, for example, many of the key business decisions are made outside of the country, and therefore, beyond the reach of unions. Additionally, the European context makes it necessary to add an additional tier that focuses on inter-industry bargaining. While many of the same environmental forces that have affected the United States are important in Europe, it is less clear cut as to what the response has been. The lack of exclusive representation makes even the distinction between a union and a nonunion plant often ambiguous, although it is clear that, in general, the transformation of industrial relations in Europe has been even more dramatic than in the United States.

Anil Verma uses his comments on the Rojot paper as a vehicle for another useful discussion of the international aspects of the KKM strategic choice perspective. In his analysis of the European situation, Verma concludes that the model is a useful diagnostic framework rather than a theory that can predict outcomes. He finds, however, that it is a significant advance " . . . because it formalizes the role of choice or discretion in industrial relations decision-making."

Fortunately, the Bargaining Group conference included Thomas Kochan, Harry Katz, and Robert McKersie. These authors of *The Transformation of American Industrial Relations* participated in the discussion and developed a paper summarizing their reactions to the critiques and expansions on their ideas. Their paper addresses the four most basic questions that were generated at the conference and in the present chapters. They first consider the matter of whether the significant changes in industrial relations constitute a transformation. They next consider " . . . the role of strategic choice versus environmental factors in shaping the course of American industrial relations; the nature, viability and fairness of nonunion personnel systems; and the international applicability of our arguments." The usefulness of their 1986 book in explaining more recent developments is then considered. They " . . . find continuing evidence that the locus of activity in American industrial relations has shifted to the strategic and workplace levels." Contrary to Block, they feel (for example) that the new and profoundly different relationship between labor and management has continued. They conclude with the important assertion that " . . . the transformed industrial relations system we described in the book provides a more suitable micro foundation for the economy and workforce of the future than either the traditional New Deal system or the cautious experimentation with a new system now underway."

In a final chapter, the editors asked David Lewin to summarize what he feels are the major research issues that come out of this debate. In a very useful synthesis of the chapters and comments, Lewin proposes how scholars may test the relevance of the propositions found in this volume. As we discuss in the rest of this introduction, this empirical work is now the most productive direction for the field to pursue.

Historical Perspective

Certainly this is not the first time that intellectual and institutional ferment have combined to compel an assessment of the status quo.

The first presidential address to the Industrial Relations Research Association by Edwin E. Witte in 1948 was entitled, "Where We Are In Industrial Relations." The "Hawthorne Studies" of Elton Mayo and his colleagues were the most widely discussed research of this era. While recognizing the importance of Mayo's findings that the production of individual workers depends on group thinking and action, Witte (1948) pointed out that:

> He [Mayo] was not the first to discover that there are group limitations to production even in unorganized plants. John R. Commons noted this fact in his report on *Regulation and Restriction of Output by Employees and Unions* which was published by the United States Bureau of Labor in 1904, and Stanley Mathewson reported the same phenomenon in his *Restriction of Output Among Unorganized Workers* in 1931. Still less was Mayo the first, to make in-plant studies in industrial relations or to conduct controlled experiments in this field.

Industrial relations phenomena can, and indeed need, to be studied from a variety of disciplinary perspectives; but if this effort is to be greater than the sum of its parts, attention must be paid to the contributions of other disciplines. If the academic field of industrial relations is anything more than just a body of subject matter, multi-disciplinary research, or at least research that is carried out with an appreciation of the insights of other disciplines, must be its cornerstone.

In order to promote this type of cross fertilization, the first annual meeting of the Industrial Relations Research Association devoted an entire session to the role of various disciplines in industrial relations research. Interested readers might enjoy going back to this volume to examine the contributions of psychology (Kornhauser, 1948), political science (Leiserson, 1948), sociology (Mills, 1948), and law (Feinsinger, 1948). The comments of discussant Benjamin Selekman (1948) are as valid today as they were in 1948.

> It is significant that, by the testimony of these papers, none of the four disciplines—psychology, political science, sociology, or law, nor in blunt truth all of them together—can as yet offer a systematic, coherent theory of human behavior for application and testing by those of us who work in the field of industrial relations. . . . The task of formulating such a theory lies ahead; and industrial relations, it seems to me, affords an especially fruitful field for exploration and collaborative analysis by all the disciplines directed toward getting on with that fundamental task.

Several years later, Lloyd Reynolds (1955) asked industrial relations researchers to contemplate how research priorities should be established from the thousands of possible topics available when one defines our field as "aspects of the employment relation." Given the enormous number of topics and limited research resources, it was suggested that scholars concentrate their efforts on those topics where certain criteria are met:

(1) The research should be *scientific* in nature, implying the generation of clear hypotheses capable of being validated or refuted from an adequate body of data;
(2) The subject should have important and continuing implications for human well being; that is, we ought to work on *big problems* and not worry so much about small issues; and,
(3) Research should be *operational* in nature and therefore make a contribution to sound public policy.

Reynolds asserted that the " . . . bane of our subject, [is] the magpie-like gathering of facts unrelated to any possibility of social action" (1955, p. 4). While it is appropriate to promote research that is relevant or "serviceable," to use the terminology of Reynolds, in our opinion, too little attention is paid to the criterion of being scientific (with its emphasis on theory development and theory testing).

This is where the work of Kochan, Katz and McKersie (KKM) has had its most significant contribution to the field of industrial relations. Clearly, the KKM transformation research meets Reynolds criteria of being scientific, aimed at the big picture and policy relevant. While many authors in this volume disagree with KKM's theoretical framework and their interpretation of events, it is the very debate about these important issues that makes this a scientific exercise and therefore one that will advance the state of our knowledge and its impact on policy.

To return to our historical review, the debate over the status of industrial relations research continued the very next year. In 1956, Richard Lester gave the profession a "progress report," noting that a close connection exists between industrial relations research and policy. While making the point that such research was coming of age, Lester pleaded for "more reflection and less concentration on fact-gathering alone" (1956, p. 2). He was very clear in pointing out that " . . . it is such general theoretical work in industrial relations that needs emphasis now" (p. 4).

Dale Yoder (1957, p. 4) reemphasized the importance of good theory when he suggested: " . . . we need more thinking and more theorizing. We will always need theory to provide us with hunches and hypotheses." It is interesting, however, to note that a basic issue emerging from an IRRA survey on Industrial Relations education in 1960 was "whether industrial relations is a discipline" (Estey, 1960, p. 98). Inherent in the answer to this question are other fundamental questions that needed to be addressed, such as: What is the field of industrial relations? Does industrial relations have its own paradigm? How much emphasis should be given to theoretical research? In 1960, the field was sharply divided on these issues.

The controversy continued. Solomon Barkin (1964, p. 2) reflecting on industrial relations research and the progress made in our field stated, "the major criticism has been that there is no all-enveloping system of analysis built on a comprehensive theoretical framework." He argued for a wholesale reexamination by researchers of industrial relations institutions, structures, policies and beliefs that would move us away from discrete descriptive reports into " . . . a program with grand design."

While some continued to argue for more theory and the creation of the discipline of industrial relations, others like George Shultz (then Secretary of Labor) maintained that "the field of industrial relations . . . is problem based. It is not a discipline in itself but rather draws on many disciplines for theory and technique to understand and help solve the problems arising in the work place, the labor market and at the bargaining table" (1968, p. 1).

In 1980, Jack Barbash wrote about values in industrial relations and advised members of the profession that: "industrial relations as a field of study . . . needs to liberate itself from obsessive reliance on mechanistic counting and theorizing and return to the value of the founding fathers of industrial relations who, if I am not mistaken, tried to get at the spirit of industrial relations."

Milton Derber (1982) had a different perspective. He noted that " . . . while facts are essential, they are not sufficient. To give them analytical meaning and to develop them as useful predictive tools, effective general conceptual or theoretical frameworks are needs. This is the facet of industrial relations scholarship that has been neglected in recent decades in the United States. . . ."

In responding to reviewers of his 1980 text, *Collective Bargaining and Industrial Relations*, Thomas Kochan stated: "whether this or some other new framework is adopted, it is clear that the fundamental challenges now confronting the American system will force equally fundamental reexamination of our research paradigm" (1982, p. 22).

In an interesting summary of some thirty-six years of industrial relations research, Kerr (1983, p. 17) stated clearly that "industrial relations research is an applied field." His view is that, as an applied field, industrial relations research is based upon facts, and researchers are obliged to collect and analyze said observations. In assessing the performance of industrial relations research, Kerr examined three criteria. First, he argued that an applied field such as industrial relations research should meet the test of providing an accurate historical and current commentary of what has happened in the field. Second, research should be useful in policy formation. Finally, industrial relations research can make contributions in the realm of theory. Theoretical contributions can come in the form of (a) testing propositions of existing theories; (b) modifying old theories or creating totally new theories; (c) bringing to the attention of the field new problems to be explained; and, (d) extending old theories into explanations of farther corners of practice. Kerr argued that industrial relations research has been clearly successful only in the last of these four areas of potential theoretical contribution. To summarize, while industrial relations research has been fairly successful in the realm of *commentary* and has had several substantial contributions to public *policy* (such as encouragement and acceptance of the trade union movement and training for disadvantaged workers), *theoretical* advance has not been a major contribution of industrial relations research.

The work of KKM does establish a theoretical framework which builds on that attributable to Dunlop (1958). As these authors state (KKM, 1984, p. 262), "we use the term 'industrial relations' to describe the broad values, laws, institutions, and practices that govern employment relationships, and in this way our research domain overlaps with that proposed by John Dunlop . . . where our framework differs from Dunlop's is through its emphasis on the need to consider both the critical features that structure U.S. industrial relations and the dynamic interplay between union and nonunion employment systems."

Perhaps Arnold Weber (1987, pp. 22-23) summed things up for us best when he stated:

> I [do not] seek to reaffirm our scientific authenticity by calling for "a shift in paradigm." The study of industrial relations has a long record of making important contributions to our understanding of basic forces that determine the character of industrial, or, if you will, postindustrial society. It has led the way in fruitful, interdisciplinary research, blending the concepts and methodologies of the various social sciences. . . . Our limitations in perceiving and understanding recent events have indicated, however, that we should not confuse maturity with unchallenged wisdom. It is unlikely that there is an equivalent

of John Maynard Keynes sitting in this audience or brooding in some distant graduate student's carrel who will stand current assumptions on their head by formulating an alternative Grand Design for industrial relations. Rather, the intellectual record of this field of inquiry reveals that we are more likely to change our focus and deepen our understanding in hard-earned increments.

Looked at in this manner, one must ask if the current work of KKM should be viewed as an example of one of Weber's "hard-earned increments" or the beginning of a new industrial relations paradigm. Are we in a period of fundamental change or, as Block has argued, are we "merely" witnessing the natural evolution of industrial relations practice to a changing environment?

Past Debates in Industrial Relations

There are several past examples of fundamental disagreements over theoretical and methodological issues in industrial relations. Perhaps this is due to the nature of the subject, where researchers from a variety of disciplines study the same problems. Whatever the reason for these controversies, for our purpose, it is instructive to briefly examine two of the most famous of these past debates—the Lester-Machlup argument surrounding the concept of marginal analysis and the Dunlop-Ross controversy about the nature of the trade union institution. A review of these exchanges may shed light on whether we have a usable theory of industrial relations and whether the current changes represent an evolution or a transformation.

The marginal productivity theory asserts that a direct relationship exists between the wage level and the quantity of employment offered by an individual firm (McNulty, 1980). On the basis of interviews with corporate executives and questionnaire responses, Richard Lester argued that demand for product was more important than wages in determining employment levels. Thus, Lester (1946, p. 71) concluded that "much of the economic reasoning on company employment adjustments to increases or decreases in wage rates is invalid, and a new theory of wage-employment relationships for the individual firm must be developed."

Fritz Machlup stated the other side of the issue a few months later. His conclusion was that the marginal productivity theory of the firm's conduct had not been shaken, discredited or disproven by Lester's analyses. He severely criticized Lester's methodology and conclusions. With regard to Lester's argument about the difficulty of calculating the exact magnitude of the significant variables in the marginalist theory, Machlup noted that " . . . the explanation of an action must often include steps of reasoning which the acting individual himself does not consciously perform (because the action has become routine) and which perhaps he would never be able to perform in scientific exactness. . . . To call, on these grounds, the theory 'invalid,' 'unrealistic' or 'inapplicable' is to reveal failure to understand the basic methodological constitution of most social sciences" (Machlup, 1946, p. 535). Other distinguished scholars found both sides of the debate wanting since they were essentially arguing the realism of the marginalist assumptions rather than the predictive power of the model (Friedman, 1953, p. 15).

Despite his stinging criticism of Lester in 1946, Professor Machlup had softened his tone quite a bit by the time of his presidential address to the American Economic Association in 1966. In this speech, he suggested that while marginalism still dominated the teaching of microeconomics, regular reports of research on alternative approaches to the theory of the firm at least imply that a " . . . superior theory may eventually replace marginalism" (Machlup, 1967, pp. 3-4).

The second controversy surrounded the issue of the adequacy of, what was then, the traditional theory for explaining labor union wage policies. John Dunlop (1944) made a strong case for the movement away from the use of purely institutional and historical methods for explaining union behavior. He favored incorporating unionism into the mainstream of economic theorizing since " . . . the trade union is clearly a decision making unit" (p. 4); and therefore a useful model of the trade union as a market enterprise could be constructed. This approach presented hypotheses that could be empirically tested.

While some scholars such as Lloyd Reynolds (1944) applauded Dunlop's work as "one of the most significant studies of wages which has appeared in recent years," other writers criticized Dunlop on the grounds that union wage policy was not amenable to " . . . the mechanical application of any maximization principle" (Ross, 1956, p. 8). Rather, Ross (p. 74) argued that while concerned with economic matters, the trade union was primarily a "political instrumentality not governed by the pecuniary calculus conventionally attributed to business enterprise." He asserted that wage determination had less to do with economics than with other social and political forces. In economic terms the Ross theory is that unions ignore, or act as if they ignore, the tradeoff between wages and employment that is implied by a negatively sloped demand curve for labor.

This debate has been reopened over the years. And although many conclude that, "[a]vailable empirical evidence is consistent with either of the original approaches" (Mitchell, 1972), a robust body of literature in labor economics has followed the Dunlop perspective.

What can we conclude from these past debates that would be useful for us as we wrestle with our current question of whether there has been a transformation of the field? Several items seem to be significant:

1. No clear winner emerged from these past debates. Fortunately, progress is not predicated on having a clear winner to such controversies.
2. These debates have spawned much useful research on the nature of the firm and the wage determination process under trade unionism. While our field has not moved on to a new paradigm, we do know a lot more about these issues today due to the research generated from these past debates.
3. The most progress can be made where researchers with the proper grounding in history and institutions combine these skills with quantitative and theoretical sophistication. A skillful blend of these components in the research process may be our surest road to progress in the field of industrial relations.

The Question of a Paradigm

To begin with, a few definitions are in order. Thomas Kuhn (1962, p. 10) defines normal science as " . . . research firmly based upon one or more past scientific achievements, achievements that some particular scientific community acknowledges for a time as supplying the foundation for its further practice." The past achievements of a field are normally recounted in textbooks or scholarly review articles. Other researchers engaged in normal science work on the further articulation of the phenomena and theories that emanate from their accepted paradigm. Kuhn refers to these types of studies as "mop-up-work" (p. 24). The basic notion is that there is a commonly accepted paradigm (to be defined below) that researchers attempt to refine and develop throughout most of their careers. Like it or not, most of us doing industrial relations research are engaging in Kuhn's mopping-up operations. Also, note that even in a pre-paradigm stage, most research will be aimed at testing conflicting claims, the ultimate goal being a "winner" theory which may emerge as the "first" or "new" paradigm.

Exactly what is meant by the term paradigm? In Kuhn's analysis, a paradigm must satisfy two essential characteristics (1962, p. 10).

First, the scientific achievement must be " . . . sufficiently unprecedented to attract an enduring group of adherents away from competing modes of scientific activity." Second, a paradigm has to be
" . . . sufficiently open-ended to leave all sorts of problems for the
redefined group of practitioners to resolve."

Normal science can also be viewed as activity geared at approach-
ing the stage of a "paradigm." Kuhn (1962, p. 33) refers to three
classes of problems that exhaust both the empirical and theoretical
literature of normal science: (1) the determination of significant
facts; (2) the matching of these facts with theory; (3) the articulation
of theory. More germane for our purposes, Kuhn (p. 48) has this to
say about pre-paradigm periods of science:

> The pre-paradigm period, in particular, is regularly marked
> by frequent and deep debates over legitimate methods, prob-
> lems, and standards of solution, though these serve rather to
> define schools than to produce agreement. . . . Furthermore,
> debates like these do not vanish once and for all with the
> appearance of a paradigm. Though almost non-existent during
> periods of normal science, they recur regularly just before and
> during scientific revolutions. . . .

Given these arguments presented by Kuhn, where are we in
industrial relations? Do we have a paradigm? Do we practice normal science? Does the KKM book represent the beginning of a
new industrial relations paradigm? Are we, as industrial relations
researchers, bound to be relegated to a life of "mopping-up" types
of research activities? These are not easy questions that yield
obvious, unambiguous answers. Rather, answers to these types of
questions are in part dependent upon our individual values and
norms as researchers and scientists. Nevertheless, there seem to be
several conclusions that are evident at this point in the evolution of
our field.

First, the field of industrial relations has never had a paradigm to
rely upon as one would find in other scientific fields such a physics,
chemistry and biology. Perhaps our best past candidate might be
Dunlop's "systems approach"; yet even here, it would be safe to say
that this framework has failed to attract an enduring group of
supporters. It should be clearly noted, however, that the lack of an
accepted paradigm does not relegate a field to the status of something less than a science. Far from this, scientific endeavor is seen as
any activity in a discipline in which progress is made. And clearly, the
Dunlop framework has been a useful descriptive tool that has
furthered the scientific study of industrial relations.

Second, given that industrial relations has not had an accepted paradigm, our discipline must of necessity be classified as in the pre-paradigm stage. If the acquisition of a paradigm and the accompanying esoteric research that a paradigm permits is seen as the sign of a mature field, industrial relations as a discipline would have to be seen as being in a developmental stage. Note that there is nothing inherently wrong or inferior about this developmental or pre-paradigmatic aspect of scientific endeavor.

Third, the work of KKM is not a new paradigm in and of itself. Recall that for a paradigm to arise, an enduring group of adherents must be swayed away from competing models of scientific activity. But, what are these competing models? The Dunlop framework, employment relations systems theory (Begin, 1989)—or, others? The point is that it is not clear what the competing models of scientific activity are and, it is certainly not established that the KKM framework has attracted an enduring group of adherents. On the other hand, it is clear that the KKM framework does satisfy Kuhn's second feature of a paradigm, that is, it is sufficiently open ended so as to leave all sorts of research opportunities for industrial relations scholars to explore.

Finally, even though not viewed as a new paradigm, the KKM framework certainly represents a healthy sign of progress in our field. Readers of this volume will have to decide for themselves if what KKM describe is in actuality a transformation of industrial relations or merely an evolutionary stage. Perhaps making even this decision is an exercise in semantic juggling. For no matter what one calls it, the KKM dynamic model of industrial relations focussing on strategic choices for unions, corporations and government does break new ground in helping us understand our changing industrial relations system. The papers presented herein are a healthy testament to the fact that industrial relations research is indeed alive and well. Only future research will enable us to state for certain the lasting impact of the KKM book. It is, however, very clear that KKM are to be congratulated on producing a volume that has already, in the short span of time since its publication, generated so much controversy and recognition. Perhaps the KKM model will eventually rise to the level of a paradigm. But even if this comes to be true, Thomas Kuhn (1962, p. 17-18) would warn industrial relations researchers that:

> To be accepted as a paradigm, a theory must seem better than its competitors, but it need not, *and in fact never does*, explain all the facts with which it can be confronted.

References

Barbash, Jack. (1980). Values in Industrial Relations: The Case of the Adversary Principle. *IRRA Proceedings*, 1-7.

Barkin, Solomon. (1964). A Current Focus for Industrial Relations Research. *IRRA Proceedings*, 2-17.

Derber, Milton. (1982). Are We in a New Stage? *IRRA Proceedings*, 1-9.

Dunlop, John T. (1944). *Wage Determination Under Trade Unions*. New York: Macmillan.

Dunlop, John T. (1958). *Industrial Relations Systems*. New York: Holt.

Estey, Marten S. (1960). Unity and Diversity in Industrial Relations Education: The Report of the IRRA Survey. *IRRA Proceedings*, 92-100.

Feinsinger, Nathan P. (1948). The Contribution of the Law To Industrial Relations Research. *IRRA Proceedings*, 14-21.

Friedman, Milton. (1953). *Essays in Positive Economics*. Chicago: University of Chicago Press.

Kerr, Clark. (1983). A Perspective On Industrial Relations Research— Thirty Six Years Later. *IRRA Proceedings*, 14-21.

Kochan, Thomas A. (1980). *Collective Bargaining and Industrial Relations*. Homewood, IL: Irwin.

Kochan, Thomas A., Robert B. McKersie and Harry C. Katz. (1984). U.S. Industrial Relations In Transition: A Summary Report. *IRRA Proceedings*, 261-276.

Kornhauser, Arthur. (1948). The Contribution of Psychology To Industrial Relations Research. *IRRA Proceedings*, 172-188.

Kuhn, Thomas S. (1962). *The Structure Of Scientific Revolutions*. Chicago: University of Chicago Press.

Leiserson, Avery. (1948). The Role Of Political Science In Industrial Relations Research. *IRRA Proceedings*, 189-198.

Lester, Richard A. (1946). Shortcoming of Marginal Analysis For Wage-Employment Problems. *The American Economic Review*, 36, 63-82.

Lester, Richard A. (1956). Progress In Industrial Relations Research and Policy. *IRRA Proceedings*, 2-9.

Machlup, Fritz. (1946). Marginal Analysis and Empirical Research. *The American Economic Review*, 36, 519-554.

Machlup, Fritz. (1967). Theories of the Firm: Marginalist, Behavioral, Managerial. *The American Economic Review*, 57, 1-12.

McNulty, Paul J. (1980). *The Origins And Development of Labor Economics*. Cambridge, MA: MIT Press.

Mills, C. Wright. (1948). The Contribution Of Sociology To Studies Of Industrial Relations. *IRRA Proceedings*, 199-222.

Mitchell, Daniel J.B. Union Wage Policies: The Ross-Dunlop Debate Reopened. *Industrial Relations, 11*, 46-61.

Reynolds, Lloyd G. (1944). Review Of Wage Determination Under Trade Unions. *The American Economic Review*, 34, 639-641.

Reynolds, Lloyd G. (1955). Research And Practice In Industrial Relations. *IRRA Proceedings*, 2-13.

Ross, Arthur M. (1956). *Trade Union Wage Policy*. Berkeley, CA: University of California Press.

Shultz, George P. (1968). Priorities in Policy And Research For Industrial Relations. *IRRA Proceedings*, 1-13.

Selekman, Benjamin M. (1948). Discussion Of The Role Of Various Disciplines In Industrial Relations Research. *IRRA Proceedings*, 229-231.

Weber, Arnold R. (1987). Understanding Change In Industrial Relations. *IRRA Proceedings*, 11-23.

Witte, Edwin E. (1948). Where We Are In Industrial Relations? *IRRA Proceedings*, 6-20.

Yoder, Dale. (1957). Research Needs For The Second Decade. *IRRA Proceedings*, 2-10

2. AMERICAN INDUSTRIAL RELATIONS IN THE 1980's: TRANSFORMATION OR EVOLUTION?

Richard N. Block

Introduction

The Transformation of American Industrial Relations by Thomas Kochan, Harry Katz, and Robert McKersie (KKM, 1986) has made an important contribution to the field of industrial relations. The book has documented many of the changes that have occurred in industrial relations in the past decade. Collecting and analyzing these practices in one volume is, in itself, an important contribution. More important, however, the book has forced researchers in industrial relations to think about the role that corporate business strategy plays in industrial relations. This represents a substantial broadening of the scope of the areas of inquiry that have traditionally been the province of researchers in our field.

The real question that must be answered regarding the book, however, is whether the practices that KKM have identified represent a true transformation in industrial relations. In order to answer this question, there must be some definition of transformation. For the purposes of this paper, a transformation will be defined as occurring when there is a fundamental alteration in the way industrial relations is conducted. By this definition, a transformation in American industrial relations occurred with the passage of the National Labor Relations Act in 1935. Prior to the passage of the NLRA, industrial relations was almost totally unilateral, with no

The author thanks Joel Cutcher-Gershenfeld, George Strauss, James Martin, Jack Knott, and the participants in the Bargaining Group Conference for their comments on an earlier draft of this paper.

mechanism for employee involvement. The government's encouragement of bilateralism in industrial relations through the NLRA, expressing the sentiment that there were circumstances in which control of the employment relationship must be shared, represented a true transformation in industrial relations.

The basic thesis of this paper is that the trends and practices that KKM identified do not represent a transformation of American industrial relations. Rather they are the inevitable result of the impact of product market changes on the industrial relations/collective bargaining system that was established in 1935 and continues to evolve. Looked at in this way, the new practices that KKM document and the focus on business strategy that is so central to the book can be placed in an appropriate historical and institutional context.

In order to understand this thesis, the second part of this paper will lay out a framework for understanding industrial relations and human resources in the United States. The third part of the paper will analyze the historical overview presented by KKM, the model that KKM introduce, and the practices that KKM document through the framework introduced. The final section will summarize and present conclusions regarding the future of the industrial relations system in the United States.

A Framework for Studying Industrial Relations Systems in the United States

A useful framework for studying the industrial relations system in the United States as it has evolved since 1935 is contained in Figure 1. That model contains four basic elements: fundamental societal values, industrial relations/collective bargaining law and the legal system, the resulting industrial relations/collective bargaining system, and the product market. The basic assertion embodied in that diagram is that, over the long run, the fundamental values of American society have been a key factor shaping the evolution of the industrial relations system. The industrial relations system that was created in 1935 was and is molded and shaped by these values. The vehicle for shaping the industrial relations/collective bargaining system is the law and legal process, which affects the parties and is affected by the parties. The impetus for bringing industrial relations issues into the legal system or for using the status granted through societal values and the legal system are the pressures placed on the industrial relations system by the product market in which firms and, by derivation, employees, compete.

Each of these factors will be discussed in this part of the paper. As societal values and the legal system have the broadest impact because they affect all employers, they will be discussed in the first two subparts. An overview of the resulting industrial relations system will be presented in the third subpart. The fourth subpart will bring in the operation of the product market.

Values in American Society

As an integral part of American society, it would be expected that the industrial relations/collective bargaining system in the United States will be influenced by the value set held by the larger societal context in which it operates. In this regard there are several fundamental American societal values that have been of particular importance to the evolution of the industrial relations/collective bargaining system in the United States.

The one value that seems to be most important is individualism. By individualism, I refer to that value in society that tends to make the rights of individuals generally superior to other rights in society. Thus, when a person or entity exercises or claims to exercise an individual right, and that individual is allegedly in conflict with some other, nonindividual right, the institutions of our society tend to favor the party claiming individual rights (Bellah, Madsen, Sullivan, Swidler & Tifton, 1985, pp. 3-5). This individualism manifests itself in two important ways that affect the industrial relations/collective bargaining system. First, it results in great value being placed on property rights as a derivative of the rights of individual owners or their designees to use and dispose of property to further their own interests, provided that no laws are violated in that use or disposition. Along the same lines, it also means that individuals are to be free to order their own economic transactions provided that no laws are broken, with a high value being placed on freedom of contract (Block & Wolkinson, 1985, pp. 43-81; Chamberlain & Kuhn, 1986, pp. 42-75; Lewin & Lipsky, 1985, p. 7; Perlman, 1966, pp. 155-162).

The great weight given to individualism and property rights provides corporations substantial freedom to pursue their interests. This results because corporations are viewed by the law as legal individuals, with most of the economic and legal rights that accrue to persons. Corporations are viewed as voluntary collectivities of individual stockholders governed through the legal mechanism of election of the Board of Directors. The corporation is also embodied with limited stockholder liability and a flexible structure, so that it can change its form and function as the interests of the stockholders,

Figure 1

FRAMEWORK FOR ANALYZING INDUSTRIAL RELATIONS
IN THE UNITED STATES SINCE 1935

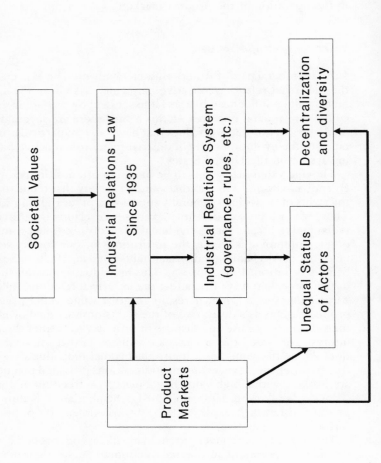

as interpreted by corporate management and the Board of Directors, dictate (Galbraith, 1967, pp. 83-96).

Thus, as a legal individual, the corporation is viewed as legally identical to a person for the purpose of engaging in economic activity. It exercises property rights to contract with individuals and other corporations for various goods and services, including labor. Although constrained in some ways by the law, fundamentally, the purchase and sale of labor is an exchange transaction and is viewed by the law in the same way as the purchase and sale of any other commodity with the special twist that it has a time dimension to it (Marx, 1967, pp. 231-302). Because the sale is a continuing one, and occurs in discrete segments, the buyer may cease purchasing it, and the seller may cease providing it, when either sees fit. Moreover, since the labor is often done on the premises of the employer, or at least with the employer's permission or sanction, the employer, exercising its property rights, controls who may enter and what may be done on the premises.

The high status given to individual rights and the status of the corporation as an individual and as distinct from its stockholder owners is in direct contrast to the status of unions. Unions are, by definition, collectivities of individuals. Their major role is collective bargaining, that is, to take an employment relationship that would otherwise be marked by individual bargaining, and collectivize it. In order for collectivizing the employment relationship to be successful, there must be some willingness to sacrifice individual interests for collective interests. But such a sacrifice is fundamentally inconsistent with the value of individualism that is so central to American society.

Placing this discussion in the context of the actors in the American industrial relations system, what becomes clear is that corporations are exercising individual and property rights, individual employees are exercising individual rights, and unions are exercising collective rights. Given the higher status of individual and property rights, one would expect that, over the long run, in the absence of any societal pronouncement (such as legislation) giving unions higher status than that to which they would otherwise be entitled, unions would be unable to thrive in the United States. As will be discussed below, that is precisely what is occurring today.

Finally, also consistent with the value of individualism, is a general reluctance to permit governmental interference with individual, property-based transactions. This is not to say that there is no government involvement in the labor market, because there is, in fact, a great deal of such involvement. Rather, it is to say that government involvement is the exception rather than rule, and that the burden is always on the advocate of government involvement to show why a system of unregulated individual transactions has generated unsatisfactory results.

Values in American Society and Industrial Relations Law

On the surface, the NLRA seemed to be a societal assertion of the legitimacy of collective bargaining and the creation of a status for unionism and collective bargaining that was roughly equal to that of employers (Block, Wolkinson & Kuhn, 1988; *NLRB v. Jones and Laughlin*, 1937). Yet, as it has evolved, the scope of the NLRA has been interpreted quite narrowly. This is because there is a fundamental inconsistency between the collective rights embodied in the NLRA on the one hand, and the high status given to individual rights on the other. Thus, when it has been claimed that the NLRA is in conflict with individual or property rights, and it is not absolutely clear from the language of the statute that Congress meant to interfere with those individual rights, the individual right will generally prevail over the collectively asserted right (Atleson, 1983; Block & Wolkinson, 1985; Block et al., 1988).

This distinction between individual, property-based rights and collective rights has manifested itself in two important ways under the NLRA that are relevant for understanding the changes that have taken place in the American industrial relations system. First, early in the administration of the Act, it was made clear that the NLRB was not to involve itself in determining the substantive terms of collective bargaining agreements (*Ex-Cell-O Corp.*, 1970; *NLRB v. American National Insurance*, 1952; *NLRB v. Insurance Agents*, 1960; *H.K. Porter v. NLRB*, 1970). The purpose of the Act was simply to determine if a unit of employees wished to be represented by a labor organization and, if so, to require the employer to negotiate with them. Consistent with the principle of government nonintervention, then, the fundamentals of the employment relationship, the actual terms and conditions of employment, were left to the parties to decide. Thus, governmental involvement with the individual, property-based employment relationship was reduced. As will be discussed below, this has important implications for the diversity of collective bargaining relationships.

A second important manifestation of this distinction between individual, property-based rights and collective rights is the greater status given to employers vis-à-vis employees and unions in organizing campaigns, and vis-à-vis unions in collective bargaining. Regarding organizing campaigns, since the early 1940's, the NLRA has consistently been interpreted in such a way as to increase the rights of employers vis-à-vis employees and unions to the point at which the employer has almost total control over the workplace during an organizing campaign. Employees generally have access to fellow employees only during normal conversation and non-working time while unions have almost no rights to reach employees at the workplace (Block, et al., 1988). Between 1941 and 1956, employers obtained the right to present their views on union activity during working hours, to present captive audience speeches, to prevent the distribution of relevant information during an organizing campaign, to deny the union the right to respond to captive audience speeches, and to exclude the union from the its property (Block & Wolkinson, 1985; Block et al., 1988; *Livingston Shirt*, 1953; *NLRB v. Babcock and Wilcox*, 1956; *NLRB v. Clark*, 1947; *NLRB v. Clearwater*, 1953; *NLRB v. Virginia Electric*, 1941).

With respect to the relative rights of employers and unions in collective bargaining, since the Fibreboard decision in 1964 (*Fibreboard*, 1964), the law has evolved in such a way as to narrow the definition of terms and conditions of employment and scope of mandatory bargaining under Sections 8 (a) (5) and 8 (d) of the NLRA. Relying on traditional notions of property rights, the law during the 1980's excluded from the scope of mandatory bargaining most managerial decisions that had a substantial impact on employment if those decisions involved major capital investment decisions or a major change in the direction of the firm. Of course, it is precisely these decisions that are strategic. The only exception to this occurs when the firm's decision turns primarily on labor cost considerations (Atleson, 1983, pp. 111-135; *First National* (1981); Sockell, 1986, pp. 19-34; *Steelworkers Local 2179*, 1987; *United Technologies*, 1984).

In essence, what has evolved is a system that operates on a premise that is analogous to the reserved rights theory of management in arbitration. The variant is that all rights are reserved to the employer except what legislation or common law has removed from it. In the absence of legal constraints, the employer can operate its business and its employment relations as it sees fit. Consistent with this notion, and excluding those cases that are characterized by clear employer discrimination, the law seems to be moving toward evaluating cases by what can best be described as an employer good faith test. When the employer acts in good faith, its interests will generally prevail.

Finally, it should be noted that the importance of the legal environment should not be underestimated. A cardinal principle of the American legal system is access, it is open to all. It covers all employers that have an impact on interstate commerce, meaning that it provides a uniform set of constraints. It is also very public, with its outcomes well documented and available to the legal community. When interests conflict, as they often will in industrial relations, to resort to the law is the accepted method of resolving the conflict. It is often not necessary to invoke a formal legal process, since, in general, the parties know the law, and need not wait for an administrative determination of rights in situations similar to those that have occurred in the past. To the extent the law favors employers, the resolution of conflicts will be in their favor.[1]

The Industrial Relations System[2]

The industrial relations system that resulted from the interaction of the law and broadly based societal values discussed above has attributes that are a manifestation of the values discussed above. The major actors in the system are as follows:

(1) A union movement that is characterized by conservative business unionism. It is fundamentally interested in furthering the interests of its members. It is flexible in that it will do what is necessary to represent its membership. It is generally accepting of the principle of private property and the basic values of society. Its primary focus is on protecting incumbent membership, and on the workplace (Perlman, 1966, pp. 237-318; Taft, pp. 1-38).

(2) Corporate and business employers that are primarily interested in the maximization of shareholder wealth. They believe that this can best be accomplished by maximizing the control of management over the allocation of corporate resources (including labor) so that decisions can be made in the best interest of the owners/shareholders. While there are exceptions, it seems reasonable to state that most businesses would prefer to operate without the constraints imposed by collective bargaining and unionization. As a rule, American management believes that it is in the best interests of the stockholders and, by implication, the employees, if management was unconstrained by collective bargaining in its decisions regarding resource allocation. In general, corporations, to the extent practicable and consistent with other business interests, will, other things equal, attempt to avoid unionization where there is no union, eliminate unionization where it exists, minimize the constraints imposed by unionization where it is not practicable to eliminate it, and attempt to obtain union concurrence in its decisions when necessary.

The general constraints of the system are as follows:

(1) An absence of government intervention in the substantive

terms of collective agreements. In general, employers and unions are able to make their own rules for the administration of their industrial relations provided that neither the process by which the rules were made nor the substance of the rules violates the NLRA or other laws. The rules are determined by the relative power of the parties (*American National Insurance*, 1952; *NLRB v. Insurance Agents*, 1960; *NLRB v. Truck Drivers Local 449*, 1957).

(2) A narrow scope for bargaining, with the scope limited to terms and conditions of employment as defined under the law. Thus, the industrial relations system in the United States evolved into one in which corporations as employers were exercising individual rights of shareholders/property owners, while unions were exercising the collective rights of employees, who, in general were not property owners, at least with respect to their employer. Given the greater status of individual and property rights relative to collective rights, it might be expected that corporations would have more status in the system than unions, and that is precisely what has occurred. This greater status gave employers more power to pursue their interests than unions had to pursue theirs. This is not to say that in every instance the employer had more bargaining power than the union. But it is to say that, overall, the industrial relations system gave greater deference to employer interests than to union interests. Since 1935, in a myriad of cases involving a clash of good faith employer and union interests, employers ultimately prevailed, and the range of union activity in organizing and the scope of matters that unions could affect in bargaining became progressively narrower. Thus, employers obtained consistently greater freedom to pursue their corporate interests free of union constraints (Block & Wolkinson, 1985; Block et al., 1988).

In addition, because of the absence of governmental involvement in the substance of collective agreements, collective bargaining was highly decentralized, and relationships took as many forms as the number of parties who negotiated them. The relationships were influenced by a wide variety of factors, such as the political and organizational constraints of the parties, the extent of union organization in the industry, the production process, the relative bargaining power of the parties in each individual relationship, and the product market.

The Impact of the Product Market

A fundamental principle of economic theory is that the demand for labor is a derived demand, derived from the demand for the product of which labor is an input. This was fundamental to Commons' classic notion that the goal of a union was to take wages out of competition by organizing all the producers in the relevant product market (Commons, 1976).

To a great extent, between 1935 and the early 1970's, the major unions in the heavily unionized sectors of manufacturing and transportation had succeeded in doing just this. The product markets in these industries were sheltered from competition from outside the organized sector, either because of an absence of foreign competition or because of regulation. Product markets were stable and generally predictable, with companies aware of the sources of competition and the rules of the competitive game. Indeed, given the small likelihood of eliminating unions and collective bargaining from the industries, firms no doubt saw an advantage in stable, uniform industrial relations across all competitors. One source of competition among them was eliminated. Thus, firms could achieve a satisfactory rate of return without the necessity of making changes in their industrial relations, as all of their relevant competitors had comparable industrial relations systems (Block & McLennan, 1985; Lipsky & Donn, 1987).

Under these product market conditions, unions negotiated relatively high wages and benefits. In the regulated industries, such as airlines and trucking, (Block & McLennan, 1985; Cappelli, 1987) increased wage costs could be passed on to the consumer through regulated pricing. In some manufacturing industries, such as auto assembly and steel, in which the product markets were concentrated among the unionized firms in the United States, the costs could also be passed on to the consumers (Block & McLennan, 1985; Katz, 1987). In other manufacturing industries, such as rubber, where there was little control of retail distribution, unions were less successful in negotiating high wage and benefit packages. Even in rubber, however, the union eliminated wage competition among the manufacturers (Block & McLennan, 1985; Karper, 1987).

Under these conditions, unions appeared to have a great deal of power. Yet, this union influence derived in substantial part because the product market strategies of the employers in such key industries as steel, autos, and transportation were often not aggressive strategies driven by competition, but passive strategies driven by concentration and regulation.[3] Where there was little price and cost pressure in the product market, there was little pressure placed on the industrial relations system. This changed in the 1980's. With deregulation and competition from overseas producers, unionized firms were required to undertake aggressive product market strategies in order to survive.[4] The system that had evolved gave organized employers the right to do this with little involvement of the union if that was their desire and if the relative power of the parties permitted them to do so. It is at this point that KKM begin to analyze the changes in practices.

Summary and Conclusions

This section attempted to lay out a framework for studying industrial relations in the United States as it has evolved since 1935. It was pointed out that the societal values of individualism, private property, and minimal government intervention in the market have a profound influence on industrial relations. It was also shown how the legal regulation of industrial relations was shaped by these values, with employers having more status than unions. The industrial relations system that resulted reflected these values and that system. It also reflected, in substantial part, sheltered product markets, which permitted substantial union wage gains, as the absence of product market pressures obviated the need for employers to reduce labor costs and resist the interests of the industrial relations system.[5]

Application of the Framework to Kochan, Katz, and McKersie

Analyzing the changes that have taken place in the industrial relations system through the lens provided by the above framework, it is clear that the employer domination of industrial relations in the United States in the 1980's, so well documented by KKM, is primarily a manifestation of the higher status of employers in the industrial relations system. The changes in the product markets required employers to be innovative and to exercise their management rights. Unions, in attempting to resist, had no status in the system that would permit them to innovate free of resistance. Employers, however, had the means to innovate through their status as legal individuals exercising property rights, and used it.

This section will use the KKM volume as data to analyze the major changes in the industrial relations system in the United States in the context of this framework. In doing so, it is conceded that it is impossible to do justice to the richness of detail in the KKM study. Yet, it is believed that the general themes of the book are accurately represented.

This section will be divided into three main areas of inquiry all based on KKM: (1) an historical overview of the evolution of the industrial relations system in the United States; (2) a discussion of the strategic choice perspective on industrial relations developed by KKM; and (3) an analysis of industrial relations practices as they have developed in the 1980's.

A Historical Overview of the Evolution of the
U.S. Industrial Relations System

In discussing the historical foundations of the current collective bargaining system in the United States, KKM point out that the NLRA, which outlines the parameters and guiding principles of the system, was the embodiment of pluralism, with collective bargaining as the cornerstone. They also state that the collective bargaining system created by the NLRA was not designed to address strategic decisions made by corporations. Rather, they state, the NLRA was focused on personnel policy and industrial relations on the shop floor. In support of this position, KKM (pp. 21-28) cite (1) the standard arbitral principle that management acts and the union grieves and (2) Hoxie on business unionism.

While a reliance on the reserved rights principle is certainly appropriate, there is nothing in the wording of the Wagner Act or the Taft-Hartley Act that expressly excluded unions from involvement in strategic management decision-making. The Wagner Act did not codify what the parties were to discuss, simply incorporating 8(5), which made it unlawful for the employer to refuse to bargain with the representative of its employees. In 1947, that section, redesignated 8(a)(5), was clarified through Section 8(d), which provided that the parties must negotiate about wages, hours, and terms and conditions of employment. But that latter phrase was never defined, leaving it to the Board and the Courts to interpret the term (*NLRB v. American National Insurance*, 1952; *NLRB v. Insurance Agents International Union*, 1960).

There is no indication that when either the Wagner Act or Taft-Hartley was being debated, Congress ever considered whether corporate strategic resource allocation decisions that affected employment would be considered terms and conditions of employment and thus subject to negotiation with a union representing employees. It seems most likely that the employment model Congress had in its collective mind was a single establishment in a fixed location with a fixed group of employees. Thus, when interpreting the intent of Congress in enacting the NLRA and Taft-Hartley, one can just as easily make the claim that corporate strategic decisions that had an effect on employment would be left to the bargaining process between the employer and the employees at that site.

It is most likely that the matter of the relationship between the NLRA as amended and corporate strategic decision-making that had an effect on employment was not raised until structural changes in the product market forced corporations to reexamine their commitment to participation in their traditional markets, and their older, more mature facilities, many of which were unionized. Thus, it may be that only when management was under pressure from outside market forces and began to make business decisions that had an effect on employees was the issue joined. The bitter debate over this issue is exemplified in the controversy surrounding Fibreboard and its progeny, in which there is a strong case made that the Congress did intend the Act to cover strategic business decisions that affect employment.[6]

Nevertheless, the institutions of the industrial relations legal system were silent on the issue. Thus, at the point of conflict, the courts fell back on society's ideology of property rights to fill the void, in essence saying that U.S. society believes in reserved management rights and property rights. In the absence of clear Congressional intent to infringe upon those, they will prevail. Since it is not clear from the legislation that Congress meant to so infringe upon management rights to operate the business, they need not negotiate with the union over the employment related effects of their strategic decisions.

Thus, one can make the case that the industrial relations legal system never explicitly addressed the matter of the relationship between corporate strategic decision-making and collective bargaining. Rather, the matter was addressed and has been regulated through established legal principles of property rights.

A Strategic Choice Perspective on Industrial Relations

The major contribution of the KKM study is their development of "a strategic choice perspective on industrial relations" (p. 3). In support of that perspective, KKM point out that industrial relations practices and outcomes are shaped by interactions of environmental forces along with the strategic choices and values of American managers, union leaders, workers, and public policy decision-makers (p. 5). In trying to analyze the relationship between the environment and the parties in the 1980's, they state that

we are not arguing that labor- and product-market changes
have independent effects or operate in a unique or deterministic fashion. Rather market forces set in motion a series of
employer and union responses. It is the interaction of market
forces and the responses of employers, unions, workers, and
government policy that together determine the outcomes of
cyclical or structural changes. Our major conclusion is that
employers adapted to labor- and product-market changes in
the post-1960 period in ways that reduced their vulnerability
to unionism while unions and government policy remained
fixed in the collective bargaining model of the new deal. (p. 13)

In view of the greater status of employers vis-à-vis unions in
society, the framework discussed above would suggest that this
outcome was inevitable. The legal individuality and property rights
of employers permitted them to act strategically, as strategic actions
imply control over resources and an absence of external constraints
over choices.

Unions, on the other hand, have no such status. Indeed, fundamentally, in the industrial relations system, they have no status
independent of the employees they represent and that status is
constrained by the property rights of management. They cannot
match an employer response because the scope of their actions vis-
à-vis the employer is severely limited. Unions can only address
issues involving terms and conditions of employment as defined
under the law. Any attempt by a union to expand the scope of action
beyond the legally defined terms and conditions of employment may
be met with resistance by the employer. The employer may simply
exercise its property rights to unilaterally implement its strategic
decision, assured that the legal system will vindicate that implementation. Moreover, as the law evolved into the 1980's, some of the
most important strategic issues to management, such as plant location and investment, issues that would have a substantial effect on
employment, were not deemed to be terms and conditions of
employment and ruled outside the domain of collective bargaining
and union action.

This is the lesson of the progeny of the Fibreboard-First National
Maintenance line of cases. If, as KKM state, unions remain fixed in
the New Deal model, it may be because the legal system that gives
them status is a New Deal system. Moreover, employers have an
interest in keeping them there, and the government has not seen fit
to change it. Employers are inherently flexible through their legal
structure and because there is little institutional opposition to their
actions. Unions, on the other hand, are inherently inflexible vis-à-

vis employers with their constrained legal status. They have institutional resistance, in the form of employers, to increasing their status.

Building on their notion of strategic choice, KKM introduce the three-tier notion of industrial relations activity (pp. 15-20). They claim there exists a long-term strategy policy making top tier, a collective bargaining and personnel policy middle tier, and a workplace organization lower tier. They say that employers, unions, and government each participate in the three tiers. This analysis seems to be an attempt to parallel employers, unions, and government; to fit unions and government into the employer's industrial relations structure. Yet, with some exceptions, neither unions nor government have a substantial impact on the strategy and policy making of the employer. That level is unfettered except for legal constraints. Under the industrial relations system in the United States, union long-term strategy is generally not aimed at firm strategy. Rather it is targeted at levels above and below the firm strategic level; at government policy and at the collective bargaining policy/personnel policy of the firms that are in its jurisdiction.

Accordingly, it would seem that a more accurate representation of the notions conveyed in KKM Table 1 (p. 17) would be depicted as in Table 1 of this essay. The major differences between this framework and the KKM framework are at the two levels above firm-level personnel policy and collective bargaining. There is very little union or governmental presence at the strategic level of the corporation. The union has been removed from this level by the law, and the principle of governmental nonintervention means that the government will not be a great check on employer strategic decision-making except to the extent that it violates anti-trust law.

This table also adds a public policy level above the strategic level. Employers, unions, and government operate in this arena as well, all pursuing their self-interest. Employers and unions each attempt to obtain public policy decisions that will aid them; employers vis-à-vis unions and other constituents (consumers, government, competitors), unions vis-à-vis employers and, on occasion, individual employees. Government is not necessarily a neutral party, as it will attempt to accommodate to the shifting political consensus to further its own interest in staying in power.

The United States Industrial System in Practice

The bulk of the KKM book explores changing practices in the industrial relations system, examining the growth of the nonunion industrial relations system, the processes and outcomes of negotia-

TABLE 1

LEVEL (of what actor)	EMPLOYERS	UNIONS	GOVERNMENT
Macro, national, societal level political policy	political activities in self-interest	political activities in self-interest	laws and regulations based on changing political consensus
Organizational strategic level	KKM	no institutionalized cell occupant; generally an empty cell (exceptions: UAW-GM neut pact, ALPH-UAL, Acustar	anti-trust policy
Personnel Policy, collective bargaining	KKM	KKM	KKM
workplace	KKM	KKM	KKM

tions, changing workplace industrial relations in the unionized sector, union attempts to engage corporations at the strategic level, and the views of workers on industrial relations systems. Each of these will be examined in this subsection.

The Growth of the Nonunion Industrial Relations System. In examining the growth of the nonunion industrial relations system in the United States at the same time that the unionized sector is declining, KKM look to changes in managerial values as indicated by the rise in influence of human resources staffs as compared to labor relations, greater attention given by chief executives to the employment function, more influence given to line managers, and management attention, and union inattention, to the behavioral sciences. They also discuss the disproportionate number of nonunion plants among new facilities and a general investment away from unionized facilities by once-unionized firms. This they attribute to the greater flexibility of nonunion (flexible, individualistic) plant industrial relations vis-à-vis union (rigid, legalistic, uniform) plant industrial relations. They note that nonunion plants have lower labor costs and appear to retain greater flexibility than unionized plants, encouraging disinvestment, over time, in the unionized sector of the firm (pp. 47-108).

The broader question suggested by these changes is not how corporations were able to stay nonunion or reduce union coverage among their employees, or even why they did it. Rather, the important question is what characteristics of the industrial relations system permitted corporations to pursue their interests at the expense of the interests of unions representing their employees? One answer may be that the industrial relations system described above makes it possible, if not inevitable, for corporations to pursue such a strategy.

Firms that were nonunion in the late 1950's could easily stay nonunion by using the plethora of weapons that had been given employers as a result of interpretations of the NLRA and the new tools of Human Resources Management (HRM) and the behavioral sciences (Foulkes, 1980). As for unionized firms, they need not have necessarily pursued a conscious strategy of union avoidance. Rather, the evidence is also consistent with the proposition that plant and product decisions were made in response to changes in the product market, and the company took the opportunity to reduce union penetration by establishing new, nonunion plants and by investing in new, modern plant and equipment away from the union (Block & McLennan, 1985; Verma & Kochan, 1985).

Thus, the shift to nonunion facilities was as much a function of the status of the parties as company nonunion strategy. Companies could deunionize because the industrial relations legal system permitted them to do so by giving them unilateral decision-making authority in matters of capital investment and limiting the union to the employees and work at a particular site. Those employees had no right to negotiate over these corporate decisions that would have an impact on their employment, if not in the short run, then in the long run by moving the most modern facilities in the company away from the union. It is the high value that the industrial relations system places on managerial freedom and the weak value associated with union protection of employee interests that permits corporations to pursue production and market strategies free of union influence. This discussion is also consistent with the revision of KKM in Table 1 shown above. The company-union intersection at the strategic level is, in essence, an empty cell.

The Process and Outcomes of Collective Bargaining Negotiations. In examining the process and outcomes and collective bargaining negotiations, KKM address three major questions. First, they ask have wage outcomes deviated significantly in the 1980's from post-World War II trends (p. 111)? The answer, however, is obvious, as it is quite clear that they have; although the reduction in inflation makes it likely that the real wage loss in the unionized sector is less then it might appear to be. More important, however, the moderating of wage increases is precisely what would be expected in the face of product market pressures. It is well established that a fundamental determinant of wages is the product market and the extent to which the union can organize it (Commons, 1976; Kochan & Block, 1977; Mishel, 1986). Product markets were generally sheltered in the organized sector, and unions had been successful in taking wages out of competition. The product market had changed by the early 1980's, however. With the shelters removed, and the entrance of nonunion and/or foreign competitors, the relevant product markets were no longer organized. Thus, there was increased pressure on wages. The fundamentals of the industrial relations system began to come into play, with actions on the part of employers to reduce costs, and unions conceding in an attempt to save jobs, consistent with their inherent flexibility and focus on job security (Perlman, 1966, pp. 237-253).

The second question asked by KKM (pp. 111-112) is what has changed? Their answer is unclear. It seems they are saying that management is more aggressive than they were in the past. But it may be that management is simply in a position to pursue its interests more strongly than in the past. In response to product market pressures, employers made decisions on business strategy that were deemed to be outside the boundaries of the employment relationship and collective bargaining. Only if the strategy necessitated negotiating with the union was the union a relevant actor. But the point is that the major decisions occurred outside of the industrial relations system as defined, providing the union little input into the decisions.

The third question (p. 112) is are these universal developments? The KKM answer is "no," which supports the notion of diversity inherent in the 1935 industrial relations system. In discussing bargaining structure and process changes, KKM first talk about decentralization of bargaining, citing steel, trucking, and autos as examples. Yet, the auto industry has recentralized its bargaining structure. Even when it was negotiating separately with Chrysler during the early 1980's the UAW never conceded that it would accept differential contracts among the Big Three in the long run. In the 1988 negotiations with Chrysler, the UAW completed the process, begun in 1984, of returning to the traditional auto industry bargaining structure of complete parity among GM, Ford, and Chrysler (Block & McLennan, 1985, pp. 352-354; Fogel, Lupo & Spelich, 1987; Fogel & Spelich, 1988; Lipert & Lupo, 1988; Lupo & Lipert, 1988; Schlesinger, 1988).

The discussion of broader corporate involvement in the IR function on management's side and attempts by management to provide more information for workers (pp. 131-134) is interesting but simply shows how external pressures from the product market forced management to look at costs in the IR function more closely than in the past. From an IR point of view, it might seem new because IR researchers have always viewed the IR system as separate and somehow different from other management functions in the firm. But due to competitive pressures, management did not see it that way. This suggests that the sheltered markets in the post-World War II era in the U.S. made it unnecessary for management to pay a great deal of attention to costs in the industrial relations system, provided those costs were equal to those of their competitors. With the decline of sheltered markets, management began to pay attention to those costs. They could be reduced by resistance or cooperation, depending on how management viewed the situation, again suggesting the diversity that can result from a decentralized IR system.

KKM discuss the decline in the use of strikes as a weapon (pp. 134-137), but, consistent with the pragmatic nature of business unionism, unions have been willing to use other tactics to force employers toward their position. The strategies of the Air Line Pilots Association (ALPA) and the United Steelworkers at Allegis/United Air Lines and Wheeling-Pittsburgh Steel Corporation, respectively, are examples (Block, Kliener, Roomkin, & Salsberg, 1987, p. 340). Recently, ALPA has been a major player in the negotiations over what will happen to Pan Am (Agins, 1988a, 1988b, 1988c; Agins & Brown, 1987; Move over Boone, 1987). This suggests that while strikes have been a traditional weapon, they are not the only weapon available to unions, and that, consistent with the pragmatic nature of business unionism, a union will use whatever it can to protect the interests of its members.

The Schneider Transport case, cited by KKM (pp. 134-137), is a case in point of a use of the established system. Product market factors (deregulation) forced the company to rethink its mode of operations in labor relations. Since there was no true institutionalization of the union in company decision-making, management could change part of its operations to independent contractors in 1982 without negotiating with the union. The law permitted the company to implement their HRM-type personnel practices with little objection from the union, with the union eventually agreeing to separate negotiations outside the National Motor Freight Agreement. Schneider Transport represents a superb illustration of what can happen in a decentralized industrial relations system dominated by management.

Changing Workplace Industrial Relations in Unionized Settings. If there has been a transformation of industrial relations in the United States, it would be expected to manifest itself at the workplace and to maintain itself over time. Thus, KKM attempt to document some of the major new workplace initiatives that have occurred over the last decade (pp. 146-177).

Many of the new initiatives that have occurred can be subsumed under the rubric "quality of worklife" (QWL). KKM discuss the history of QWL and the marginal estimated effects of QWL on product quality and labor efficiency in two unionized auto plants (pp. 146-157). These results suggest that the benefits of QWL may not be perceived by the parties as being worth the potential compromise to their internal integrity. The union is interested in protecting its members and management is interested in furthering the interests of the shareholders.

KKM's discussion of changes in the collective bargaining relationship between Xerox and the Amalgamated Clothing and Textile Workers Union (pp. 162-168) indicates the importance of job security guarantees. Their analysis indicates that while QWL may have served as the vehicle by which the agreement could be reached, job security is still the key to obtaining union cooperation. The 1984, 1985, 1987, and 1988 auto agreements which contained job security guarantees are further evidence of this.

The discussion of QWL suggests that Commons and Perlman have much to say about what is occurring in industrial relations. Commons points out the importance of the product market in collective bargaining. Unions, he says, want to take wages out of competition, essentially requiring employers to compete in the product market on some basis other than wages. The notion is that the union is attempting to insulate itself from the vagaries and uncertainties of the product market. This is the basis of job security agreements. The union is providing the company with the capability of adjusting its labor requirements to the product market while, at the same time, minimizing the effects of those adjustments on its membership. In other words, through job security guarantees, the union is attempting to do what Commons said it did through organizing all suppliers of the product—insulating its members from the product market.

Perlman and the notion of scarcity consciousness and work rules is also important here. Perlman stresses the concern of workers about rules that will maximize employment opportunity and attachment to the firm. This, in essence, is what unions are doing through job security provisions. Consistent with the notion of the importance of job security, the December 1984 Packard Electric-IUE wage concessions and employee involvement in business decisions, discussed by KKM (pp. 168-171), had as its foundation enhanced job security provisions. Again, we see that what is happening can be explained through traditional collective bargaining theories, frameworks, and assumptions. This further reinforces the notion that what KKM discuss is not a transformation, but simply an aspect of the evolution of the industrial relations system that was created in the United States between 1935 and 1955.

KKM also discuss less successful examples of QWL. They attribute the lack of success of Labor Management Participation Teams (LMPT's) at U.S. Steel and Jones and Laughlin (now LTV Steel) to the decisions of the companies to adopt a strategy of technological change and workforce reduction to improve its competitive position through productivity increases and cost decreases (pp. 171-173). The important point here, however, is that there were no job security promises, thus the QWL process floundered, as there was nothing for the union to gain. The employer's interest in shifting resources out of steel production was the driving force in the industrial relations system. Given the worldwide overcapacity in steel in the early 1980's and the general technological backwardness of the unionized integrated steel companies in the United States (Barnett & Schorsch, 1983), this was a rational strategy, from the point of view of management and the stockholders. But it was not a strategy that would foster a successful QWL program or collective bargaining innovations. If the union would give up some of its internal integrity through new collective bargaining innovations, it must gain something; that is, enhanced job security. In the absence of enhanced job security, there is nothing in it for them.[7]

Union Engagement of Strategic Business Decisions. In discussing union involvement in corporate business decisions, KKM discuss the difficulty that has been encountered when unions attempt to become involved in corporate business strategy. KKM state this is because of mind sets growing out of the New Deal collective bargaining system (pp. 178-180). Yet, such difficulty is precisely what would be expected if the industrial relations system conformed to that outlined above. The barriers to greater union involvement are more fundamental and structural than simply attitudinal; rather they derive from the nature and status of unions and management in the industrial relations system as it has evolved.

Unions and management each have their own constituency. Management is responsible to the shareholders and unions to their membership. Since, at its basis, the employment relationship is an exchange, market transaction, there is a fundamental conflict of interest between employees and shareholders. Other things equal, higher wages, greater benefits and more employment security increase the cost of doing business, thus resulting in lower profits for the shareholders. Because unions represent employees, and management is hired to act in the interest of shareholders, to the extent that the union appears to become involved in management decision-making, there is the potential of being perceived, correctly or not, as acting in the interests of the shareholders and contrary to the interests of its constituency. Similarly, management, because it represents the interests of shareholders, is reluctant to share power with employees, a group whose interests might be antithetical to that of management.

The industrial relations system is built upon this conflict of interest, and the actors in the system act in a way that is consistent with this system. Therefore, to share power in management decisions is a rare occurrence mainly because it is inconsistent with the legal statuses of the parties to collective bargaining.

Thus, it is not simply attitudes that have made it difficult for the union to become involved in corporate business decisions. Flexible, business unionism would be able to overcome these attitudes and share power if it were in the best interests of the union membership. Corporate management clearly has the authority to involve the union in corporate decision-making if it believed that it was in the best interest of the shareholders. The fact that there is such a reluctance on the part of the both parties suggests that such power sharing is inconsistent with the institutional structure of the industrial relations system.

Relying on quotes from union leaders, KKM suggest that there is some realization on the part of union leaders that they must influence strategic management business decisions (pp. 181-182). Yet, the system makes it difficult for them to do this. The national retail food industry joint committee has been limited to broad questions that might have an effect on employee relations, but has not been able to address either underlying structural problems of erosion of market share of unionized firms and local, store-wide issues (KKM, pp. 182-187). This may be not only because the collective bargaining system cannot address these issues, but because the market for retail food is primarily local rather than national (despite the prevalence of national and regional chains), limiting what can be addressed at the national level to industry level problems (health and safety, pensions, effects of technological change). This example again demonstrates how the product market drives the industrial relations system.

The Tailored Clothing Technology Corporation and its joint experimentation with a sleeve making machine is closer than the other examples to union involvement in corporate strategic decision-making (KKM, pp. 187-189), but clothing manufacturing has traditionally been a special case in industrial relations. Union involvement in stabilizing the industry goes back to the 1920's as a result of the large number of small employers in the industry (Millis & Montgomery, 1945, pp. 404-407). This phenomenon, which is simply a manifestation of the basic product market characteristic of ease of entry, still exists today in the context of imports. The major threat to the American clothing industry is from low-priced low-wage imports that are not produced by the American firms (Block & McLennan, 1985). Thus, American firms and the clothing union have joined together in an attempt to limit imports.

Other cases discussed by KKM also support the enduring nature of the traditional statuses of the parties. The general employee disinterest in board representation described by KKM in their discussion of Western Airlines (pp. 191-193) indicates the strength of the traditional system defined by the legal statuses of the parties. There was reluctance on the part of the employees to act in a way that is inconsistent with this status. In some sense, they wanted what unions have traditionally wanted—more monetary compensation, in this case through profit sharing, since wage increases were not tenable. This suggests that unions do not forget that they represent their membership, who are not owners, and that the notion of conflict of interest is still deeply embedded in the system. Institutional status is still crucial.

KKM's discussion of the Teamsters' stock ownership principles for troubled over-the-road trucking companies (pp. 193-195) also indicates the reluctance of unions to give up their traditional status. The principles operate on the basis of limited engagement. The Teamsters seem to prefer that management run the business. The KKM discussion of the Litton industries' corporate campaign ends with the point that the union was unable to affect basic business strategies of Litton (pp. 195-197).

The KKM discussion of the Fiero plant labor relations (pp. 198-199) is interesting but, of necessity, does not address the March, 1988 announcement that the plant will close in August, 1988 (Lippert). Whether or not GM and the union can develop a plan to permit the plant to remain open represents a major test of the new relationship between GM and the UAW.

American Workers and Industrial Relations Institutions. KKM discuss survey results of attitudes of American workers on industrial relations institutions. Although much of this discussion does not address systemic questions and is outside the scope of this paper, one point seems relevant. They state that surveys indicate that American workers are essentially pragmatic in their approach to jobs; they are interested in strategic issues just so long as they can help to attain specific goals they want (pp. 210-213). Thus American workers are instrumental in their views of industrial relations institutions and practices. In this sense, traditional pragmatism of American unions is consistent with this worker view. The American labor movement, as represented by the AFL, succeeded (existed) by being nonideological and pragmatic.

This suggests that there is still much to be learned from Perlman's notion of organic labor. Unions are democratic institutions and represent the views of their membership. To the extent that workers are reluctant about worker/union involvement in corporate decision-making, unions would be expected to be reluctant about it.

Conclusion

The fundamental point of this paper is that the industrial relations practices that have developed over the last ten years and that have been identified by KKM as a transformation in industrial relations are primarily a result of the evolution of the industrial relations system that was established in 1935 and the adaptation of this system to a change from sheltered product markets to competitive product markets. If this is true, then it is reasonable to believe that it will require a fundamental alteration in the institutions of the industrial relations system if the United States is to move away from employer dominance of industrial relations.

It is appropriate to apply this notion to KKM's conclusions. KKM assume that American firms will continue to be under intense competition, and that they will tend to be high wage, high cost producers who must rely on technology to provide a competitive edge. Unions will be unable to take wages out of competition by organizing the product market, since product markets often cross international boundaries. KKM also believe that broader participation in decision-making makes more sense than less participation, given the fact that the market changes and the technological responses cut across all levels of the firm (pp. 227-230).

Drawing on the framework of employer dominance discussed in the paper, it should be pointed out that more employee participation may make sense from an objective point of view, but it may or may not make sense from the point of view of the firm depending on the firm's situation. Firms that have chosen a strategic response that involves labor are more likely to need employee participation and cooperation than firms that have chosen a different strategic response. Thus, KKM do not address the more fundamental question of whether or not workers' jobs should depend on the employer's perception of its interest.

In discussing updating the goals of national labor policy, KKM state that flexibility is more important than stability (p. 231). Yet one might also say that institutionalizing unionism through stability will lead to flexibility. A union is more likely to be flexible to the extent its leadership believes that its institutional security will not be threatened. We need stability in the status of unions so that there can be flexibility within individual relationships.

Most of the KKM discussion on reforming the election process deals with the remedies for activity that is currently illegal (pp. 233-234). Yet, it is clear that election activity that is legal also strongly favors employer interests by giving employers greater status in the system. They also discuss legal impediments to labor-management cooperation created by the NLRA (pp. 234-236). It should be noted, however, that the 1986 U.S. Department of Labor report on labor-management cooperation showed that the Board and Courts have been able to distinguish between true employee participation and "participation" that is really dominance (U.S. Labor Law, 1986).

In this regard, however, an important question is whether the law is simply objective or whether it is what the parties make it through their activities and challenges in the legal system. In general, it can be argued that the decentralized NLRA collective bargaining system can accommodate these individual differences in representation provided that it is structured in such a way so that the union and the employer have equal status regarding matters of employment.

This suggests the importance of institutionalizing unions as an essential actor in a pluralistic industrial relations system. Flexible unionism presupposes secure unionism. If we truly want union flexibility to meet the needs of the firm, we need management willingness to recognize the union's legitimacy to meet the needs of the union and its members. This may take society forcing management to accept the legitimacy of unions as a legitimate actor in the firm's industrial relations system where the union represents employees and as at least a potential representative of employees in other situations.

KKM point out that partially unionized firms can either continue to slowly deunionize by investing away from the union or can invest in the union sector by obtaining cooperation from the union (pp. 242-245). In the absence of external (that is, legal) pressure the firm is unlikely to move toward the union unless its strategy so dictates. Again, because of the empty cell at the strategic level, the firm drives the system.

In their discussion of the impact of competition on the human resource policies of nonunion firms, they point out that in firms in which Human Resources (HR) executives have influence and in which HR policies are deeply ingrained in corporate values, there will be concern for employees' interests (KKM, p. 246). But this is not necessarily the case for other firms. Again, this raises the question of whether the interests of employees should be subject to the random occurrence of HR-oriented values among employers. Employees of such employers will not need a union, but employees in other firms might. It is important that there be a viable union option.

It is unlikely that firms that currently have enlightened HR policies will shift away from such policies even in the absence of a viable union option. Rather, in the absence of a viable union option, it is most likely that firms will have less incentive to pay attention to employee interests. A series of marginal decisions will be made that are adverse to employee's interest. In metaphorical terms, the fabric of HRM policies would not be immediately cut into little pieces. Rather, there would be a continual fraying of the edges and unraveling. But, over time, the result could be the same. There will simply be less concern for the interests of employees, and more concern for the interests of other corporate constituencies in many small corporate decisions.

Finally, KKM discuss four scenarios for the future of the United

States industrial relations system: (1) continuation of current trends; (2) labor law reform of the type proposed in 1977-78; (3) diffusion of labor-management innovations; and (4) new organizing strategies (pp. 250-253). In the absence of a substantial change in the status of unions, scenario 1 is most likely, and scenario 3 unlikely since there is no incentive for nonparticipants to accept the changes. Scenario 4 is unlikely to be successful, given the current status of unions. Scenario 2, as they say, will not make a great deal of difference by itself.

If unions are to remain a viable option for unrepresented employees and a major actor in the industrial relations system, we must develop a legal system in which the union and the employer have equal status in addressing issues that are crucial to both of them. It seems unlikely that a strong vigorous labor movement that represents the collective interests of employees can thrive under a system in which the greatest status is given to individual and property rights. Fundamental changes in the legal system are necessary if unions are to be made a coequal actor with corporations in the industrial relations system.

Notes

1. This notion has grown out of discussions between the author and Professor Myron Roomkin of Northwestern University.
2. The basic framework to be used in this subpart is derived from Dunlop (1970).
3. There were exceptions. During the 1970's, the apparel and textiles industries were driven by imports, and the rubber tire industry was driven by the development of the radial tire. See Block and McLennan (1985), and Karper (1987).
4. These phenomena are quite similar to the widening of the market described by Commons in his classic "shoemakers" article (1976).
5. This discussion has focused, in part, on the legal system for regulation of the employment relationship through collective bargaining. The employment relationship can also be regulated by laws protecting the individual rights of employees. Laws barring discrimination on the basis of race, gender, age, etc. are examples of this type of regulation. Such regulation, increasingly common in the United States, is based on an individualistic model of the employment relationship, consistent with the theme of individualism discussed above. It is also consistent with the concept of reserved management rights; management may do what it wishes unless there is legislation barring such action. See the discussion above.
6. See, for example, Justice Brennan's dissent in *First National Maintenance Corporation v. NLRB* (1981).

7. In the auto industry, which has tended to move toward more cooperative relations with the UAW, the union has been able to use the possibility of withdrawal from cooperative programs as a weapon. In March of 1988, Chrysler abandoned an attempt to sell Acustar, its parts subsidiary, when the UAW strongly objected. Among the weapons the UAW used was a threat to withdraw from cooperative programs. See, for example, Fogel & Lupo (1988a, 1988b, 1988c); Fogel, Lippert, Lupo & Spelich (1988); Fogel, Lupo & Spelich (1988a, 1988b); Spelich (1988).

References

Agins, T. (1988, January 6). Pan Am may get labor cost concessions; Changes in senior management planned. *The Wall Street Journal*, p. 2.

Agins, T. (1988, January 11). Federal mediators expected to release Pan Am, Teamsters from contract talks. *The Wall Street Journal*, p. 4.

Agins, T. (1988, January 13). Pan Am expects '87 loss to top prior estimates. *The Wall Street Journal*, p. 6.

Agins, T., & Brown, F.C. (1987, December 24). Merger proposal with Braniff fails; Pan Am renews effort for concessions. *The Wall Street Journal*, p. 2.

Atleson, B. (1983). *Values and Assumptions in Labor Law*. Amherst: University of Massachusetts Press.

Barnett, D.F., & Schorsch, L. (1983). *Steel: Upheaval in a Basic Industry*. Cambridge, MA: Ballanger.

Bellah, R.N.; Madsen, R.; Sullivan, W.M.; Swidler, A.; & Tipton, S.T. (1985). *Habits of the Heart: Individualism and Commitment in American Life*. Berkeley: University of California Press.

Block, R.N.; Kleiner, M.M.; Roomkin, M.; & Salsburg, S.W. (1987). Industrial relations and the performance of the firm: An overview. *In* M.M. Kleiner, R.N. Block, M. Roomkin, & S.W. Salsburg (eds.), *Human Resources and the Performance of the Firm*. Madison, WI: Industrial Relations Research Association.

Block, R.N., & McLennan, K. (1985). Structural change and industrial relations in the United States' manufacturing and transportation sectors since 1973. *In* H. Juris, M. Thompson, & W. Daniels (eds.), *Industrial Relations in a Decade of Economic Change* (pp. 337-382). Madison, WI: Industrial Relations Research Association.

Block, R.N., & Wolkinson, B.W. (1986). Delay in union election campaign revisited: A theoretical and empirical analysis. *In* D.B. Lipsky & D. Lewin (eds.), *Advances in Industrial and Labor Relations, 3*. Greenwich, CT: JAI Press.

Block, R.N; Wolkinson, B.W.; & Kuhn, J.W. (1988). Some are more equal than others: The relative status of employers, unions, and employees in the law of union organizing. *Industrial Relations Law Journal, 10*.

Capelli, P. (1987). Airlines. *In* D.B. Lipsky & C.B. Donn (eds.), *Collective bargaining in American Industry*. Lexington, MA: Lexington Books.

Chamberlain, N.W., & Kuhn, J.W. (1986). *Collective Bargaining.* 3rd ed. New York: McGraw-Hill.

Commons, J.R. (1976). American shoemakers, 1648-1895. *In* R.J. Rowan (ed.), *Readings in Labor Economics and Labor Relations,* (3rd ed.) Homewood, IL: Irwin.

Dunlop, J.T. (1970). *Industrial Relations Systems.* Carbondale: Southern Illinois University Press. (Original work published 1958).

Ex-Cell-O Corp., 185 NLRB 107 (1970).

Fibreboard Paper Products *v.* NLRB, 379 U.S. 203 (1964).

First National Maintenance Corp. *v.* NLRB, 452 U.S. 666 (1981).

Fogel, H.; Lippert, J.; Lupo, N.; & Spelich, J. (1988, March 4). Chrysler Corporation to keep Acustar, dump 4 plants. *Detroit Free Press,* p. 1A.

Fogel, H., & Lupo, N. (1988, February 5). Iacocca says Acustar may be sold. *Detroit Free Press,* p. 4B.

Fogel, H., & Lupo, N. (1988, February 11). Locals warn Chrysler on Acustar sale. *Detroit Free Press,* p. 1A.

Fogel, H., & Lupo, N. (1988, February 18). Strikes planned to protest sale of Acustar. *Detroit Free Press,* p. 5C.

Fogel, H.; Lupo, N.; & Spelich, J. (1987, October 9). GM, UAW reach tentative contract. *Detroit Free Press,* p. 1A.

Fogel, H.; Lupo, N.; & Spelich, J. (1988, March 4). UAW claims victory in Chrysler's decision. *Detroit Free Press,* p. 17A.

Fogel, H.; Lupo, N.; & Spelich, J. (1988, March 6). Acustar: Chrysler blinked. *Detroit Free Press,* p. 1H.

Fogel, H., & Spelich, J. (1988, September 18). Ford guarantees jobs for 104,000 workers. *Detroit Free Press,* p. 1A.

Foulkes, F. (1980). Large nonunionized employers. *In* J. Stieber, R.B. McKersie, & D.Q. Mills (eds.), *U.S. Industrial Relations 1950-1980: A Critical Assessment* (pp. 129-157). Madison, WI: Industrial Relations Research Association.

Galbraith, J.K. (1967). *The New Industrial State.* New York: Signet Books.

H.K. Porter Co. *v.* NLRB, 397 U.S. 99 (1970).

Karper, M.D. (1987). Tires. *In* D.B. Lipsky & C.B. Donn (eds.), *Collective Bargaining in American Industry.* Lexington, MA: Lexington Books.

Katz, H.C. (1987). Automobiles. *In* D.B. Lipsky & C.B. Donn (eds.), *Collective Bargaining in American Industry.* Lexington, MA: Lexington Books.

Kochan, T.A., & Block, R. (1977). An interindustry analysis of bargaining outcomes; Preliminary evidence from two-digit industries. *Quarterly Journal of Economics, 91*(3).

Kochan, T.A.; Katz, H.C.; & McKersie, R.B. (1986). *The Transformation of American Industrial Relations.* New York: Basic Books.

Lewin, D., & Lipsky, D.B. (1985). Current research on industrial relations regulations, bargaining, theory, progressive discipline, and occupational influences on unionism. *In* D.B. Lipsky & D. Lewin (eds.), *Advances in Industrial and Labor Relations, 3.* Greenwich, CT: JAI Press.

Lippert, J. (1988, March 2). GM to idle Fiero plant kill model. *Detroit Free Press*, p. 1A.

Lippert, J., & Lupo, N. (1988, May 8). UAW and big three score. *Detroit Free Press*, p. 1F.

Lipsky, D.B., & Donn, C.B. (eds.). (1987). *Collective Bargaining in American Industry*. Lexington, MA: Lexington Books.

Livingston Shirt Corp., 107 NLRB 400, 33 LRRM 1156 (1953).

Lupo, N., & Lippert, J. (1988, May 5). Chrysler, UAW reach agreement. *Detroit Free Press*, p. 1A.

Marx, K. (1967). *Capital vol. 1. A Critical Analysis of Production*. New York: International Publishers.

Millis, H.A., & Montgomery, R.E. (1945). *The Economics of Labor: Volume III Organized Labor*. (pp. 404-407). New York: McGraw-Hill.

Mishel, J. (1986). The structural determinants of union bargaining power. *Industrial and Labor Relations Review, 40*.

Move over Boone, Carl and Irv—Here comes labor. (1987, December 14). *Business Week*, p. 124.

NLRB *v.* American National Insurance Co., 343 U.S. 345 (1952).

NLRB *v.* Babcock and Wilcox Co., 351 U.S. 105 (1956).

NLRB *v.* Clark Bros. Co., Inc., 163 F.2d 373 (CA 2, 1947).

NLRB *v.* Clearwater Finishing Co., 203 F.2d. 93B, 32 LRRM 2084 (CA 4, 1953).

NLRB *v.* Insurance Agents International Union, 361 U.S. 477 (1960).

NLRB *v.* Jones and Laughlin Steel Corp., 301 U.S. 1, 33 (1937).

NLRB *v.* Truck Drivers Local 449 ("Buffalo Linen"), 353 U.S. 87 (1957).

NLRB *v.* Virginia Electric and Power Co., 314 U.S. 469, 9 LRRM 405 (1941).

Perlman, S. (1966). *A Theory of the Labor Movement*. New York: M. Kelley. (Original work published 1929.)

Schlesinger, J. (1988, October 9). GM, UAW reach tentative pact; Officials say it is similar to Fords'. *The Wall Street Journal*, p. 2.

Sockell, D. (1986). The scope of mandatory bargaining: A critique and a proposal. *Industrial and Labor Relations Review, 40*.

Spelich, J. (1988, March 5). Chrysler turned downed $1 billion of Acustar. *Detroit Free Press*, p. 1A.

Steelworkers Local 2179 *v.* NLRB ("Inland Steel Container Co.") 822 F.2d. 559, 125 LRRM 3313, (CA 5, 1987).

Taft, P. (1952). Theories of the labor movement. *In* G.W. Brooks, M. Derber, D.A. McCabe, & P. Taft (eds.), *Interpreting the Labor Management Movement*. Madison, WI: Industrial Relations Research Association.

United Technologies, 269 NLRB 891 (1984).

U.S. Labor Law and the future of labor management cooperation, BLMR 104, Bureau of Cooperative Labor-Management Relations, U.S. Department of Labor, 1986.

Verma, A., & Kochan, T.A. (1985). The growth and nature of the nonunion sector within a firm. *In* T.A. Kochan (ed.), *Challenges and Choices Facing American Labor*. (pp. 89-117). Cambridge, MA: MIT Press.

COMMENTS ON BLOCK'S ANALYSIS

James E. Martin

I AM PLEASED TO BE A discussant of the paper "American Industrial Relations in the 1980's: Transformation or Evolution?" by Richard N. Block (1990, chap. 2), which examines the book, *The Transformation of American Industrial Relations*, by Thomas Kochan, Harry Katz, and Robert McKersie (KKM), 1986. In their book, KKM argue that the massive changes in industrial relations that they document are a transformation, while Block argues that such changes represent an evolution. Block has placed himself in an unenviable position. In less than 50 pages, he attempts to lay out a framework for understanding industrial relations, analyzes the approximately 250 pages of the KKM book, and presents some conclusions concerning the future of the industrial relations system in the United States. Given that Block analyzes the KKM book in some detail, discussing material from every chapter, I am in a rather difficult position of being a discussant of a discussant. I will attempt to present and evaluate the relative strengths of some of the major positions where Block and KKM differ.

Block's definition of a transformation as "a fundamental alteration in the way industrial relations is conducted" can be understood in his example of the "transformation" which occurred in industrial relations in this country with the passage of the National Labor Relations Act. His basic thesis is that the practices and trends identified by KKM as part of a major change in industrial relations did not represent a transformation, but rather were "the inevitable result of the impact of product market changes on the industrial relations/ collective bargaining system that was established in 1935 and continues to *evolve*" [emphasis added]. In contrast, KKM argue:

> the changes which occurred in the early 1980s reflect deep-seated environmental pressures that had been building up

gradually as well as organizational strategies that had been evolving quietly for a number of years. Moreover, we shall argue that to fully understand and interpret current developments requires a fundamental rethinking of industrial relations theories and a broadening of the scope of what managers, union leaders, and government policy makers traditionally envision as the domain of industrial relations professional activity (p. 4).

To shed light on the Block-KKM differences, it is useful to discuss what would be a transformation of industrial relations as opposed to an evolution. In my opinion, examples of three transformations, that is radical rapid changes in both the nature and environment of industrial relations, would be: 1) European style laws mandating co-determination; 2) laws outlawing collective bargaining; or 3) laws mandating collective bargaining. Examples of changes that are evolutions of industrial relations, that is, changes that move it further along paths it has already started, can be found in the conclusion of the KKM book. In that conclusion they discuss four plausible scenarios as to what may occur in the future to U.S. industrial relations. They identify the four alternatives as: 1) continuation of the current trends; 2) labor law reform similar to what was proposed in 1977-78; 3) diffusion of labor management innovations; and 4) new organizing strategies, as part of a potential continuing "evolution" of industrial relations. As each of these four scenarios represents movement along the paths upon which various facets of industrial relations have already been shifting, they would each be an evolution. Thus, I agree with Block's assessment that what KKM have discussed is an evolution of industrial relations and not a transformation.

Both Block and KKM conclude that management now has the dominant role in the industrial relations system. However, they appear to differ in their views of how management arrived at that position. Block argues that it always was that way under the framework that he describes in the beginning of his paper, where "all rights are reserved to the employer except what legislation or common law has removed from it." Under a sheltered product market, before strong foreign competition and deregulation become factors, Block argued management had passive product market strategies. With the changes in the 1980's, management had to undertake aggressive product market strategies in order to survive. He concludes this portion of his paper with the argument that the industrial relations system that had evolved gave employers who desired to do so the right to undertake massive changes with little union involvement if the relative power of the two parties permitted them to do this. In contrast, KKM argue that a shift took place, and that this shift was attributable in large part to a change in the implementation of different managerial values. KKM document this shift in their Chapter 3, "The Emergence of the Nonunion Industrial Relations System." They argue that line management (as opposed to industrial relations managers) always preferred to operate in a nonunion setting, and that "changes in the environment since 1960 served gradually to increase both the opportunities and the economic incentives for firms to act on these preferences" (p. 65). With such opportunities, KKM noted that the power of line managers over human resource management issues increased. The KKM view, however, is not inconsistent with Block's view, as KKM also discuss changes in the product market structure which then affected strategic business decisions. While I tend to agree more with Block's viewpoint, I believe he might have strengthened his paper by including greater discussion of the nonunion sector, as it currently appears to be strongly affecting the unionized sector.

Block further argues that the system continues to evolve. A persuasive example Block uses is related to the KKM discussion of the changes in the usage of strikes as a weapon in collective bargaining in Chapter 5. KKM note that the number of strikes have declined, there has been a change in strike outcomes, and the way in which strikes are conducted has changed. While KKM may have taken these changes in strike activity as a result of the transformation of industrial relations, Block suggests that in many situations, strikes have been replaced by other union weapons. Block sees that as being consistent with the pragmatic nature of business unionism, with a union using whatever tools it can to protect the members' interests. Thus the United Automobile Workers could threaten to withdraw from the Quality of Work Life projects at Chrysler if the company sold its Acustar parts subsidiary. This example and the others referenced by Block appear to be the evolution of a union strategy with different tactics, rather than a transformation.

Other papers presented at this conference also discuss major changes in industrial relations which can be analyzed in light of the Block-KKM differences. For example, Roomkin and Juris (1990, Chap. 5) discuss trends in the steel industry that appear to have continuing effects on the industrial relations system in that industry. Their analysis suggests that if the protective tariffs which act to restrict steel imports were to be removed, one result would be a massive change in industrial relations in that industry. While such a change might be considered as a transformation by some industrial relations scholars, Block would not consider it a transformation because it would only represent an example of product market changes driving the industrial relations system.

In summary, Block has presented an interesting and well argued commentary on what is likely to be one of the most important books in the industrial relations field this decade. Whether one agrees with KKM or Block, the KKM book, the Block paper, and the others presented at this conference have advanced the debate over the future of industrial relations practice, theory, and policy. Block's paper and the KKM book will help to increase understanding of the massive changes occurring within the US industrial relations system and highlight the diversity of that system. Both are supportive of the conclusion that if industrial relations scholars do not expand their view to include the nonunion sector and more about management as an initiator, they will exclude a large portion of the major changes affecting the workplace.

References

Block, R.N. (1990). American industrial relations in the 1980's: Transformation or evolution? *In* J. Chelius & J. Dworkin (eds.), *Reflections on the Transformation of Industrial Relations*. Metuchen, NJ: IMLR Press.

Kochan, T.A.; Katz, H.C.; & McKersie, R.B. (1986). *The Transformation of American Industrial Relations*. New York: Basic Books.

Roomkin, M.J., & Juris, H.A. (1990). Strategy and industrial relations: An examination of the American steel industry. *In* J. Chelius & J. Dworkin (eds.), *Reflections on the Transformation of Industrial Relations*. Metuchen, NJ: IMLR Press.

3. AN ORGANIZATIONAL SYSTEMS PERSPECTIVE ON THE TRANSFORMATION OF INDUSTRIAL RELATIONS

James P. Begin

THE BOOK *Transformation of American Industrial Relations* by Kochan, Katz, and McKersie (KKM, 1986) has generated substantial discussion as to the extent and stability of the transformations they have described. How permanent are the decentralization of bargaining structures, the flexible work rules, the worker participation and labor-management cooperation systems, the pay-for-knowledge or pay-for-performance compensation systems, and the decline in union membership that have characterized the transformation identified by KKM? This chapter will utilize recent developments in organizational theory to develop a systems model for integrating industrial relations and human resources concepts. This integrating framework will in turn be used to evaluate the cause and stability of the transformation in American industrial relations we are observing.

The basic difference between the systems approach developed here and the approaches of Dunlop (1958), KKM, and Beer, Spector, Lawrence, Mills, and Walton (Beer et al., 1985) is that this chapter introduces organizational level variables these authors tend to treat as black boxes. For example, how do organizational contingencies such as age, size, power relations, and technical systems affect organizational design and the derivative employment relations system (ERS)? How are technical systems and organizational design influenced by the environmental contingencies (for example, product and factor markets, unions, and government control) confronted by organizations? This paper ties these two questions together in the following manner: Are there systematic relationships between organizational and environmental contingencies that impact the design of organizational ERS's in predictable patterns?

This approach goes beyond the essentially descriptive theories employed by the other authors noted because it is designed to test and develop specific hypotheses about the linkage of environmental and organizational contingencies to the design and impact of organizational ERS's. The Strauss paper (1990, chap. 4), drawing on Osterman, touches on this approach by describing four types of ERS's (unstructured, craft, traditional, high commitment). These models are similar to the four models developed below (simple, professional, machine, adhocratic). However, the four ERS models described in Strauss are not systematically linked to the environmental and organizational contingencies in which they evolved, with the result that we have no understanding of the forces which led to the creation of the four different models.

The application of the framework developed below to the KKM book produces the general conclusion that the transformation has been restricted to the types of manufacturing bureaucracies commonly organized by unions in this country, and that the transformation of employment systems in these organizations, which is still in its early stages, is only as stable as the underlying environmental and organizational forces that created the changes.

This paper will first develop a general model derived from organizational theory. A summary of the characteristics of the transformation described by KKM will then be presented, followed by an application of the model to the findings of KKM.

The Model

The work of Henry Mintzberg entitled *Structure in Fives: Designing Effective Organizations* (1983) inspired this perspective about employment relations systems. The central thesis of his book is that organizations, in developing congruence between organizational design (particularly the technical systems used to produce their products or services) and the external environment, evolve into five basic configurations: simple structure, machine bureaucracy, professional bureaucracy, divisionalized form, and the adhocracy.[1] In developing his work, Mintzberg synthesized the theoretical and empirical literature on organizational design. From the literature and his own research, he hypothesized relationships among environmental and organizational contingencies and organizational design features such as work coordination (direct supervision, mutual adjustment, standardization of work, skills, or outputs), job specialization (horizontal and vertical), training and indoctrination, formalization of behavior (organic or bureaucratic), unit groupings (market or functional), unit size, planning and control systems, liaison devices, and decentralization (horizontal and vertical). He develops specific hypotheses relating environmental and organizational contingencies to the above design characteristics. For example, he postulates that old organizations are bureaucratic, that complex technologies require decentralization of authority to professionals, that governmental regulation centralizes authority, and that market diversity produces divisionalization by markets. He further postulates that these hypothesized relationships interact in a manner that produces a limited number of organizational designs or configurations. The following discussion only provides a brief overview of his complex, comprehensive organizational systems approach.

Modifying Mintzberg (1983), this paper predicts that the five organizational configurations he identifies produce four basic types of employment relations systems (ERS's) at the organizational level. These systems yield distinct differences in the nature of the employees, the employee decision-making procedures, the employment rules, and the impact of these rules on the organization. The four hypothesized configurations are: simple ERS, machine ERS, professional ERS, and adhocratic ERS.

At the outset, it is recognized that combining all ERS's into four basic configurations produces broad generalizations that can mask the substantial variations occurring within each basic configuration across organizations. Nevertheless, there is a benefit to first visualizing our field in broad theoretical terms. It is hoped that other researchers will refine and extend the arguments and ideas presented here. Each of the four basic configurations will be described, related to their basic organizational and environmental determinants, and, finally, related to where they fit into the life cycle of organizations.

The Four ERS's: A Description

The four ERS configurations are defined in terms of the environmental and organizational contingencies that drive the ERS authority distribution, the ERS decision content, and the impact of ERS's on the individual, organization, and society. The *environmental* contingencies consist of the predictability of the environment including the demand for the product or service (stable or dynamic or hostile),[2] the sophistication of the technical knowledge required to operate in the environment (simple or complex), the diversity of the markets, and the power relations in society. The *organizational* contingencies consist of the age, size, the degree of regulation of the technical system (unregulated, regulated, machine controlled),[3] and the power needs of the managers.

It is expected that the unique interaction of these environmental and organizational contingencies will develop distinct patterns of ERS designs and impacts. ERS *authority distribution* is comprised of the source of authority within an ERS, including the role of employees in decision making with or without unions. The degree of specialization of ERS functions within organizations is also part of this dimension. ERS *decision content* is comprised of the types of ERS rules, for example, performance appraisal, selection, recruitment, union policies, compensation, training. ERS *impact* is defined using the terminology of Beer et al. (1985), where ERS outcomes are evaluated in terms of their effect on worker commitment to the organization, worker competence, organizational cost effectiveness, and organizational goal congruence as indicated by the absence/presence of conflict within the organization. The environmental and organizational contingencies and the ERS dimensions yield the following patterns as managers and owners make strategic decisions to establish congruence among the environment in which their organizations operate, the design of their organization, and the design of their ERS system for regulating relations with their employees.

Simple ERS's arise where a dynamic (unpredictable) environment demands that ERS rules be flexible to permit fast responses to change, but the technical knowledge is simple enough and the organization small enough that the power in the organization can remain in the hands of the entrepreneurial top managers. Coordination of work is accomplished through direct supervision. Employees have little formal authority, but if given informal authority, worker congruence and commitment is high and unionism low. The ERS rule scope is narrow, and the ERS rules that exist are organic ("organic" has the opposite meaning of "bureaucratic" in that it means that rules, if they exist at all, are loose and informal). For example, in a simple ERS there are few formal selection, job allocation, job security, training, performance appraisal, career development, job analysis, or compensation rules. ERS functions where they exist are not specialized and are usually performed by line managers or subcontracted. Pay is usually job performance based. Employment security protections are not rationalized. An automobile agency headed by an entrepreneurial leader is an example of this type of organization. The "unstructured" internal labor market described in the Strauss paper (1990) is very similar to the simple ERS.

Machine ERS's arise in organizations operating in environments that are stable (product demand and factor supply is predictable) and simple (the technical knowledge is well understood). The organizations are old, large, and use highly regulated, but non-automated technical systems to produce the product. Significant authority in the organization is held by technicians (job analysts, industrial engineers) who set the highly specialized work standards used to control worker performance. In instances where market diversity creates divisions, there is a limited vertical decentralization of power to division heads whose performance is carefully controlled through formal performance control mechanisms. Because of these performance controls, organizational theory predicts that all divisionalized ERS's in time evolve into machine ERS's. For example, many institutions of higher education have developed machine ERS's as the performance controls instituted by statewide coordinating boards have led to the centralization of authority and development of bureaucratic rules.

There is very little vertical decentralization of authority to employees in machine ERS's, except in the commonly occurring, unionized machine ERS. Unionism is high because of the stress (low congruence) created by the tightly controlled human behavior inherent in highly specialized job design systems. High grievance and strike rates are also expected. Bargaining structures are centralized to the industry level to eliminate the destabilizing effects of labor market competition. Employees or unions have little participation in strategic decisions or job level decisions. Worker participation at the job level is unstable because of the low skills required by the job designs, and because authority is generally highly centralized.

In general, machine ERS's are very bureaucratic with many formal work rules, although the selection process, training process, and planning process are highly informal or nonexistent due to the low skills of the workers. Job design, job evaluation, compensation systems, work rules, job allocation mechanisms, grievance procedures, contingency benefits and job security rules are highly formalized and specialized—job control at its best. The ERS function has a large, specialized staff. Because workers control the speed of the machines, to provide worker incentive to produce, wages are usually based on hourly rates and often include incentive compensation based on the quantity of product produced. Rates are set using bureaucratic time study procedures. In short, the relatively stable market environment of the machine ERS has permitted such organizations to surround their highly regulated and well-understood (simple) technologies with extensive rules and regulations.

The result of the rule-bound ERS is that the organization is not adaptive to change. Because of the nature of the work, and of the presence of unions, wages and contingency benefits are high. Congruence, competence, cost effectiveness, and commitment are low. Machine ERS's develop in large manufacturing organizations such as auto or steel. The "traditional" internal labor market described by Strauss is similar to this configuration, but as we have seen here it is traditional only to organizations experiencing certain types of environmental and organizational contingencies.

Professional ERS's arise in environments where the knowledge is complex, but the markets stable. The technical systems tend to be unsophisticated and non-regulating, and the age of the organization older. Higher education institutions, for example, deal with complex knowledge, but the demand for higher education is predictable since the number of births for a given entry class are known far in advance and births shift marginally from year to year. The complexity of knowledge causes decision making on many issues, including many of strategic value to the organization, to be decentralized to experts. Because the markets are predictable, professional organizations can standardize, and because the knowledge is also complex, the work can be coordinated by highly specialized skills rather than by direct supervision or standardization of work processes or outputs. The skills are usually imparted by outside organizations through substantial training or apprenticeship programs. Therefore the selection process has to be sophisticated to judge skill levels, and often involves peer review. Some organizations even subcontract the selection process, for example, construction firms use union hiring halls. Training and career development once workers are on board is unsophisticated and informal. Market stability contributes to this situation since there is no need to respond to rapidly evolving skill needs. Professional ERS's need limited employment relations staff since work is not standardized, many policies are informal, and authority on hiring and performance appraisal is decentralized to skilled professional workers. Compensation is based on knowledge, and in the pure form, increases are based on merit. Job allocation procedures are informal or nonexistent due to the high degree of specialization and market stability. The decentralization of authority on hiring and promotions to knowledge experts requires extra effort to ensure compliance with affirmative action goals, so affirmative action procedures tend to be specialized and formalized.

Work rules are informal since the production processes are difficult to rationalize. For example, every move of a professional in a classroom, on a construction site, or in an operating room cannot be exactly specified by rules. The subjective nature of output measures makes performance appraisal subjective and less formal. The stable markets permit high job security and therefore high employee commitment. The decentralized authority contributes to high congruence. Unionism, therefore, is low. The organizations tend to be inflexible to change due to the specialized nature of the skills. Hospitals, universities, and construction firms are examples of organizations with professional ERS's. The "craft" internal labor market described in Strauss is most similar to this configuration, although the meaning of craft is too narrow for all of the occupations included within many professional ERS's.

Adhocratic type ERS's arise where the markets are dynamic and the knowledge required to function in the markets is complex. Alvin Toffler used the term "adhocracy" in his book *Future Shock* (1970) to describe organizations that must innovate to survive unpredictable markets. Such organizations are often young. Because innovation requires complex knowledge, authority in an adhocracy is decentralized to the experts, as in a professional ERS. The support staff (marketing and research functions) is considered the key part of the organization because that is where the knowledge exists to drive the creative processes of the organization. The dynamic nature of the environment requires organic systems that permit adhocracies to respond quickly to changes. Communications are informal and the coordination of work is by mutual adjustment, not by direct supervision, or standardization of skills, work processes, or outputs.

The adhocracy separates the innovative activities from the negative bureaucratic influences of production work by (1) isolating the production functions (for example, newspapers isolate the collection and writing of news from the repetitive and standardized processes for printing and delivering newspapers), (2) subcontracting the production work (NASA subcontracted most of the construction work on the space programs), or (3) fully automating the production processes so that they can run by themselves to preset standards (an automated oil refinery). Subcontracting or automating the operating core provides an organization substantial flexibility.

Basically, the adhocratic ERS work rules must be organic since the organization needs flexibility to respond to the dynamic environment. The scope of ERS rules is broad, but informal. In this sense it is the exact opposite of the machine ERS, with there being a minimum number of job descriptions, performance appraisal rules, and job allocation rules, for example. The complex knowledge requires skilled support staff, and, where the technical system is highly automated, skilled production employees. These skill levels require ERS policies that select from national markets. Training and human resource planning is also more developed in adhocratic ERS's since there is more labor market competition for skilled workers. The need to respond to changing situations also creates a greater need to provide ongoing training. Career development does not get high priority due to the dynamic nature of the organizations and the resulting mobility of employees across jobs.

Adhocracies are more democratic since authority is decentralized to the workers who possess the power of knowledge in the support staff or the production operation where technical systems are fully automated. The ability of unions to organize adhocratic ERS's is diminished since conflict is lower where there is worker participation, and where automated technical systems have replaced human workers performing repetitive tasks. Highly skilled and highly paid workers who also have excellent benefits are also more difficult to organize. So, overall, high congruence diminishes employee needs for unions. Where unionized, the power of unions is decreased since automated equipment can be operated during strikes, for example, in oil refineries and telephone communications.

There is high employee commitment to the organization, in part because of the high degree of employment security if the organization is profitable. Salaries are based on knowledge, with group incentives based on unit or organizational performance.

Examples of adhocratic ERS's are engineering and architectural firms, NASA, communications companies, plastics companies, oil refineries, and computer firms. The "high commitment" internal labor market described in Strauss is closest to this model. However, both the professional and adhocratic ERS's provide high worker commitment to the organization. Furthermore, it is clear that the high commitment model is not a new type of internal labor market (except for former machine ERS's), but has always existed under specific environmental and organizational contingencies. Without these contingencies, organizational theory predicts that the high commitment model would be unstable.

ERS Life Cycles

Figure 1 illustrates the life cycles of the four ideal ERS's. Organizational theorists have concluded that organizations and their derivative ERS's start as either a simple configuration or the adhocratic configuration if the technical knowledge is complex. The arrows in Figure 1 then indicate the changes in contingencies that will drive an ERS in one direction or the other over time. As the initial organizational configurations grow older and larger, they become more bureaucratic, and the ERS's should change accordingly. The Ford Motor Company, for example, started out as an adhocratic configuration headed by an entrepreneur, Henry Ford. As it evolved its

Figure 1
LIFE CYCLES OF ERS CONFIGURATIONS

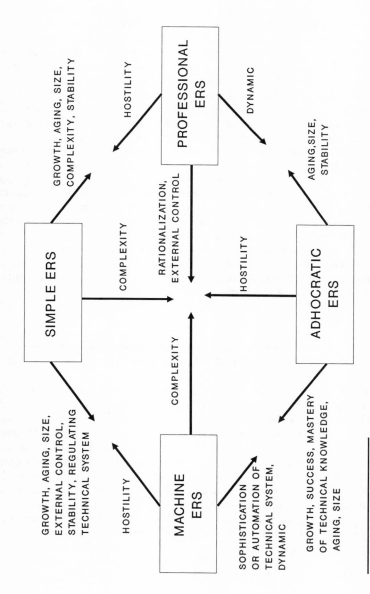

Source: Adapted from Figure 13-1, Mintzberg (1983), p. 287. Reprinted with the permission of Prentice-Hall, Inc., a Division of Simon and Schuster.

mass production technical system which divided work into repetitive, simple functions, the company became, in a stable environment, a machine bureaucracy. As its markets diversified to include other types of autos and products, the company developed a divisionalized machine bureaucracy. In recent years, a recession combined with increasing foreign competition have made the environment more dynamic, and some features of an adhocracy have started to appear in auto companies. The GM Saturn plant which will decentralize decision making to the workers in the operating core in the context of a highly automated technology is an example. Flexibility in job assignments and compensation systems planned at the Saturn plant are other examples of an adhocratic ERS configuration.

It can be expected that a company whose ERS is not congruent with the changing environmental and organizational contingencies that it confronts will find it difficult to survive. For example, an organization bound by bureaucratic ERS rules developed in a stable environmental context will find these rules will hinder the organization's flexibility in adapting to a dynamic environmental context. Thus, the rules must be altered or the organization must make other strategic decisions in order to survive.

A limitation of the four internal labor market models described in Strauss is that there was no discussion of the relationship of the models to each other in terms of the impact of time on the evolution of internal labor markets.

The Transformation of Industrial Relations—
The KKM Description

The transformation described by KKM fits very comfortably within the ERS configurations derived from organizational theory. Although using a somewhat different format, KKM considered most of the variables considered by organizational theory. KKM use a dynamic, strategic choice decision-making model which focuses on the dominant role of employers in strategically adapting the organization and its ERS to its changing environment. Using this model, KKM conclude that there are four scenarios that address the future of unions. The scenarios range from the one they feel most likely to occur (the continuing decline of unions until they represent only specific enclaves such as the public sector or the auto industry) to one which they feel is least likely to occur (labor law reform enhancing organization and the spread of unions to other sectors). The KKM model is basically a contingency model that describes how employers, operating through their peculiar value systems, adjust technology, organizational structure and policies, and market policies to ensure survival under changing market conditions. The model presented here is also a contingency model, but it is less descriptive in that it opens up the black box that has represented organizational structure and policies in much industrial relations theory and research. The model attempts to predict ERS patterns based on unique combinations of environmental and organizational contingencies, something that neither the descriptive Beer et al. (1985), Dunlop (1958), or KKM approaches attempt to do.

KKM, using data primarily from manufacturing and transportation industries, describe how companies in these industries, under pressures of economic change, are shifting away from an ERS in which employee decision making through unions was restricted to mid-level bargaining issues, and was highly centralized. The emphasis of work rules was on bureaucratic job control mechanisms. The workers in these organizations were highly unionized. In other words, the authors were describing the process of change in machine ERS's that were driven by basic changes in the environmental contingencies confronted by the organization. Before the changes, the environmental contingencies could be characterized as stable (demand was predictable) and simple (technical knowledge was well understood). Most of the organizations were also old and large. The effect of the changing environmental contingencies, as described by the authors, was reinforced by the emergence of aggressive anti-union strategies employed by management, strategies which included enlightened human resources policies like worker participation.

KKM And Organizational Systems Theory— A Congruence?

A comparison of the two approaches to understanding the nature, causes, extent, and stability of the ongoing transformation indicates a great deal of congruence. However, the organizational systems perspective appears to provide a much more thorough explanation of the causes and extent of the transformation as well as a clearer vision of the stability of the changes.

For large, old manufacturing companies, the transformation described by KKM essentially fits the path predicted by organizational theory. In other words, under increasing international competition in relatively free markets, the environmental contingencies for many manufacturing companies have shifted from stable to dynamic, and simple to complex (as companies have turned to high tech to obtain a competitive edge). To survive under these new contingencies, strategic changes had to be made to organizational ERS's. As predicted by the model, the new ERS's of surviving manufacturing organizations are beginning to look like adhocratic ERS's. Many companies also pursued the strategic policy of shifting production to greenfield sites or overseas to achieve cost savings and to rid themselves of bureaucratic work restrictions. They also subcontracted manufacturing work, often to foreign companies.

The result of these strategic decisions was the loss of highly unionized positions, and thus a decline in union membership in the labor force. The predicted difficulty of unions in organizing workers in the professional and adhocratic ERS's of a service economy in an environment where values and government rules are not totally supportive of unions, prevented the unions from recouping their membership losses. Companies also introduced more automated technical systems that often substituted fewer, more highly skilled jobs for routine blue collar work. Flexibility had to be substituted for bureaucratic job control mechanisms. A quid pro quo for achieving this increased flexibility was increased worker participation at the job level (a management objective) and increased worker and union participation at the strategic level (a union objective). These mechanisms increased worker commitment to the organization, further undermining worker support for unions, particularly where there had been none before.

These decentralized models also contributed to organizational flexibility by enhancing innovation. Job security guarantees also accompanied many of these changes; indeed, the increased flexibility made them easier to implement. Work teams with a few, broad job descriptions, have been substituted for numerous, highly specialized job descriptions that limited the ability of employers to assign workers flexibly. Compensation systems also became more flexible under pay for knowledge and pay for performance plans. Flexibility was also achieved through the decentralization of bargaining to the company level or even lower—the connections between settlements were diminishing, thus permitting companies more flexibility in adapting settlements to their particular environmental contingencies.

KKM and organizational systems theory describe the transformation in similar terms. However a unique contribution of organizational systems theory in understanding this transformation is its illustration that for some time there have been ERS's that have provided professional and craft employees with substantial looseness on how they go about their work as well as participation in a range of work place decisions. The key contingency driving this configuration was a technical system that could not be highly regulated and thus required highly trained workers whose advice the managers had to rely upon to run an effective organization. Adhocratic ERS's have been around a long time as well, driven by dynamic and complex markets. These ERS's have minimized the effect of inflexible bureaucratic processes and structures on the creative processes required for survival by truncating the bureaucratic manufacturing processes (AT&T's isolation of Bell Labs from the operating companies is an example) or automating them (oil refineries and the communications industry). So the issue as clarified by organizational theory is not whether a new type or organizational form will evolve and survive; the alternative ERS configurations have existed for some time. The issue is whether the professional and adhocratic ERS's will become the predominant organizational configurations in our society. An examination of the extent and stability of the contingencies producing the transformation is helpful in addressing this question. The discussion below will also highlight to a greater extent than KKM the role of societal values in creating and stabilizing the transformation of ERS's.

With respect to the extent of the transformation, organizational systems theory helps us see more clearly that the transition to a different type or types of organizational configuration(s) is still at a very early stage in this country, particularly when compared to other industrialized societies. The auto industry appears to have made the greatest changes at this point. But as we have seen, the transportation and steel industries are at an earlier stage of change. The communications and rubber industries have also done little to alter ERS's except to devise market strategies which, in the case of the rubber industry, had the effect of undermining union penetration (Lipsky & Donn, 1987). The discussion below of the stability of the transformation will illustrate the very important role of the technical system in also determining the degree of the transformation.

How permanent is the transformation? The answer is that it depends on how stable the respective underlying contingencies are. For several decades the predominant ERS in manufacturing and transportation has been the machine ERS. Will changes in technical systems or other organizational contingencies like age, size, and management power needs permit a permanent shift to professional ERS's? Similarly, will changes in environmental contingencies such as the predictability of markets, complexity of technical knowledge, or power relations in the environment permit a permanent shift to adhocratic ERS's?

Organizational systems theory is very helpful in producing the following generalizations: the decentralization of authority to workers with respect to all three levels of decision content, strategic, mid, and job level, and the development of flexible work and compensation systems will depend on (1) the degree of technological change, (2) the stability of societal and management beliefs about the value of employee participation and unions, and (3) the stability of the environmental conditions producing the transformation, particularly foreign competition.

Technological Change

As we have seen from organizational systems theory, it is the power of knowledge that ensures the stability of worker participation. Therefore, to the extent that technical systems require skilled workers, worker participation is of value to an organization. In those industries where technological change has and will occur we can expect that the ERS's will decentralize power to the employees in order to ensure efficiency. However, many organizations have made strategic choices in response to their peculiar market structures that did not include significant technological change. For example, technological change in the steel, airline and other industries has been slow, so the transition to the new ERS will also be slow. Any changes in worker authority driven by environmental contingencies alone will be unstable since the underlying technical system has not changed. Strong management values supporting worker participation will enhance its development and stability, but in the long run worker participation in a *wide* range of organizational decisions must be embedded in the power of knowledge.

A key difference in the transformation between the manufacturing and transportation industries is that the managers in some manufacturing companies adjusted the technical system in a way that supported the changes; that is, the introduction of advanced technologies along with significant job redesigns increased the knowledge required of the workers. Accordingly, in the context of changed management values about the advantages of giving workers power, many of the changes supported by automated technical systems may be stable even when the market environment stabilizes. Organizational theory predicts that, otherwise, there will be a return to the machine ERS's which have dominated American employment relations. It should be noted that the major actors in the steel industry did not adapt to a more dynamic environment by making significant technological changes. Rather, the industry, according to Roomkin and Juris (1990, chap. 5) found market niches that enabled them to profitably survive on a smaller scale, and thus reduced the pressure to force more substantial ERS changes. Perhaps this is the reason that the basic ERS transformation under way in the auto industry was never matched by most large steel firms.

The transportation industry, particularly the airline industry, does not fit the machine ERS configuration exactly because many of the employees in the operating core of the organization (the production level) are highly skilled, and have a higher degree of authority on the job because their every move is not prescribed by detailed work rules. However, job allocation and work load rules are highly bureaucratic. And the requirement for safety saddled such organizations with exhaustive regulations developed mostly by the government. This government regulation, not only of the production processes but also of the market, reduced considerably the degree of competition and thus stabilized the airline environment. Consequently, the machine ERS evolved in the airline industry because of stable environmental contingencies created by government control. Deregulation destabilized the markets by increasing competition. Indeed, the rapid deregulation not only created dynamic markets, but hostile markets.

Massive mergers, deriving form strategic management decisions unhindered by government control, have reintroduced a degree of stability into the airline market environment. Since the technical systems of the airlines were essentially unchanged during the market crisis, organizational theory would predict that the machine ERS would once again dominate that industry, particularly if the decentralization of authority to workers was not thoroughly institutionalized. If authority decentralization was institutionalized, then the professional bureaucracy may evolve. However, the unchanged nature of the technical system (which is still strongly underpinned by government safety regulation—manning is still largely determined by the government and not the employers, for example), and the independent nature of the work, indicate that strategic and job level participation will be minimal in the long run. As a result, unions will probably continue to be the predominant choice for representing worker interests to employers and governments in the airline industry. This example illustrates how important the technical system is in determining the nature of the ERS. This factor, along with the fact that the ERS changes under deregulation were more of an early transition than a transformation, would indicate that any changes that did occur may be unstable.

The outcome in the trucking industry may be different since the large number of employers has apparently not diminished enough to stabilize the industry. And employers have not had the strategic option to change the technical system. As long as the market retains its dynamic character, KKM's prediction that union membership is not likely to recover, at least in this industry, will hold.

In general, if, because of technological change and/or dynamic markets, the professional and adhocratic ERS configurations become much more predominant in our society, then union penetration will continue to decline and not recover. The theoretical explanation for this is that the higher worker commitment and high congruence of these ERS types will diminish worker interest in collective participation through unions. The inability of unions to organize these configurations over time provides significant empirical support for this prediction. It should be noted that public sector union penetration, while falling off to some extent in recent years (Burton & Thomason, 1988), will remain high relative to the private sector since government organizations have been and will remain public machine bureaucracies. Even where employee skills might dictate greater authority, the size and age of public organizations, bureaucratic civil service protections against patronage, and the substantial policy and budgetary authority possessed by politicians will keep power centralized and ERS policies highly formalized. This organizational configuration, as we have seen, is conducive to unionization.

Stability of Contingencies

Adhocratic ERS's are inherently unstable because size, age, market concentration, and market diversity will create pressures towards control by formal rule, a factor that will move adhocratic ERS's towards either a machine ERS (if low skills are required in the operating core) or a professional ERS (if complex skills are still required). Environmental contingencies also stabilize over time as markets become more predictable; for example, the industry becomes more concentrated. An example of this is the airline industry where governmental deregulation creating a dynamic environment was met by strategic organizational decisions to merge. The direction of ERS evolution is key because professional ERS's theoretically are more likely to sustain participatory mechanisms, as discussed above. Also key to industries that, unlike most transportation companies, are confronted with expanding foreign competition is the length of time it takes for international markets to stabilize. In a relatively free market environment, it could take several decades for this to occur. Thus the transformation towards professional or adhocratic ERS's is likely to proceed and stabilize under this sce-

nario. But governmental interference in the operation of international markets could play a major part in moderating the effect of
foreign competition, thus moderating the degree of the transformation.

Stability of Values

   Organizational systems theory highlights the importance of the
power relations in larger society and the power needs of managers
within organizations in shaping the evolution of ERS configurations.
Management anti-union power needs (described in detail by KKM)
are unlikely to change at the organizational level. Furthermore,
power relations in the larger society reflecting a strong individualistic orientation (not emphasized to a great degree by KKM) are
unlikely to change sufficiently to give the unions the leverage they
need to organize professional and adhocratic ERS's. Therefore,
union penetration will not recover unless the machine ERS with low
worker commitment and low congruence again becomes the dominant configuration in our society. It is perhaps the individualistic
value system driving our society's negative orientation towards
unions that distinguishes us from other industrialized societies
where losses in union penetration so far have been smaller or nonexistent. Clearly, values about unions shape the initial dimensions of
the ERS system in a particular country, state, or community, and the
system so shaped changes very slowly and thus limits the strategic
responses of the parties to change. In this country, for example, a
decentralized bargaining structure in the context of a weak national
union confederation and strong regulatory protections of management's rights to influence organizing drives does not produce an
adaptable labor movement. In other industrialized Western countries, a centralized, political union movement and the longstanding
unionization of occupations and companies not heavily unionized in
this country makes the union movement more adaptable, in part,
since the service and professional workers that are becoming more
dominant are already heavily unionized. KKM's work would have
benefited from a greater comparative analysis of this type. Work on
the differences in Canadian and USA ideologies as an explanation
for the varying success of unions in preserving past gains or expanding in response to new challenges reinforces the need to consider the
important impact of societal values and the public policies they drive
(Meltz, 1985).
   If markets become truly internationalized, then values may change.
Alternatively, if our government becomes a dominant force in
setting organizational employment relations policy, as is the case in

other industrialized countries, decision making within organizations
will become centralized and formalized, thus creating low commitment, low congruence environments more conducive to unionization. But it will take changes of these proportions to alter the basic
policy structure, just as it took an economic depression to create the
final impetus towards the New Deal bargaining system. Without
these changes, neither management, societal or individual values are
likely to change sufficiently to give unions the leverage they need to
unionize ERS's that increasingly look less like machine bureaucracies.

A Final Comment

Organizational systems theory has contributed to our understanding
of the causes, degree, and stability of the transformation in ERS's by
emphasizing the importance of assessing the stability of the changes
in environmental and organizational contingencies that created the
ERS changes. This approach is helpful in developing needed linkages between strategic organizational decision making and the derivative ERS's, a need recognized by KKM (p. 455). The result of
this analysis for the future of the transformation is mixed, and, in the
final analysis, depends upon one's views of how stable the changes in
environmental and organizational contingencies now underway will
be. A high degree of technological change will drive the transformation, and stable societal values concerning unions and the stable
public policies that they produce will inhibit the ability of unions to
adapt. Continuing foreign competition will drive the transformation
in industries affected by that competition. But the absence of
government control of mergers would tend to offset the dynamic
effects of deregulation, and the presence of government control of
international markets would moderate dynamic market effects. The
most likely outcome for unions is exactly that predicted by KKM:
they will continue to exist in certain enclaves (the public sector,
airlines, steel, auto, for example), but they lack the adaptability to
respond to the environmental and organizational contingencies they
will face in the decades ahead.

Notes

1. The divisionalized form of organizational configuration identified by
   Mintzberg is collapsed into the other configurations because, as described in more detail below, the machine, professional, and adhocracy
   configurations can exist in divisionalized form if the organizations

diversify their markets. Indeed, the divisionalized forms are the most commonly occurring in large organizations in our society.

2. Just as organizational theorists do not like the way that economists conceptualize organizational variables (if they do at all), the economists among us will not be too happy about the way that organizational theorists conceptualize economic variables. Clearly economic concepts of market stability such as degree of industry concentration, product differentiation, and barriers to entry and exit are useful for describing market variations, and refinements of this model should draw upon these concepts. It should be noted, however, that Mintzberg is grouping together all environmental factors into one variable, including not only product markets, but also factor markets, government regulation and union activities. In one variable, he is attempting to get a total picture of the outside world. It is also worth noting that cyclical markets under Mintzberg's definition are not dynamic to the extent that they can be anticipated. Seasonal markets are an example. And auto and steel markets have varied in a regular cyclical pattern for decades, thus permitting the parties to develop an ERS which reflects these regular changes. Supplementary unemployment benefits in the auto industry are an example.

3. Mintzberg distinguishes between the complexity of the knowledge involved in the products and the technical system used to produce the product on that basis that they are not necessarily directly related. In the auto industry they are related. An auto is a complex instrument, for example, but the knowledge is well enough understood so that the technical system is arranged in repetitive form. Complex knowledge, however, does not always lead eventually to repetitive technical systems where work is highly specialized. For years, institutions of higher education have delivered complex knowledge with simple, unregulated technical systems.

References

Beer, M.; Spector, B.; Lawrence, P.R.; Mills, D.Q.; & Walton, R.E. (1985). *Human Resource Management: A General Manager's Perspective.* New York: Free Press.

Burton, J.F., & Thomason, T. (1988). The extent of collective bargaining in the public sector. *In* B. Aaron, J.M. Najita, & J.L. Stern (eds.), *Public Sector Bargaining.* Washington, DC: BNA Books.

Dunlop, J.T. (1958). *Industrial Relations Systems.* New York: Holt.

Kochan, T.A.; Katz, H.C.; & McKersie, R.B. (1986). *The Transformation of American Industrial Relations.* New York: Basic Books.

Lipsky, D.B., & Donn, C.B. (eds.). (1987). *Collective Bargaining in American Industry.* Lexington, MA: Lexington Books.

Meltz, N. (1985). Labour Movements in Canada and the United States. *In* T.A. Kochan (ed.), *Challenges and Choices Facing American Labor.* Cambridge, MA: MIT Press.

Mintzberg, H. (1983). *Structure in Fives: Designing Effective Organizations.* Englewood Cliffs, NJ: Prentice-Hall.

Roomkin, M.J., & Juris, H.A. (1990). Strategy and industrial relations: An examination of the American steel industry. *In* J. Chelius & J. Dworkin (eds.), *Reflections on the Transformation of Industrial Relations.* Metuchen, NJ: IMLR Press.

Strauss, G. (1990). Toward the study of human resources policy. *In* J. Chelius & J. Dworkin (eds.), *Reflections on the Transformation of Industrial Relations.* Metuchen, NJ: IMLR Press.

Toffler, A. (1970). *Future Shock.* New York: Bantam Books.

4. TOWARD THE STUDY OF HUMAN RESOURCES POLICY

George Strauss

THIS PAPER IS CONCERNED as much with the transformation of academic industrial relations as with changes of Human Resources Management (HRM) in the real world.[1] It consists of two parts. The first and shorter argues that if IR is to continue to thrive as an academic field it should broaden its scope; it should focus less exclusively on union-management relations and instead reassert the jurisdiction over the personnel field (now HRM) that it exercised in the 1950's. In particular it should be concerned with what I might call macro-HR or HR policy. Difficult as this may be for some of us, we must explore what Garbarino (1984) calls "unionism without unions." And we should pay more attention to managers, professionals, and unorganized white collar workers, particularly as the distinctions among occupations decline in a computer age.

The second and longer part of the paper discusses two sets of human resources issues which are critical for management today and which deserve greater attention from IR academicians.

Why A Broader Academic Focus Is Needed

Labor-Management Relations

Let me start with the somewhat obvious observation that unions have lost membership, clout, and significance, and as a consequence union-management relations have become less attractive for students to study. Further, this doleful situation is not likely to change much in the near future. In addition, somewhat ironically, as collec-

tive bargaining has contracted in the real world, IR academicians
have made things worse for themselves by contracting their field—
which once viewed the entire employment process as its domain—
to include today primarily labor-management relations.[2]

Human Resources

Meanwhile, enrollment in Human Resource courses has been
booming and academic job openings in the field have gone begging.
Faculty drawn from other fields have been assigned (and forced) to
teach HR. In graduate IR programs the portion of students with
psychology backgrounds has increased, whole those with economics
undergraduate majors has gone down.

The switch to HR reflects changes in employment opportunities.
At Cornell, for example "of those ILR School graduates who enter
directly into the job market . . . fewer than 25 percent obtain
positions that bring them into contact with union-management
relations. The other 75 percent obtain jobs where they are involved
in the management of non-union personnel systems" (Rehmus,
1985). Thus, reacting to market pressures, some IR departments
have renamed themselves HR or at least incorporated HR in their
name. Similarly, the Industrial Relations Center Directors (a hither-
to informal group that meets with the IRRA) recently decided to
formalize themselves and to adopt a new title which refers to both
Industrial Relations and Human Resources.

Nevertheless, regardless of its broader pretensions, HR's heart—
at least as it is taught in most schools and as covered in most
textbooks—remains what used to be called Personnel. For my taste
it is too narrow:

(1)   Its texts are too cookbooky, too methodological. They tell
you what to do or what the alternatives are—but they pay little
attention to the political problems of implementation.

(2)   Many of the same criticisms may be directed to its research.
The typical research project is concerned with the development of
techniques for use in such functions as testing and performance
evaluation. Normally it makes careful use of control and experimental groups (often of students). But there is little research on how to
implement these techniques effectively.

(3)   Being directed chiefly toward how-to-do-it, HRM frequently ignores the broader implications for society of the techniques it espouses. Thus, it often seems manipulative and pro-
management.

(4)   The various parts of the field are poorly integrated: there is

little discussion of the possibility, for example, that if you use profit sharing rather than piecework you might also want a different kind of selection and induction system. In short, it is more concerned with tactics than with strategy.

(5)   The field is too psychological. It ignores developments in the world at large, such as changes in demography or technology.

(6)   The field seems directed toward staff specialists rather than line managers.

Organizational Behavior

OB, of course, has also boomed since IR's Golden Age in the 1940's, and it has taken away IR's teaching slots in many universities. OB derived in part from IR (via Personnel) and younger IR people today are making increasing use of OB concepts and research methodologies, especially in studies of union membership commitment and of voting behavior in NLRB elections (Lewin & Strauss, 1988).

Yet OB has become increasingly theoretical since the days of Likert and McGregor. Concepts such as the population ecology of organizations or the social construction of reality have little direct application, though they certainly contribute to our understanding of the real world.

Labor Economics

Labor economics is another thriving field, intellectually if not in student demand. At one time Labor Economics and Industrial Relations were almost interchangeable terms. Gradually they grew apart (from 1966 to 1984 the percent of members of the national Industrial Relations Research Association who call themselves labor economists fell from 23% to 7%).

Some important work continues to be done that links IR and labor economics. Freeman and Medoff's *What Do Unions Do?* (1984) has been justly praised, even though some of it is based on pre-concession-bargaining data and so needs redoing. Nevertheless this landmark study hardly represents the mainstream of labor economics today.

The mainstream has become heavily theoretical and/or quantitative. Much of its effort has been to explain, in neo-classical economic theory, regularities which economists find disturbing but which mainstream IR people feel they have understood all along, for example, (1) why the wage rates for any given occupation differ so widely in the same community, or (2) why employers are prepared to pay wages higher than the market-clearing rate. Little of this research has practical application; most of it ignores collective bargaining.

Nevertheless work of this sort helps integrate labor economics with economic theory and so raises labor economics' status. In so doing it makes use of a variety of innovative new concepts, such as efficiency wages, agency theory, gift exchange, moral hazard, implicit contracting, shirking, and the like. Even when labor economists merely restate old verities,[3] they do so with a precision that makes new insights emerge. Long before Newton, people knew that apples fell. But by explaining gravity in mathematical terms, Newton laid the groundwork for modern physics.[4]

Indeed a new field, the Economics of Personnel, is in the making.[5] Two new texts (Kleiner, McLean, & Dreher, 1988; Mitchell, in press) are designed to tap the thriving HRM market, while a third, by Edward Lazear, is in the works. Thus there is danger that, by combining Labor Economics with HRM, mainstream IR will be outflanked and isolated (though both completed texts include considerable traditional IR material).

Among the attractive features of this new economics of personnel are that it (1) forces economists to test their hypotheses more realistically[6] and (2) brings their contributions to the attention of mainstream IR. The challenge for mainstream IR is to take advantage of this.

Combining HRM and IR

Meanwhile, faced with declining student interest in straight IR, IR groups in business schools such as Harvard, MIT, Columbia, and Northwestern have been experimenting with courses which combine IR and HRM (with perhaps some labor economics). Harvard has already produced a casebook (Beer, Spector, Lawrence, Mills & Walton, 1985) with a heavy emphasis on how human resource problems are handled in unionized companies. At MIT Kochan and Barocci have written a text with many cases, *Human Resources Management and Industrial Relations* (1985).

There are some problems with this approach if done too mechanically. Viewing the course as half one thing and half another won't work; there must be some integrating scheme. Further, traditional HRM people tend to be psychologists, IR people may overemphasize collective bargaining; to date only a few people have been

trained to teach both halves of the course. At least on the HRM side
the elements of these courses I've seen have been too concerned
with tactics rather than strategy.

Nevertheless this is the right approach. IR should concern itself
with broad issues of HRM in both the union and non-union sectors,
leaving theoretical analysis to OB and labor economics that the nitty-
gritty of selection and training to traditional, psychologically oriented micro-HRM.[7] For my taste, IR should be concerned primarily
with firm-level (and union-level) policies, though it certainly should
not ignore national policy issues, such as various forms of government regulation. It should view collective bargaining as *one* method
of dispute resolution (in my opinion the preferable one), but not the
only one.

The relationship between IR and the more basic disciplines
should be a bit like Geology's relationship to Physics and Chemistry.
Physics and Chemistry may be all that's required to describe an
individual rock, but to find gold you must understand the relationships among rocks, and this requires Geology (Arrow, 1985). Similarly Economics, OB and micro-HMR can all contribute to our
understanding of the employment relationship, but IR's job is to pull
the parts together and to analyze their application in specific situations.

Below I provide a sampler of important macro-HRM issues that
are of critical importance today for management and *should* receive
the attention of IR academicians. At present they are likely to be
covered tangentially, at most, by OB, labor economics, labor history, traditional IR, or micro-HRM. My discussion seeks to do two
things. First, it takes up the practical problems, as seen by practitioners. Secondly, it illustrates how theoretical concepts, taken from the
basic fields, might contribute to our understanding (and even solution) of these practical problems.

I will discuss these issues under two heads, employment systems
and justice systems. I do this because these two "systems" capture a
considerable portion of the issues I would like to consider.

Employment Systems

Just as Kochan, Katz, and McKersie (KKM, 1986) argue that
management can engage in strategic choice with regard to its labor-
management relations, so it has some choice in its overall HR policy.
Perhaps the best publicized strategic choice faced by management
today is whether to install "high involvement," "strong culture," or
high commitment macro-HR policies. Such policies have received
much recent attention (some of it almost evangelical) in the academ-

ic, quasi-academic, and popular literature (for example, Lawler, 1986) and have been adopted—in form at least—by a considerable number of well known companies (KKM, 1986). Taken as a whole, these policies constitute an *employment system*.[8] (HRM people might call it a "career ladder" and economists might view it as a "labor market structure".)

In my view the implications of this system may profitably be analyzed by contrasting it with the major alternative systems available. Thus my discussion below contrasts the high commitment employment system with three major alternatives (see Table 1). In so doing it notes how the choice of employment systems has implications for overall managerial strategy.[9]

Unstructured

The first employment system is the purely competitive unstructured labor market in which wages are set by supply and demand and workers have no expectation of continuing employment. In pure form this market exists only in textbooks, since even the agricultural labor market (Fisher, 1953) has structures for job seeking and recruitment. However, Doeringer and Piore's (1971) secondary labor market resembles the purely unstructured one.

Employers make use of this market chiefly when the work is routine, requires little training, can be easily supervised, and is not excessively disrupted by high turnover. "Theory X" motivation may be appropriate here.

Craft or Occupation

Second is Kerr's (1954) craft labor market, seen best (or perhaps only) in unionized construction. Here the union is the "port of entry." In theory training is provided through union-controlled apprenticeship. Job classifications are relatively broad, with all members of a given craft assumed to be capable of performing every job in the craft's jurisdiction. Mobility is horizontal, from employer to employer. Psychological attachment is to the occupation, not the employer.

During the nineteenth century, terms of employment were imposed unilaterally by the union. Today these terms are bargained, but union-management relations are frequently harmonious (particularly in smaller firms). Fringe benefits, though improving, tend to be less generous than in manufacturing.

TABLE 1
ALTERNATE EMPLOYMENT SYSTEMS
(also known as labor market models or career ladders)

	Unstructured	*Craft*	*Traditional Internal*	*High Commitment*
job descriptions	none (broad)	broad	narrow	broad
work rules protecting jurisdiction	no	yes	yes	no
pay based on	job	knowledge	job	knowledge and organizational performance, e.g. profit-sharing
port of entry	diffuse	union	company	company
job security	none	low	depends on seniority	high
employee mobility	unstructured	lateral between employers	vertical by seniority	largely lateral within company
handling of employment fluctuations	layoffs and hires	layoffs and hires	overtime layoffs	hiring and firing peripheral employees
training	none	apprenticeship general	understudy specific	varied, but high specific
supervision	close	loose	close	loose
autonomy	none	high	low	high
employee identification	none	with craft	weak, with company	strong, with company
mgt-worker distinction	sharp	weak	sharp	weak
union-mgt relations	none	self governing or cooperative	adversarial pluralist	cooperative unitary
fringe benefits	none	moderate	good	excellent

All journeymen are paid the same, regardless of their particular assignment. Thus their pay is based on their skill, not their immediate job. Economists might argue that craftsmen's high wages are justified to reduce shirking (though I think union bargaining strength provides a sufficient explanation). Implicit contracting doesn't work here, since employees have short-term jobs.[10]

In terms of their employment system self-employed professionals (or professionals working as subcontractors) are much like craftsmen, although their training tends to be academic rather than through apprenticeship. Instead of a union, they may have a professional association which may police entry, standards of performance, and even employment conditions. Craftsmen working full-time in manufacturing enjoy some of the employment conditions of their brethren in contract construction (Strauss, 1963). Further, as I discuss below, the craft employment system is quite consistent with what has been called "network organization" (Miles & Snow, 1986) and "flexible specialization" (Piore & Sabel, 1984).

The craft-professional system yields high wages, but employers gain through the quick availability of trained, reasonably well motivated employees who are prepared to work for short periods.

The Traditional Internal Labor Market

What I'll call the traditional internal labor market (TILM) (which Kerr, 1954, calls the production and Osterman (1988) calls the industrial system) is unique to the U.S. (Stark, 1986). Europe (Katz and Sabel, 1985), Japan (Koike, 1984), and Australia (Curtin, 1987) have somewhat different systems.

TILM's origins lie deep in history (and should be studied by our students). Elements of the system were adopted to reduce turnover in the 1910's and to prevent unionization during the 1920's and 1930's (Jacoby, 1985). They were extended and elaborated by the War Labor Board and further codified and rigidified by union pressures in the 1940's and early 1950's. Thus in most plants, by the late 1950's, a complex system of written rules and past practices was in place, strongly protected by stewards, an increasingly legalistic grievance procedure, and arbitration. Indeed the US's uniquely strong shop-level union organization was both a cause and effect of the TILM (Brody, 1988a). However, non-union companies adopted systems which were almost as rigid.

The key elements of the TILM are thin job progression ladders consisting of narrowly defined jobs, with movement up and down the ladder being determined largely by seniority. Elaborate job bidding and bumping procedures are required to convert the principle of seniority into practice. Training costs are minimized since adjacent jobs are closely related to each other, so promotion may require only a marginal increase in skill. Nevertheless, because of union (and sometimes engineering) insistence, the requirement of each job is specified in considerable detail, and a worker holding one job is not permitted to do the work of another. Much of this rigidity is justified as providing predictability and preventing favoritism or speedup. The net effect is to provide each worker a "private property" right (Kerr, 1954), if not in his or her own job, at least in his or her own position on the progression ladder.

Separate wage rates are determined for each job and differentials are jealously maintained. Although the company's freedom to move workers from job to job is greatly restricted, it retains almost complete freedom to adjust levels of total employment, so long as seniority rules are religiously obeyed. In effect, companies give up flexibility in job assignment to retain flexibility in setting employment levels. Note: this is a result which the median voter hypothesis predicts. As long as less than half the work force is laid off, the median voter would prefer having other people laid off to modifying his or her own job progression rights.

The TILM is of course consistent with efficiency wage and implicit contract theories. (Indeed one reason for inventing these theories was to explain the TILM.) From the point of traditional OB theorists, such as Likert and McGregor, the TILM does little to foster motivation or psychological commitment to the organization as a whole, but these may not be essential as long as jobs are routine. TILM's rigid rules are quite consistent with "adversarial labor relations" and "mature collective bargaining" within a pluralist system. (Had either side rejected the pluralist consensus the rules would not have been accepted as quite so legitimate.)

The TILM functions moderately well in handling fluctuations in output as long as product mix and technology are reasonably stable. It is poorly designed for the kinds of rapid technological and market changes that have occurred since 1975. It is badly suited for QWL and other experiments in worker participation which call for a less rigid approach to job duties.

High Commitment System

High commitment labor market policies are, of course, a major alternative to TILM. By high commitment policies I mean those designed to develop broadly trained, highly motivated employees who identify with the organization and who are prepared to exercise high orders of discretion. Along with this comes a commitment from the organization to provide job security and the opportunity to develop a satisfying *career* (not just a job). Key components of this policy are the following:

a. broad job classifications and substantial opportunities for partici-pation, including QWL, job involvement groups, and the like; responsibility given to teams, rather than individuals;
b. lifetime employment and if this is not feasible, strenuous efforts to moderate the impact of economic fluctuations;
c. a heavy stress on both skill and attitude training; elaborate initiation procedures designed to indoctrinate new employees with the organization's values; and
d. new forms of compensation—such as profit sharing and pay-for-knowledge—which are based on factors other than job title and which are designed to foster increased motivation and/or organi-zational commitment.[11]

High commitment organizations take seriously Barnard's (1938) admonition that managers should be "shapers of shared values." They do so through various forms of ceremonial and symbolic activities (Peters & Waterman, 1983). These include award ceremo-nies, company symbols and slogans (for example, "quality comes first") and the like, all designed to link the employee to the organiza-tion. In this way they utilize "a basic social psychological mechanism that results in strong control" (O'Reilly & Kelley, 1988). For exam-ple, there are elaborate selection procedures. These can be justified on the grounds that once hired, an employee is employed for life. In addition, the firm looks upon careful selection as a symbolic means of telling new employees how important they are.

High commitment policies require heavy investments in human resources and high "efficiency wages" (indeed a good part of their justification can be found in "efficiency wage" theory). Much of their popularity comes from the fact that they are presumed to be among the secrets of Japanese success. They are also consistent with the revival of the view that corporations have multiple "stakeholders," not just their stockholders.

Some of the leaders in this movement, IBM and Hewlett Packard, for example, are non-union. However, the plans for GM's new Saturn Division and the avowed policies at the NUMMI plant in Fremont, at Xerox, and at National Steel show that equally innova-tive plans can be adopted in genuine collaboration with unions. There is nothing basically inconsistent between high commitment and collective bargaining. In fact the chances of HP and IBM backsliding from their present high resolves would be much reduced were they unionized.

Firms have adopted such policies for a variety of reasons: one reason is that with broader job classification and less fear of layoff, employees may adopt more easily to long-run technological change or short-run changes in production demand. In some unionized cases, greater job security may be part of a carefully bargained new relationship. Almost everywhere employers hope that increased opportunities for participation will result in a more cooperative, productive work force. Certainly these qualities are especially important in technologies where initiative is required and shirking is difficult to detect. Thus it is no coincidence that elements of high commitment policy are almost standard practice in the Silicon Valley.

In short, employers hope that high commitment policies will result in more efficient use of personnel, less resistance to change, higher motivation, more team spirit, better quality, higher productivity and lower costs. Some employers hope also to weaken unions.

High commitment policies are not completely new. Public-sector, bank, and public utility employees have traditionally enjoyed high levels of job security. Other elements of high commitment policy (but not necessarily life time employment) have been adopted by a long list of high culture firms, such as detailed in Peters and Waterman (1983). What may be new is (a) the adoption of high commitment as an integrating philosophy which provides a focus for HR policies generally and (b) the more frequent application of these policies to blue-collar workers.

Despite their seeming attractiveness, I think high commitment policies have been oversold. For reasons I describe below, I expect them to spread only slowly. In their pure form they may cover only a relatively small portion of the workforce. One reason is that substantial security of employment is required to make it work. Without such security workers' motivation, flexibility and loyalty to the firm is unlikely to develop. If employees lack *employment* security, they may well insist on the kind of *job* security provided by narrow job classifications and output restrictions.

(1)   In many businesses lifetime employment may be difficult to maintain. It requires stable or more likely growing employment. Perhaps high commitment is a luxury that only secure oligopolists can enjoy.

(2)   For most firms the only way to provide lifetime employment is the Japanese way through what Osterman (1988) calls the "core-peripheral system." Peak workloads are handled through overtime

and subcontracting and through employing large numbers of temporary, part-time and on-call employees, most of whom are women or
illegal migrants. Such "peripherals" have none of the benefits enjoyed by core employees.[12] In slacktime the core of lifetime employees are protected, but the subcontractors and peripherals are
quickly let go. The result is a two-class system. You have a core of
contented loyal regular employees and a periphery of discontented,
disloyal peripherals. This is hardly a stable situation. Though peripherals may be difficult to unionize, this may not be impossible.

True, there may be some people who for lifestyle or family
reasons (or to prevent burnout) prefer to maintain flexibility in their
work attachment, and may actually prefer temporary employment.
Others may prefer to switch jobs and employers often, perhaps
because they see this as contributing to their personal growth (Miles,
1988). I suspect their number is small and that most people would
prefer secure, permanent employment. Thus the supply of peripherals may shrink in time of full employment, even if companies
demand them more.

Further, peripheral employees may be prone to shirk. Prevention
of shirking may be particularly difficult in those companies for which
high commitment policies are most desirable. In short there are
limits to the extent to which peripherals may buffer uncertainties.

(3) As Miles and Snow (1986) argue, there may be a counter-
trend, away from stable organizational forms toward loosely knit, ad-
hoc relations among small firms who form consortiums to perform
single tasks and then dissolve, perhaps to reform again, with slightly
different members, to perform different tasks. As evidence of this
they cite the recent growth in outsourcing of parts and of subcontracting for staff and computer services. Such a "network organization" (or "flexible specialization") is apparently characteristic of the
Italian textiles industry (Piore and Sable, 1984). It has long existed in
US construction and recently in movie producing. While work of
this sort may provide job satisfaction, job security is not among its
strengths. Network organization of skilled or professional workers
suggest a craft employment system.

(4) In unionized companies the high-commitment system is
predicated on the continuance of a cooperative, nonadversarial
relationship in which the union is (in theory) an (equal?) partner in
all key decisions. As the MIT group has been studying, such
relationships are difficult to develop and maintain (Strauss, 1988a).
They require considerable decentralization of collective bargaining,
an abdication by higher union leadership of many of its traditional
functions, perhaps even more substantial changes in the role of
lower level supervisors, the development of new skills generally—

and above all, high levels of sensitivity and trust. This is a long list of requirements. But each is critical. If any one is absent, the whole house of cards may collapse. Indeed, it is far too easy for each side to revert to its pre-cooperative behavior, for example, for management to pay large bonuses to its executives while asking for continued worker pay concessions.

At best, a high commitment system plus union-management cooperation at all three KKM levels, represents an extension of democracy. In practice, I suspect (Strauss, 1988a) the success of high commitment will be accompanied by a weakening of unions and even, as in Japan, their transformation into company unions. (I am personally conflicted by this, because I believe strongly in both unionism and participation and believe that *in principle* each should strengthen the other.)

(5) High commitment suffers from other limitations. It assumes that workers value autonomy and participation, that they are prepared to be emotionally committed to their company, and that managers at all levels are willing to surrender a significant part of their authority. None of these assumptions are universally valid.

In practice high commitment may amount to little more than paternalistic manipulation. Sometimes, to achieve commitment, companies engage in ethically questionable training techniques.[13]

(6) Finally, high commitment has met Wall Street, and Wall Street won. (The takeover, leveraged buy-out, and downsizing wave of the last few years has left many firms with a desperate need for cash flow.) This had led many presumably high commitment firms (for example, AT&T) to welch on their implicit contracts and to liquidate their human assets.[14] Not only are skilled managers, professionals, and workers thrown on the ash heap, but expensively nurtured "corporate cultures" are quickly shattered. Commitment and loyalty are difficult to maintain. This breach of faith may trigger KKM's Scenario I, a revival of union strength.

In short, high commitment is a *system*. Weaken any major part of it and the whole system may collapse.[15]

To conclude this section, IR people need to look beyond the details of the collective bargaining arrangement to the wider employment system in which it is embedded. The high commitment system represents an integrating concept around which many currently pressing macro-HRM employment issues may be centered. The transformation from TILM to high commitment systems in both union and nonunion companies requires the same careful multi-level, multi-method research which KKM have applied to the transformation of collective bargaining. We need more evidence, for example, as to the conditions which are appropriate for high commitment and the techniques required for its successful introduction.

Justice Systems

Even though unions have lost strength, the demand for what Barbash (1988) calls "justice" has not. Justice is certainly a major issue for IR practitioners, and macro-HR courses should consider various systems of justice, not just those sponsored by unions. The day when the typical labor law book devoted 15 chapters to collective bargaining law and only two chapters to "protective legislation" is long past.

Pressures for increased employee rights are coming from a variety of sources: Congress, state legislatures, the courts, (although not the Reagan presidency) and ethnic, women's, and older worker's organizations.[16] As unions continue to weaken, society has increasingly turned to the law to stem abuses.[17] Since 1960 Congress and the courts have had a greater impact on human resources policies than anything unions could do. Indeed the "transformation of industrial relations" caused by equal employment legislation since 1962 may be greater than that caused by union decline. Certainly it has affected more workers.

True, President Reagan was elected on a platform calling for deregulation, and his Presidency has been marked by considerable slackening of the rigor with which the *executive* branch has sought to enforce the laws. But the laws themselves have been little changed; nor have the courts greatly changed their interpretation of them. Indeed, even under Reagan, Congress has done more tightening than loosening,[18] the state legislatures keep on legislating, and as this is written there is a tremendous log jam of bills which have gone part way through the federal legislative process. These deal with such topics as minimum wages, parental leave, plant closures, polygraphs, toxic risk notification, catastrophic health insurance coverage, continued life insurance coverage for retirees whose employers have fallen into bankruptcy, and "double breasting" in construction. Regardless who is President in 1989 much of this legislation will pass.

Even without new legislation, courts have been active fashioning new employee rights, for example with regards to drug testing. Similarly, the erosion of the employment-at-will doctrine has already heavily involved courts in company personnel practices. And management has had to spend much time trying to justify its decisions in an increasingly litigious society.

Forty years ago it was the union movement which took the

initiative and came up with new ideas. Even in their weakened form unions are still influential in setting agenda for reform. They are the main force today, for example, behind proposed plant closing legislation. Nevertheless, many of the changes I see in the future will come from the women's agenda (if not from the women's movement itself). These include comparable worth, flextime, the freedom to move in and out of the labor force, and above all, child care. The new, new (post-1982) feminist is interested not just in equality on the job, but in equality *plus* the chance to bring up a family without unduly harming her career.

Beyond this, there appears to be a continuing upgrading in society's expectations as to how workers will be treated, especially in large organizations.[19] Illustrative of this increased interest is the organization (outside the academic IR establishment) of a new professional association, the Council on Employees' Responsibilities and Rights, with its own journal and annual meeting.

Reacting to these pressures some companies have gone further than the law requires. They have done so in part to protect themselves from regulation, in part to ward off unions and other pressure groups, and in part because employee rights are consistent with high commitment policies (as well with both efficiency wages and implicit contracts.)

The demand is for both substantive and procedural justice.

Substantive Justice

Substantive justice can be an all-embracing term. Nevertheless, there are changes in emphasis over time.

The 1970's were the decade of equal employment. They forced a radical change in the procedures used to select, evaluate, and promote employees at all levels, as well as significant increases in the employment of women and ethnic minorities in occupations that were once all white-male.

But the legally mandated adjustments in company policy have already been made. Organizations have learned how to live under equal employment rules and yet preserve a degree of flexibility. For this reason, business has shown little interest in following the Reagan administration's call to dismantle the affirmative action machinery. As stressed earlier, the laws are still in place. Through judicial inertia and the operation of formal and informal seniority systems, the number of minorities and especially women in higher paid jobs should continue to increase.

Major current equal-employment issues relate to the handicapped, the aged, and comparable worth. As to the latter, the courts appear to have shied away from imposing job evaluation schemes, but some progress toward comparable-worth is being made in the government sector through lobbying and collective bargaining. The private sector will move more slowly.

But the enthusiasm for equal employment has been lost. It is last decade's cause. The real hot issues for the next few years relate to individual rights (especially privacy) and fringe benefits.

Job Rights and Privacy

The typical issues here involve drug and AIDS testing, smoking, polygraphs, whistle blowing, confidentiality of personnel files, and letters of recommendation. Standards are rapidly changing. Who could have predicted a few years ago that the right not to be bothered by cigarette smoke would be widely protected by law, that employers would be prohibited from testing for a major disease (AIDS) as part of routine physical exams, or that a firm's ability to test its employees for drug usage would trigger a considerable (so far unresolved) social debate? Looming on the horizon are challenges to personality tests on grounds of privacy (not just equal employment).

Fringes

Along with wage concessions, the spread of fringes has slowed down considerably. I suspect this is only temporary. In any case, even if the level of fringes remains unchanged, an aging workforce will make pensions and medical care increasingly expensive.

There are numerous issues of social policy in this area. The big question, of course, is that of fringes versus take-home pay. Fringes are based on workers' needs while take-home pay is based on their contributions. What should be the tradeoffs between these two? The issue is likely to arise with regards to child care (which some see as the major issue of the 1990's). Whether paid for by the employer or by the government, child care will be terribly expensive. Increased female labor force participation, particularly of women with children, has changed the terms of many debates.

Then there are more technical questions, for instance those relating various approaches to containing medical costs and the impact of such containment measures on the quality of medical care.

An emerging issue concerns sick leave. In many organizations employees are allowed to use their sick leave to take care of their new born babies. There is considerable pressure to extend this right, step by step, to cover sick children of all ages, sick spouses, sick significant others, and sick parents. Policing this is difficult. Further, such a policy may arguably be said to discriminate against single workers, gays, and even males generally. Would it be fairer to fold sick leave into vacation pay and treat them the same? Such a proposal might make for an exciting class discussion.

Procedural Justice

Among the union's primary functions is to provide individual workers a chance to "have their day in court."[20] As Garbarino (1984) points out, the collective bargaining model of representation has been meeting heavy competition from what he calls the legal, administrative (company), and civil service models. Illustrative of this is the growing number of unfair dismissal cases taken to the courts. Meanwhile numerous companies have established ombuds or grievance procedures, some with impartial arbitration. Whistle-blowing is becoming increasingly accepted. In a high commitment system, voice is a critical substitute for exit.

But are these new systems as efficient (in terms of cost) or as effective (in terms of remedying injustice) as the union grievance procedure? Certainly the courts are expensive. In company-run grievance procedures, the unrepresented worker may be easily overwhelmed; while ombudspersons may help, rarely will they be as diligent in protecting workers' rights as independent union stewards. The company personnel manual will rarely provide as definitive a bill of rights as the union contract. Thus, as the AFL-CIO Donahue Committee suggests, there may be an important role for unions in acting as advocates for individual workers' rights under both "administrative" (company) and legal systems. Still this Legal-Aid-Society role is a pale substitute for participation in determining the substance of these rights.

Teaching and Research

Justice issues pose real problems for practitioners. How might academicians teach and research them? Let me suggest four related approaches, although there are many others.

(1)   One approach is via business ethics. What standards should be applied to determine an employer's social responsibilities to its employees? In my view, it should be required to bear at the least the

costs of its externalities and perhaps more. Presumably, if a manufacturing process causes cancer, then the manufacturer should bear the full costs of that cancer. But since the costs of human suffering are impossible to quantify objectively, we come to another question: how should this cost be calculated? Or is reparation not meaningful, only prevention? And should the cost of eliminating cancer be balanced against the possible costs of unemployment (which are also externalities) if the cancer-causing process is shut down?

Beyond externalities, what are the employers' social obligations to employees? For example, what is the social rationale for requiring employers to hold jobs open for pregnant women or to provide assistance to AIDS patients?

(2)   How are employment-rights policies implemented? How should they be? Union policies are implemented through collective bargaining and the grievance procedure—and IR students study these intensively. As Peter Feuille has argued, IR students might also examine the bargaining process which underlies most EEOC enforcement efforts. What has been the union's role in different kinds of EEOC cases? Unfair dismissal cases are now handled by the courts. How does this work in practice? What better mechanisms can be devised?

For example, formal ADR (alternate dispute resolution) procedures, such as mediation, are being used increasingly widely to settle family and environmental disputes. At present a high percentage of EEOC and NLRB cases are disposed of informally (that is by bargaining), but third parties are rarely brought in to mediate. Would ADR be desirable here? A related question: how effective are ombudsmen and nonunion grievance procedures? (Peterson and Lewin, 1988).

(3)   What has been the impact of the various justice policies? For example, the macro-impact of equal employment, in terms of overall employment patterns and distribution of income, has been thoroughly studied. And there have been numerous articles by psychologists and lawyers on how to live with equal employment rules. But the organizational impact of these rules has been hardly examined. A few hypotheses as to their consequences: there has been a tremendous increase in paper work; internal company rules have proliferated; the power of the human resources department has increased; and organizations have become accustomed to dealing with a larger number of interest groups and government departments.

(4)   The foregoing approaches related to my final question, which is the most difficult of all: what are the costs and benefits of various measures to provide substantive and procedural justice?

Conclusion

I have argued that academic IR should reassert its traditional jurisdiction over the entire employment relationship. But to do this
requires new paradigms, new sets of questions and analytic models. I
suggest that many of these can be derived from labor economics,
organizational behavior, and organizational sociology as well as
micro-HRM.

I have covered (quite lightly) a number of topics which are
important for practitioners today and which a broadened IR course
might cover. (I much prefer the title IR to HR Policy). Further I have
tried to illustrate how such a course might draw upon the disciplines
mentioned above.

I've left a great deal out. At the least, a broadened IR course might
consider recent and perspective changes in labor supply (for example, the aging of the baby-boom generation) and demand (for
example, new technologies and the growth of network organization). Certainly it should deal with compensation, especially new
forms such as profit sharing and payment for knowledge. It would
discuss the various forms of participation, both union and nonunion. Further each of these topics might be considered in the
context of alternative employment and justice systems.

A broadened conception of IR might reflect the reality that the
major human resources problems faced by the American economy
are not likely to be resolved through union-management negotiations. Yet, drawing upon their multi-disciplinary background, IR
scholars may contribute to the understanding and solution to the
new dilemmas faced which our society faces in much the way they
contributed in the past to the analysis of collective bargaining.

Notes

1. My thanks to James Dworkin, Herbert Heneman III, and Jack Fiorito
   for helpful criticism. For a more extensive discussion of some of the
   issues raised here, see Strauss (pp. 91-118; 1988b).
2. In the words of a perceptive labor historian, "Industrial relations itself
   shrank down into a kind of minidiscipline, confined as before to the
   union sector, but striving belatedly to assert its credentials as rigorous
   social science" (Brody, 1988b).
3. Most of the new labor economics can be found in Slichter, Healy &
   Livernash (1960), but they put it in simpler language.
4. My main reservation is that many of the assumptions made by contemporary labor economists are wildly unrealistic, at times as if Newton

assumed apples went up rather than down. Even where these assumptions are not wholly wrong, they sometimes abstract away such large portions of reality that they end up being more wrong than right. I am distinctly uncomfortable, for example, with the assumption that all unemployment is voluntary or that an institution's behavior should be analyzed as if it were determined by the sum of its members' preferences (or those of its median and even marginal member).

5. See, for instance, "The New Economics of Personnel" (1987), the proceedings of a conference sponsored by the Goldwater Foundation and Arizona State University. None of the papers deal with unionism. Parenthetically, the sponsorship by the Goldwater Foundation is somewhat appropriate. We have gone a long way since the days when most labor-economists were left-wingers.

6. Most of these personnel economists' hypotheses deal with the relationship between the behavior of firms and their own employees, yet traditionally these were tested by data which aggregates the behavior of employees of a number of firms and/or by industry level data. Encouragingly, this is changing.

7. I view IR and macro-HRM as being broader fields than what has begun to be called "strategic human resources management." The latter tends to be concerned with such subjects as long-term manpower planning and cost-benefit analyses of the various services provided by HR departments (Dyer, 1984; Lengnick-Hall & Lengnick-Hall, 1988). Macro-HR would be concerned with such issues as job design, motivation, corporate culture, as well as representational systems.

8. My analysis borrows heavily from Paul Osterman's work, especially his forthcoming *Employment Labor Markets and Employment Policy*. The term "employment systems" is his. My limited contribution is to stress the OB implications of the alternatives, especially those relating to commitment and motivation. My thinking has also been greatly influenced by David Brody and Sanford Jacoby.

9. Aside from choice of employment systems, management may also choose among motivational strategies, for example, traditional (autocratic), human relations (paternalistic), and human resources (Theory Y).

10. On the other hand the closed shop requires employers to hire older, less efficient workers at the same wage as younger ones.

11. The new approaches to compensation put "pay at risk." Thus high commitment systems may increase job security but reduce pay security. Some employees may feel this is an unfair tradeoff.

12. Unskilled peripherals belong to unstructured labor markets, more skilled ones perhaps to the craft or professional markets.

13. "Employers are increasingly making use of training programs designed to improve motivation, cooperation, or productivity through the use of various 'new age' techniques," says the EEOC (1988; *Daily Labor Report*, April 11, 1988). "For example, a large utility company [Pacific T&T] requires its employees to attend seminars based on the teaching of a mystic, George Gurdjieff, which the company claims has improved

communications among employees." The EEOC questions whether such programs may violate religious freedoms.

14. Despite the Japanese management fad, US managers had traditionally focused on immediate payoff. Flipping through recent *Wall Street Journals*, I note that "institutional investors [are showing] increased impatience with companies that aren't producing short-term profit gains" (April 11, 1988, 1) and that "GM Officials Get Short-Term Incentives Despite Plan to Emphasize Long Term" (April 18, 1988, 4).

15. Let me be more specific. The high commitment system consists of at least three critical elements (inputs): (a) job security, (b) participation, autonomy, or some other source of task identification, and (c) trust, plus, in a unionized situation, (d) good relations at all three KKM levels. Its outcomes are higher productivity, etc. I hypothesize that if any one of the inputs are weakened, the outputs will be substantially reduced.

16. The American Association of Retired People may have as much clout as any union.

17. Unions do best in protecting their own members. The groups that recent legislation has tried to protect are for the most part non-union.

18. Laws passed in the 1985-86 Congress prohibited mandatory retirement in most occupations, required continued health plant protections and pension accruals for employees who work beyond normal retirement age, permitted employees to extend their health benefits for at least 18 months after layoffs, and prohibited employment of illegal immigrants.

19. What sociologists call the "institutional environment" (Scott, 1987) is placing increasing restrictions on human resources practices.

20. The 1977 Quality of Employment Study found that union members ranked the handling of grievances as their first priority for union attention (Kochan, 1979).

References

Arrow, K. (1985, May). Economic history: a necessary though not sufficient condition for economists. *American Economic Review, 75, Part II,* 320-323.

Barbash, J. (1988). A department for protecting workers' equity, *Monthly Labor Review, 3*(2), 3-10.

Barnard, C. (1938). *The Functions of the Executive.* Cambridge, MA: Harvard University Press.

Beer, M.; Spector, B.; Lawrence, P.R.; Mills, D.Q.; & Walton, R.E. (1985). *Human Resource Management: A General Manager's Perspective.* New York: Free Press.

Brody, D. (1988a). *In dubious regard: trade unions and the American public.* Working paper.

Brody, D. (1988b). *Labor history, industrial relations, and the crisis of American labor.* Working paper.

Curtin, R. (1987). Skill formation and the enterprise. *Labour and Industry*, *1*(1), 8-38.

Doeringer, P., & Piore, M. (1971). *International Labor Markets and Manpower Analysis*. Lexington, MA: Heath.

Dyer, L. (1983). Bringing human resources into the strategy formulation process. *Human Resources Management, 22*, 156-169.

Equal Employment Opportunity Commission. (1988, April 11). Policy statement on 'new age' training programs which conflict with employees' religious beliefs. *Daily Labor Report*.

Fisher, L. (1953). *The Harvest Labor Market in California*. Cambridge, MA: Harvard University Press.

Freeman, R.B., & Medoff, J.L. (1984) *What Do Unions Do*. New York: Basic Books.

Garbarino, J.W. (1984). Unionism without unions. *Industrial Relations, 23*, 40-51.

GM officials get short-term incentives despite plan to emphasize long term. (1988, April 18). *Wall Street Journal*, p. 4.

Institutional investors are showing increased impatience with companies that aren't producing short-term profit gains. (1988, April 11). *Wall Street Journal*, p. 1.

Jacoby, S. (1985). *Employing Bureaucracy*. New York: Columbia University Press.

Katz, C., & Sabel, C.F. (1985). Industrial relations and industrial adjustment in the car industry. *Industrial Relations, 24*, 295-315.

Kerr, C. (1954). The Balkanization of labor markets. *In* P. Webbink (ed.), *Labor Mobility and Economic Opportunity*. Cambridge, MA: MIT Press.

Kleiner, M., McLean, R. & Dreher, G. (1988). *Labor Markets and Human Resources Management*. Glenville, IL: Scott Foresman.

Kochan, T.A. (1979, April). How American workers view labor unions. *Monthly Labor Review, 102*, 23-31.

Kochan, T.A., & Barocci, T. (1985). *Human Resources Management and Industrial Relations*. Boston: Little, Brown.

Kochan, T.A.; Katz, H.C.; & McKersie, R.B. (1986). *The Transformation of American Industrial Relations*. New York: Basic Books.

Koike, K. (1984). Skill formation in the U.S. and Japan, a cooperative study. *In* M. Aoki (ed.), *The Economic Analysis of the Japanese Firm*. Elsevier.

Lawler, E.E. III. (1986). *High Involvement Management*. San Francisco: Jossey-Bass.

Lengnick-Hall, C., & Lengnick-Hall, M. (1988). Strategic human resources management: a review of the literature and a proposed typology. *Academy of Management Review, 13*, 454-470.

Lewin, D., & Strauss, G. (1988). Behavioral research in industrial relations: introduction. *Industrial Relations. 27*(1), 1-6.

Miles, R. (1988). Adopting to technology and competition: a new industrial relations system for the 21st century. Working paper.

Miles, R., & Snow, C. (1986). New concepts for new forms. *California Management Review, 28*(3), 62-73.

Mitchell, D.J.B. (in press). *An Economic Approach to Human Resource Management*.

The new economics of personnel. (1987). *Journal of Labor Economics* 5(4).

O'Reilly, C., & Kelley, W.A. (1988). The human resources priorities of Japanese firms at home and abroad: psychological consequences. Working paper.

Osterman, P. (1988). *Employment Policy and Internal Labor Markets*. Oxford: Oxford University Press.

Peter, T., & Waterman, R. (1983). *In Search of Excellence*. New York: Harper & Row.

Peterson, R., & Lewin, D. (1988). *The non-union grievance procedure*. Working paper.

Piore, M., & Sabel, C. (1984). *The Second Industrial Divide: Possibilities for Prosperity*. New York: Basic Books.

Rehmus, C. (1985). Report from the dean. *ILR Research, 2*(2), 3.

Scott, W.R. (1987). The adolescence of institutional theory. *Administrative Science Quarterly, 32*, 493-511.

Slichter, S.; Healy, J.; & Livernast, E.R. (1960). *The Impact of Collective Bargaining on Management*. Washington, DC: Brookings Institution.

Stark, D. (1986). Rethinking internal labor markets: new insights from a comparative perspective. *American Sociological Review, 51*, 492-504.

Strauss, G. (1963). Occupational associations and professionalism. *Industrial Relations, 2*, 7-31.

Strauss, G. (1987). The future of human resources management. *In* D.J.B. Mitchell (ed.), *The Future of Industrial Relations*. Los Angeles: Institute of Industrial Relations.

Strauss, G. (1988a). Workers participation and U.S. collective bargaining. *Handbook of Organizational Participation*. Oxford: Oxford University Press.

Strauss, G. (1988b). Industrial relations as an academic field: What's wrong with it. *In* J. Barbash (ed.), *Theories and Concepts in Comparative Industrial Relations*. Columbia, SC: University of South Carolina Press.

COMMENTS: THE WIDER BOUNDS OF IR SYSTEMS

Jack Fiorito

As is CHARACTERISTIC OF Professor Strauss' work, his paper (1990, chap. 4) is thoughtful and provocative. I substantially agree with its principal thesis, that IR (industrial relations) as an academic field needs to reassert its traditional broader jurisdiction. This broader jurisdiction is coincident with the employment relationship rather than union-management relations. I differ with Professor Strauss in terms of how we conceptualize this broader jurisdiction. I also disagree with some lesser points in the paper, but by far my main concern involves the issue of a conceptual framework.

Professor Strauss correctly identifies the need for an integrating scheme through which the fields of IR and HR (human resources) might be combined. Absent a coherent and plausible integrating scheme, any attempt by IR scholars to reclaim the HR domain is likely to be viewed as an unjustified "turf-grab," or even an act of desperation on the part of academics who had the misfortune and/or poor judgment to hitch their wagons to what appears a declining "industry"—unionism. Two concepts, employment systems—with an emphasis on the emerging "high commitment system" (HCS)—and justice in employment relations, are suggested by Professor Strauss as issues for a broadened study of IR. These two ideas can be useful devices for illustrating, on the one hand, variations in important employment dimensions, and on the other, the notion that there is a demand for workplace justice that will be met by some means other than market forces, whether it be via unions, legislation, or court actions. These concepts fall far short, however, of providing an integrating framework for the study of employment relations.

Paul A. Jarley and Cheryl L. Maranto provided many helpful comments on the ideas in this paper.

Will the Real IR Systems Framework Please Stand?

The good news is that an integrating framework for the study of employment relations already exists. I refer to the familiar but often bastardized "Industrial Relations Systems" framework outlined by Professor Dunlop (1958), and to its legitimate progeny.[1] In their haste to identify some of the dramatic changes in IR of recent years, Kochan, Katz, and McKersie ("KKM," 1986) and associates (for example, Kochan, McKersie, & Cappelli, 1984)[2] have at times confused IR changes with the question of the IR systems framework's continued relevance.[3] But as Professor Kochan noted during discussion at this conference, one can conclude that the IR system has transformed (or merely evolved) without necessarily concluding there is a need for change in our basic conceptual framework.

What KKM have justly criticized is a simple-minded but popular bastardized version of the IR systems framework that is limited rigidly to three actors (management, government, and unions) who engage in (or in the case of government, regulate) collective bargaining (only) to produce a contractual web of rules, while each actor accepts completely the legitimate role of other actors. Environmental or contextual factors in this bastardized IR systems framework are excessively deterministic, leaving virtually no range for actor discretion, including management's "strategic choices." This is hardly an adequate integrating framework for the study of employment relations, and it is this constraining "paradigm" if we may call it that, from which Professor Strauss rightly argues we break away.

The *real* IR systems framework is considerably broader than this caricature, which has been attacked by KKM. The real IR systems framework may specify employees as a fourth actor, as Dunlop notes that his "hierarchy of workers does not imply formal organizations" (Dunlop, 1958, p.7). It probably specifies shared ideology as necessary for system stability or equilibrium, and consequently system instability arises as a consequence of inconsistent actor beliefs, which in turn may be driven, although not precisely determined, by contextual factors such as product markets.[4] It most certainly does not imply a passive view of management, as Cochrane refers to the "replacement of the labor movement with industrial managers and professional workers as the vanguard of the future" as one of the three major ideas in Kerr, Dunlop, Harbison, and Myers' (1960) *Industrialism and Industrial Man* (Cochrane, 1979, pp. 118-119), a volume clearly intertwined with Dunlop's *Industrial Relations Systems* (1958).

The real IR systems framework is hardly deterministic. For example, in wage determination an IR scholar would presumably turn first to economic theory for guidance: Economic theory suggests that product markets establish an upper bound for wage rates while labor markets set a lower bound. The two would be coincident under perfect competition, but not in general, and thus there is already a source of discretion. Unlike some economists, IR scholars are unlikely to assume perfect competition and thus this discretion is nontrivial. Further, IR scholars are likely to recognize that noneconomic considerations such as choices of referents might affect actual wage rates, introducing further uncertainty, and possibly further discretion.

The issue of determinism in the IR systems framework also requires recognition of the distinction between short and long term forces. Contextual factors might indeed tend to be given in the short term. Via what one could call strategic choices, however, in the long term the actors may be able to alter their sensitivity to particular influences or the nature of the influence itself.[5]

Most importantly, the real IR systems framework does not equate IR and collective bargaining. Since Dunlop's aim was to provide a framework useful for understanding IR in its various forms throughout the world, it would be particularly odd if he were to yoke his framework to collective bargaining. The IR systems concept easily enough accommodates the notion of multiple rule-making processes, including individual bargaining, legislation, judicial processes, unilateral management (or union) processes or self-management. For that matter, why not hybrid processes which combine basic types of rule-making processes? Professional sports presents an example combining collective and individual bargaining. Strictly speaking, doesn't our legal framework's treatment of bargaining subject types (mandatory, permissive, illegal) effectively yield a process combining unilateral management and collective bargaining rule-making, even though we may tend to call this combination "collective bargaining" (only)? Is today's participative-management-but-on-management's-terms in nonunion situations essentially a unilateral management process or a hybrid? This is a most important point to which I will return more fully in a moment.

I seem to have digressed substantially from the subject of Professor Strauss' paper. But in fact, Professor Strauss' paper puts the issue of an integrating framework for understanding employment relationships at center stage. The work of KKM, the main topic of this conference, has suggested at times that the contemporary relevance of the IR systems framework is in doubt. The point of my digression is to argue that KKM's challenges to the systems framework have been generally unpersuasive. The essence of this position has been taken by others at this conference and elsewhere (for example, Block 1990, chap. 2, Lewin 1987, Roomkin & Juris 1990, chap. 5,

Stepina & Fiorito 1984). Usually, however, the issue is cast simply in terms of whether IR *systems* are changed or changing, or whether the KKM framework represents something fundamentally new, without substantial attention to the (at least) implicit alternative of the IR systems framework. This may be a case of failing to see the forest for the trees: we are so accustomed to thinking in terms of the ideas embodied in the IR systems framework that we are hardly aware of it.

I join KKM's other critics in noting that the KKM work represents a significant contribution even if it falls short of providing a persuasive new paradigm for the study of IR.[6] For example, although Dunlop (1958) stressed the multiple levels at which the IR systems concept might be applied, the KKM notion of simultaneous consideration of multiple levels within the firm (strategic, bargaining/personnel, workplace), and possible inconsistencies across the levels is important and novel. (Block's [1990] "political level" needs to be added to the model, however.) In addition, even if Dunlop's framework does not encourage neglect of management's IR role, nevertheless that neglect occurred, and the KKM work begins to rectify the problem. In general, and as this last example illustrates, to the extent the narrow *bastardized* IR systems concept described earlier has come to prevail, the KKM work is useful in pointing out the severe limitations of *that* framework.

Reasserting the IR Systems Boundaries

How does Professor Strauss' call for a new integrating framework square with the preceding digression on the IR systems concept? My argument is, again, that the real IR systems concept is in fact the framework sought. If we look carefully at the high commitment system (HCS) which is elaborated upon in Professor Strauss' discussion of employment systems, and the discussion of justice in employment relationships, the essential and common element is the emphasis on a process for establishing the terms and conditions of employment that is different from but parallel to collective bargaining.

What is most fundamental about the HC employment system described by Professor Strauss is that it is essentially a unilateral rule-making system. Employee commitment is sought to achieve unity of purpose (for example, organizational prosperity, shareholder wealth), loyalty, and effort on behalf of the employing organization. Employee participation is sought, true, but on management's terms and only to a limited degree. Acceptance of managerial authority is still a dominant management goal, but now the device of preference is commitment rather than coercion or passive consent. Even if we conceive of the HCS as partly unilateral and partly self-management the main point is still valid: The essential character of the HCS lies in its rule-making process.

What is most fundamental about Strauss' discussion of justice is not that justice is sought—surely unions feel that they seek workplace justice! What is most fundamental about the justice system is the process involved in determining workplace outcomes ("rules" in a broad sense). Strauss' discussion of justice confuses the distinct rule-making processes of legislation (or the Webbs' "legal enactment") and adjudication (courts, arbitration, etc.), but a common characteristic these two distinct methods share with collective bargaining is their non-unilateral character. In theory, both the legislative and adjudicative rule-making processes remove the determination of rules from the immediate power circumstances of the parties, and at the same time subject the determination of rules to a relatively substantial measure of public interest.[7] The important distinction between the legislative and adjudicative processes is that the former clearly fashions substantive rules while the latter's principal function is to apply rules fashioned elsewhere.

Things start to get more interesting if we combine KKM's levels of analysis (strategic, collective bargaining/personnel policy, workplace), Block's (1990) macro or political level, and multiple rule-making processes. This yields a matrix of levels by processes. This matrix suggests a number of interesting questions, including the following:

1. Why do nations choose different processes for particular levels? For example, why is peak-level collective bargaining or consultation important in Japan and Canada but not the U.S.?
2. Why, within a given nation, are different processes favored for different levels of decisions? For example, why are many strategic level issues effectively excluded from collective bargaining (through the bargaining subjects typology; see Block, 1990), while lower level issues are subject to collective bargaining?
3. Why are different types of issues subject to different rule-making processes? For example, in a nonunion situation why might management delegate performance appraisal and individual salary adjustment recommendations to a peer process as part of a participative team concept, but maintain strict unilateral determination of the actual salary schedule?

The main point is that this levels-by-process conception leads us to ask questions of general interest in employment relations, both union and nonunion. In particular it encourages us to ask *why* a particular rule-making process is chosen. Since the rules (in the broad sense of outcomes) themselves may be very sensitive to the process used to determine them, the choice of process seems a useful focal point in the study of Industrial Relations. Indeed, this question may be more fundamental than the more familiar one of how variations in IR system elements affect outcomes, since in a sense the rule-making process is a mechanism for converting inputs and contingencies into outcomes. Research on this topic, the question of why particular rule-making processes are used in particular circumstances, might represent a significant step for the field of IR, and one which might help it reassert jurisdiction over the employment relationship beyond union-management relations.

Other Issues

As noted earlier, there are other points in Professor Strauss' paper that merit attention. Two of the additional issues that concern me deal with IR's relation to other subject areas. One of these involves the need for IR to draw upon other disciplines, and the second concerns the appropriate theoretical focus of IR vis-à-vis other disciplines.

First, let us consider Professor Strauss' observation that IR needs to draw upon other disciplines such as labor economics, OB, organizational sociology, political science, and micro-HRM. This notion is so obviously a part of traditional IR, and so important, that some elaboration is warranted. The notion of IR as a system intertwined with the economic and social system, etc., is clearly part of Dunlop's original conception, and is also manifested in the structure of academic programs at many of the IR institutes established in the 1940's and 1950's.

Considering the context in which Professor Strauss makes this observation, it seems his point is that scholars who study union-management relations (an IR subfield) less clearly evidence the interdisciplinary (collaboration by scholars in different disciplines) or multidisciplinary (a single scholar drawing upon multiple disciplines) tradition of earlier IR scholars: They tend *not* to read the *American Economic Review*, the *Journal of Applied Psychology*, the *American Sociological Review*, or the *American Journal of Political Science*. Likewise, the readers of these journals who are interested in IR problems tend not to read the *Industrial and Labor Relations Review* or *Industrial Relations*. It is not less true now than thirty or forty years ago that IR problems cut across disciplinary lines. Yet according to Professor Strauss we now seem to observe less interdisciplinary study, which would seem to imply that important aspects of IR problems will be overlooked.

I'm not entirely sure that multidisciplinary IR research has declined, although interdisciplinary IR research probably has. I suspect the latter is partly a reflection of increased specialization, perhaps interacting with rising academic standards for promotion and tenure. In short, I think it was easier to be interested in IR and yet "pass" for an economist or psychologist thirty or forty years ago. It was easier then for a sociologist and economist to discuss IR problems because their respective disciplines' terminologies had not become so distinctive; their paradigms were less developed. Now it is extremely difficult for one to simultaneously maintain a command of a field's current paradigm and of IR knowledge. To encourage two young assistant professors from different disciplinary backgrounds to pursue their joint interest in IR problems via collaboration might be very bad advice from a promotion and tenure perspective. Publications from this joint work in IR journals are likely to be discounted by senior colleagues in both of the respective disciplines.

The irony is that there is generally a louder cry now for interdisciplinary study than in the past—there seems to be a growing perception of interdisciplinary study as a solution for the adverse effects of increased specialization in academic endeavors. Yet some of the programs designed to promote interdisciplinary study seem to be self-defeating: For example, one such program (at a major university) offering funds stipulates collaborating faculty *must* come from more than one department—too bad for departments (such as an IR department) which might be interdisciplinary or multidisciplinary in the first place! And who hasn't heard some variant of the horror stories surrounding efforts by an IR institute to recruit a faculty member in IR acceptable to one or more "true" disciplinary departments?

Are these horror stories indicative of a basic tension between the notions of interdisciplinary and multidisciplinary study in IR? That is, a general phenomenon seems to be one of hiring from the contributing disciplines to produce multidisciplinary graduates. But then who hires these graduates? The problem may be more apparent for union-management relations students than HR students for now, but in principle it concerns all of IR. Professor Strauss seems to favor a more interdisciplinary model but at the same time is quite critical of our colleagues in the contributing disciplines (for example, labor economics); he is inconsistent on this point. If we truly accept the pure interdisciplinary model, the logical conclusion might be to phase out IR (and HR) Ph.D. programs.

I suspect, however, that increased specialization has made the pure interdisciplinary model obsolete. The criticisms of the contributing disciplines expressed by Professor Strauss begin to touch on the problems inherent in these disciplines' studies of IR. In many instances the elegant theoretical model entails excess baggage that obscures rather than enlightens while attempting to fit problems and facts into its predetermined mold. (See Kerr 1983 for discussion of related issues in a labor economics context).

I feel that we should try to make sure the IR doctoral students have a significant strength in one of the contributing disciplines. Among other virtues, this should help to insure that IR gleans the best of the work in these areas that applies to IR. But we should not ask them to demonstrate the same "naiveté" or "theoretical purity" (depending on one's perspective—one might alternatively choose between "irrelevance" or "rigor") as doctorates in the contributing discipline. By trying to force our field to be interdisciplinary to some degree, we may at least maintain a multidisciplinary character. That is, bringing together an IR-economics doctorate and IR-psychology doctorate may not guarantee interdisciplinary research that is judged favorably by economists or psychologists. It may, however, tend to produce IR research which appropriately reflects the relevance of both psychology and economics to IR problems.

So, yes, we do need to continue to draw upon other disciplines, but we should also recognize that specialization increases as sciences develop. Consequently, we should not be surprised that IR has "grown away" from its parent disciplines. Nor should we be surprised that disciples of the parent disciplines regard us as wayward children.

On a second but related issue, Professor Strauss suggests that in combining HRM and IR, we should concern ourselves with the broad issues in both union and nonunion sectors, leaving theoretical analysis to OB and labor economics, and the nitty-gritty how-to-do-it issues to traditional micro-HRM. Earlier sections of this paper have dealt with combining HRM and IR, but what about the issue of leaving theory to others? This argument is intertwined with the last, but also raises additional matters. If Professor Strauss' reference to "theoretical analysis" is to deductive formalism, I heartily agree— that should be left to those in the contributing disciplines more concerned with elegant theoretical structures. IR per se should stay true to its problem-oriented nature. This implies a greater emphasis on inductive research methods and applied theory, and in this sense I agree strongly with Cappelli (1985). This doesn't make IR atheoretical, however.

On the other side, the nitty-gritty micro-HRM issues are largely measurement issues. It is in fact rather accurate to describe much of what is called HR today as measurement issues. A typical policy issue that is of concern to IR is whether pay should be linked to performance. The HR field seems at times to lose sight of the issue and become preoccupied with measuring performance as if doing so were the end objective. Under the rhetoric of "utility" analysis (an unfortunate choice of terms, perhaps, from a economics perspective), our HR colleagues have begun to ask the right questions, such as whether it is worthwhile to use ability test scores as selection criteria.

Conclusion

As I stated at the beginning of this paper, Professor Strauss' work is generally provocative, and this instance is no exception. Questions are raised regarding an integrating conceptual framework for the study of employment relationships. Questions raised about the relation of IR to other disciplines and the role of theory in IR and related disciplines go to the very heart of IR as an academic field.

Professor Strauss suggests that IR needs to reassert jurisdiction over the employment relationship, including much of the subject matter commonly referred to as HR. I agree with this aim, but I differ with Professor Strauss on means. His employment systems and justice notions might be useful pedagogical devices, but they do not add up to an integrating framework. The often maligned IR systems framework, properly specified, holds more promise in this regard.

Issues concerning the relation of IR to its contributing disciplines, the nature of theory in IR, and multidisciplinary and interdisciplinary research have been and will remain contentious matters for the IR field. They have certainly not been resolved here, but I commend Professor Strauss for raising them. It is a most appropriate time for a healthy debate of these issues.

Notes

1. I refer particularly to a version of the IR systems framework taught by Professor Milton Derber in his IR Theory seminars at the University of Illinois. The main contrasts with the popularized version of Dunlop's framework are the specification of four actors (adding employees), recognition that collective bargaining is but one possible rule-making process, and a broad concept of "rules" as the dependent variable,

wherein the term is synonomous with outcomes, including compensation, employment security, industrial democracy, job satisfaction, and the more familiar and narrow concept of rules per se. In Professor Derber's model, industrial democracy is the outcome of principal concern. There are certainly other offerings in this vein (e.g., Craig 1975), but most of the published work on conceptual frameworks appears in non-U.S. sources.

2. For convenience I will use the KKM initials to represent the work of the Sloan School IR group more broadly hereafter. Peter Cappelli is of course a principal "associate" who merits mention.

3. KKM (1986) are more careful about this distinction than the earlier Kochan et al. (1984) article. The notion that KKM's work challenges the continued relevance of the IRS framework, however, seems to remain widespread.

4. Lewin (1987) develops a critique of the KKM framework which raises several of the same issues raised here and in Stepina and Fiorito (1984). Lewin focuses particular criticism on the "strategic" aspects of the framework. See also Block (1990), and Roomkin and Juris (1990).

5. It is easy to think of increased product market competition of recent years as narrowing management's short term discretion, forcing consideration of strategic choices such as plant relocation, union avoidance rather than accommodation, and changing business lines. See Lewin (1987), especially pp. 8, 19, and 35, and Block (1990).

6. At times, the IR systems framework seems *too* general, in the same sense as economic's utility theory. If the IR systems framework were regarded as a true *theory*, this degree of generality would be more troubling.

7. An interesting aside might be the question of whether collective bargaining's general neglect of the public interest (that is, collective bargaining as a bilateral process) is a reason for public disfavor of unions. Lipset (1986) notes that the public perceives business and unions as self-interested groups, but the public nevertheless perceives that business advances the public interest. Does this perception include business' preferred unilateral rule-making in employment relations? Does the public's perception of unions as self-serving without public benefit include collective bargaining as an inseparable part of unions?

References

Block, R.N. (1990). American industrial relations in the 1980's: Transformation or evolution? *In* J. Chelius & J. Dworkin (eds.), *Reflections on the Transformation of Industrial Relations*. Metuchen, NJ: IMLR Press.

Cappelli, P. (1985). Theory construction in IR and some implications for research. *Industrial Relations, 24*, 90-112.

Cochrane, J.L. (1979). *Industrialism and Industrial Man in Retrospect*. New York: Ford Foundation.

Craig, A.W.J. (1975). A framework for the analysis of industrial relations systems. *In* B. Barret, E. Rodes, & J. Beishon (eds.), *Industrial Relations and the Wider Society.* (pp. 8-20). London: Collier Macmillan.

Dunlop, J.T. (1958). *Industrial Relations Systems.* New York: Holt.

Kerr, C. (1983). The intellectual role of neorealists in labor economics. *Industrial Relations, 22,* 298-318.

Kerr, C.; Dunlop, J.T.; Harbison, F.; & Myers, C.A. (1960). *Industrialism and Industrial Man.* Cambridge, MA: Harvard University Press.

Kochan, T.A.; Katz, H.C.; & McKersie, R.B. (1986). *The Transformation of American Industrial Relations.* New York: Basic Books.

Kochan, T.A.; McKersie, R.B.; & Cappelli, P. (1984). Strategic choice and industrial relations theory. *Industrial Relations, 23,* 16-39.

Lewin, D. (1987). Industrial relations as a strategic variable. *In* M.M. Kleiner, R.N. Block, M.J. Roomkin, & S.W. Salsburg (eds.), *Human Resources and the Performance of the Firm.* (pp. 1-41). Madison, WI: Industrial Relations Research Association.

Lipset, S.M. (1986). Labor unions in the public mind. *In* Lipset (ed.), *Unions in Transition: Entering the Second Century.* (pp. 287-321). San Francisco: Institute for Contemporary Studies.

Roomkin, M.J. & Juris, H.A. (1990). Strategy and industrial relations: An examination of the American steel industry. *In* J. Chelius & J. Dworkin (eds.), *Reflections on the Transformation of Industrial Relations.* Metuchen, NJ: IMLR Press.

Stepina, L.P., & Fiorito, J. (1984). *Strategic Choice and Industrial Relations Theory: A Comment.* Unpublished paper.

Strauss, G. (1990). Toward the study of human resources policy. *In* J. Chelius & J. Dworkin (eds.), *Reflections on the Transformation of Industrial Relations.* Metuchen, NJ: IMLR Press.

5. STRATEGY AND INDUSTRIAL RELATIONS: AN EXAMINATION OF THE AMERICAN STEEL INDUSTRY

Myron J. Roomkin and Hervey A. Juris[1]

THE PURPOSE OF THIS VOLUME and the symposium from which it arose is to celebrate, evaluate, and possibly extend the work by Kochan, Katz, and McKersie (1986) reported in *The Transformation of American Industrial Relations* (KKM). This volume, a collection of papers in the *Industrial and Labor Relations Review* (April 1988), and a chapter by Lewin in the 1987 annual research volume of the Industrial Relations Research Association are ample evidence that KKM have stimulated a great deal of interest. However, KKM's thesis—that major and permanent changes have taken place in American industrial relations—has also produced a large amount of criticism by some who have taken issue with their thesis and with their methodology.[2]

In this paper, we will examine some of the ideas expressed in KKM and in a preliminary way examine the extent to which their ideas help us to better understand the evolution of industrial relations in the contemporary U.S. steel industry. When we first agreed to write this paper, we were in the process of negotiating a study of employee relations innovations in the steel industry, which we felt would provide data for this paper. Unfortunately, due to delays in starting this project, much of what we say about the applicability of this framework to the steel industry is based on secondary sources.

KKM's Contributions

There are several important contributions in KKM. We wish to highlight three. First, KKM reemphasizes the fact that management is an active partner in industrial relations and collective bargaining, a fact that scholars who came of age in the 1960s and 1970s too often may have overlooked. It is probably because of the success of unions under what KKM call the New Deal model that the field concentrated so extensively in the postwar era on the union as an institution and on collective bargaining as a process in which unions seemed to be the prime mover and management a more passive reactor. To be sure, industrial relations scholars paid lip-service to the notion that management acted and the union reacted. But the reality, especially in the concentrated manufacturing industries and other traditional sectors, was one of the acquiescent, price-taking employer.

Second, KKM provides an "ecology" of industrial and employee relations for the period from the 1930s to the 1980s. That is, it provides a cohesive framework, more accurately a story, to describe the evolution of industrial relations practices. A central component of this framework was the existence of the nonunion alternative, either in the totally or partially unionized company, where management actively determined the terms and conditions of employment. These nonunionized operations and their economic performance in increasingly competitive markets served as invidious comparisons, motivating managers to introduce similar workplace practices in unionized settings.

Third, KKM identifies a diminished role for industrial relations professionals in the making of employee and industrial relations policies. The making of decisions in this area, according to KKM, is moving both up and down within the organization, but most important, away from the industrial relations establishment of the company. This change in the locus of decision-making came about in part, they say, due to the resistance of industrial relations professionals to workplace innovations, the growing participation of line managers in industrial relations issues at the workplace, and the participation of corporate executives at the highest levels of the organization in formulating employee relations policies to support business policies—what KKM call the strategic level.

KKM's contribution, however, is more than just a descriptive account of developments in the past few years. It is also a theory that seeks to explain the changes that have taken place in longstanding patterns of behavior and to identify behaviors that are ripe for change. Like many new theories, it seeks to displace established notions. In the area of industrial relations, the received paradigm has been one of institutional adaptation to environmental change, following the work of John Dunlop (1958). KKM emphasizes the role of the manager as decision-maker and initiator as a distinguishing characteristic, and for better or for worse have seen their theory labeled as a theory of strategic change. It is worth a moment to review the two orientations.

Adaptive Systems

The adaptive systems approach attempts to explain the substance of an existing web of rules, and accounts for changes in the web of rules as a function of the environment and the actors. In this framework, industrial relations practices change when conditions in the environment are altered exogenously or the needs of the actors change. The mechanism for change is co-determination through collective bargaining. Collective bargaining is a mechanism for reconciling divergent interests on the basis of the relative power of the parties to the bargain. While a particular contract may leave one side unhappy with the outcome, in the long run at least, all participants understand that their ability to improve upon the outcome depends upon developing alternative sources of power. Stability of this system is determined by the parties' satisfaction with the process and by stability in the environment which creates sources of power for the parties.[3]

Strategic Change

In comparison with the adaptive model, the strategic change model implies that industrial relations practices are a product of management decisions about the operation of the business. Management initiates and industrial relations and employee relations practices are derivative. Or, management might make certain decisions about the nature of industrial relations to support a business decision directly. In this framework, predictions about the evolution of industrial relations practices should focus on the business decisions of the firm, particularly the identity of those who make those decisions, that is, the executives and line managers who have the responsibility for giving their firms strategic direction. The strategic change model does not negate the power relationships of the adaptive model, rather it tries to refine who or what gets the process of change going.

Difficulty in Testing The Theories

The goal of all theory-building is to specify relationships between causes and responses (Blalock 1964, pp. 15-16). In this pursuit, it is better to identify such relationships in terms of precise mathematical expressions, rather than in terms of probabilities. The latter specifies statistical associations between causes and results and makes an explicit allowance for "other factors," "noise," and "errors." The former does not recognize these factors; instead, all possible categories of the response are determined by identified causes—hence the name deterministic models.

The research heritage of industrial relations has been probability modelling, for well known reasons. Most of our theory comes from institutional analyses and is not precise.[4] Moreover, we have an abundance of theories instead of a consensus theory. As a consequence, there has been a preference to address issues as empirical rather than theoretical questions.

If industrial relations is to progress as a field, it is appropriate to ask that our empirical work rest on stronger and more precise theoretical foundations. Following Lewin (1987), scholars should specify the conditions under which business decisions influence particular industrial relations practices, on an *a priori* basis. Without such precision, it is extremely difficult to determine whether we are testing the theory of strategic change or the paradigm it could replace.

Efforts to give this theory more precision must deal with several methodological and conceptual problems, some of which have been discussed by Thurley and Wood (1983, pp. 197-224). As others have already noted (Christiansen, 1983; Kalwa, 1985; Lewin, 1987), the first problem is: what is meant by the term "business strategy"? The literature on strategic planning uses the term to define both the process by which a firm selects strategies and the substance of the strategies selected by that process.

Because employee relations and industrial relations questions relate to the management of human resources, and because the demand for human resources is derived from the demand for the product or service produced, we believe that the substance of business strategy is the more relevant definitional path to pursue. We adopt the definition of strategy used by our colleagues in the department of business strategy: Strategy is the selection of markets in which a firm desires to compete and the methods by which it will compete. This definition is not without its problems for someone hoping to test a deterministic model, but it offers researchers advantages as well.

A focus on product markets and modes of competition has the advantage of being results and outcomes oriented. It is not necessary to assume that firms are rational in the selection of their strategies, that their judgments are informed, or that their selected strategies relative to alternatives are the best fit with their business goals. In fact, firms make mistakes in selecting a business strategy. But for testing purposes, it is only necessary to worry about whether the industrial relations strategy is appropriate to the markets selected and the competitive advantage exploited in those markets.

Business strategies are difficult to compare and evaluate, because a particular strategy can be the product of widely differing circumstances. Firms evaluate strategic alternatives in different ways. They use different time horizons for achieving business goals and different costs of capital. Companies also display differing sensitivities to stock-holders and other stake-holders in identifying options, selecting strategies, and implementing business changes.

Another problem with the proposed definition of business strategy is that it is not clear how much change in the markets selected or in the methods selected for competition is required to motivate changes in the employee or industrial relations practices of a company. For example, the capturing or preservation of one percentage point of market share can have widely different costs and consequences across companies and across industries.

In addition, questions exist about the locus of decision-making with respect to business and industrial relations issues. Even though firms are sometimes willing to describe to outsiders the formal methods of decision-making, very often informal processes are the truly influential ones. This is particularly important in assessing the influence of industrial relations and human resources executives in business decision-making because usually these groups are kept out of the formal processes. Once again, we are left to infer the true goals from the revealed behavior instead of the actual decision. This is analogous to Mintzberg's (1978) distinction between intended and realized strategies.

Last, strategy is not always set by the business planners. While planning and decision-making on business plans were relatively centralized in the 1970s and early 1980s, in the past few years, we have seen a tremendous decentralization of planning along with a growing emphasis on business performance through flexibility. Both of these trends make it harder to identify the specific business intentions of a company or even to talk about a business strategy for a company. The decisions we have defined as business strategies are very often set through a series of decisions involving line and staff managers at several levels of the firm—senior executives, planners, financial analysts, division or product market managers (sometimes also strategic business unit managers) and plant-level managers.

The concept of an industrial relations strategy is equally perplexing. Is it the decision to remain nonunion? To become nonunion? To avoid strikes at all costs? To break pattern bargaining? If these are strategies, are they pursued as ends in and of themselves or are they pursued because they aid in carrying out a business strategy?[5] Is an employee or industrial relations strategy necessary to having a successful business strategy?

One must also consider whether unions come to the table with no strategy in mind or whether they, too, have strategic objectives—goals which they intend to achieve, for example, Juris (1969). All of these considerations complicate the modeling of a deterministic strategic choice model.

An Application to the U.S. Steel Industry

In this section, problems of doing research on the strategic change model are illustrated by examining strategic business decisions and industrial relations practices in the domestic steel industry. As a test case, the steel industry is particularly appropriate. It has been one of the significant and traditional sectors for collective bargaining in the United States, and in several ways meets KKM's definition of a sector whose industrial relations has conformed to the New Deal metaphor.

The specific questions we would address are: Can one determine what product markets individual firms are in and what methods they are using to compete in those markets? Is there a link between product market strategy and industrial relations strategy in the basic steel industry? Can one test KKM's strategic choice framework in this industry?

Business Strategies of the Steel Companies

In this section, we examine the steel industry from the perspective of our substantive definition of strategy—that is, the markets in which companies compete and the ways in which they compete in those markets. We interviewed company executives, trade journalists, industry analysts, industry consultants, and steel industry association executives. This was not a random, scientific sample, but it did include some of the major actors in the industry.

We found that interviewees were able to describe the strategic *problems* facing the industry and to a lesser extent strategic problems faced by different types of companies, but the details of business strategies in specific companies were either unknown or unknowable to persons outside the individual companies, even to industry analysts.

Still, the information we received is useful in helping to understand the context in which steel companies make product market and competitive status decisions. For the industry as a whole, our interviewees generally agreed on the pertinent strategic business issues and the way that these business issues have changed over the years. All of them agreed that steel has gone through three phases: prior to the 1970s as a classic oligopolistic industry which emphasized stability and shared markets; a period between the 1970s and the mid-1980s when the central problem was overcapacity as a result of declining demand for the product and rising imports, during which shared markets gave way to competition (Barnett & Schorsch 1983; Kalwa, 1985); and a current period in which there is undercapacity associated with the success of import restrictions, rising profits, and a possible worldwide shortage of steel (Marcus & Kirsis 1987, p. 25).

At the level of the individual company, information on the specific ways in which firms are reacting to these realities is very hard to come by. Companies in this industry are more suspicious than most of releasing such information because of longstanding fears of antitrust action. One is left to infer the business strategy (markets and methods of competition) unless one can get the company to share the information.

Our reading and our interviews do suggest that strategies in the industry vary by whether the company is a small manufacturer (known as a minimill) or a large integrated manufacturer.

Minimills. Minimills are small units which melt scrap to get raw material and have traditionally fabricated product for local markets only. They tend to be nonunion, low-cost competitors who have cut into the markets of traditional integrated producers. Recently, minimills have begun to compete more broadly in regional markets by establishing satellite facilities for finishing steel. From a strategy perspective, products from minimills represent an invidious comparison to products from integrated producers sold in the same markets.

Integrated producers. Even though the integrated producers (such as U.S. Steel, Bethlehem, LTV, and to some extent Inland) all appear to be competing in product markets similar to one another by emphasizing price, customer relations, and product quality, it was not clear to our observers whether the relationship among producers was best described by the term "competition." It is not so much that the integrated producers are competing against one another as it is that each has picked a niche and a set of customers it seeks to satisfy.

For integrated producers, profitability in the period of overcapacity was to be found in "flat" products: sheets and rolled steel for the appliance and automobile industries. According to our sources, each of the major producers looked at existing plant and equipment and sought that combination of existing facilities which would let them produce a quality product at a reasonable price—that is, to find the "sweet spot" of production which capitalizes on the unique efficiencies of their particular production lines and maximizes utilization. Companies with more than one line (or facility) had greater flexibility in this search.

Having selected a product market, integrated producers then identified a set of customers whose needs best fit with the mill's productive capacity and strengths. The impact of customer needs on the choice of products produced is more than just a distinction between the requirements of the automobile and appliance industries. Within each of these markets, specifications with respect to product, service, and quality have been set by individual companies. If a particular producer were to abandon a customer, it is not at all clear that a large number of other producers could fill that customer's requirements given the differences in "sweet spots" among the various producers and facilities. In this sense then, this is a niche market.

In addition to flat products, the integrated producers have traditionally competed in structural steel and distressed products including bars and wire. In contrast to the market for flat products, the market for structural (or long) steel has been and continues to be overdeveloped. Excess capacity has motivated firms to search for greater market share by emphasizing the control of costs and product quality.

The integrated manufacturers who produce bar, wire, and other distressed products are facing considerable competition for a market that has low margins. From the viewpoint of business strategy, there is considerable motivation to get out of these businesses either by selling, spinning-off, or closing facilities. Unfortunately for the companies, they have little choice but to keep such facilities open, because there have been few buyers and potential pension funding liabilities make closing the plants prohibitively costly.

Future considerations. What developments in this industry and its environment are likely to require further changes in the business strategies now in place? As the business environment shifts from over- to under-capacity, the makers of flat products will have to decide whether and how to expand production capabilities. Choices include creating new facilities or modernizing old facilities. Because of the integrated nature of production, it is very difficult to modernize just a small portion of an existing facility. Thus there is a lot of interest in launching so-called market-mills, which would be small specialized production plants supplied by the larger parent facility.

On the other hand, undercapacity may be a moot point. Perhaps the most important competitive factor facing the industry is the expiration this year of the Voluntary Restraint Agreements that have protected the industry from increasing competition from foreign steel-makers. Without such an agreement, competition in the industry will dramatically increase, forcing these companies to reassess the viability of certain product lines and facilities.

Another environmental factor affecting production is the development and spread of new technologies. Techniques are apparently available which will allow minimills for the first time to produce flat steel products and compete with the integrated producers more directly in their most profitable markets (Rothman 1988). Still another innovation, in the planning stage, but one with profound implications for competition among the integrated producers, would shift the way in which steel products are designed and sold. Conventionally, customers purchase different steel components from different producers. Nucor—an innovator in the industry—is considering bidding on the design, fabrication, and delivery of all the steel products in a project as a package deal. All of these represent potentially significant changes in business strategy and by derivation potentially significant changes in industrial relations strategy as well.

Industrial Relations Strategies
of the Steel Companies

It is our belief that industrial relations practices in the steel industry since the 1930s have been influenced by strategic considerations, business decisions, and business decision-makers. Recall that it was Myron Taylor as president of U.S. Steel who recognized the wisdom of recognizing the union and that Benjamin Fairless, who presided over U.S. Steel some years later, who recognized the disutility of confrontation and the importance of stability in labor relations. Acceptability of the union at the highest levels has never really been shaken, despite the industry's contractions and the growth of a nonunionized alternative in the minimills.

This is not to imply that the companies have avoided militancy in

industrial relations, or embraced the union; rather, industrial relations strategies have assumed the legitimacy of the union and the
goal has been to curtail union power so that it does not impinge upon
management's objectives. Thus, during the oligopolistic period, the
labor relations goal was to confront the union's control over the
ability of the companies to manufacture steel by shutting down
operations. In the overcapacity period, the goal has been to address
the labor cost excesses. The real tests for the integrated producers
will come in the current period and the next few years, when
companies have to decide whether and how to expand production,
or when tariff protection ends, or when technology results in new
sources of domestic competition on price and quality. To date, no
integrated producer has embarked upon a nonunionized greenfield
operation, although there has been outsourcing of work to nonunionized
employees, especially in the areas of plant maintenance and
construction.

The steelworkers union has gone along with, and contributed to,
this strategic orientation. It accepted the wisdom of coordinated
bargaining and then centralized bargaining for the major producers,
even at the cost of reducing local autonomy and considerable
pressure from the rank-and-file for self-determination.

Government, too, has been a strategic ingredient in steel industry
labor relations. Livernash's (1961) study of government's intervention in steel industry collective bargaining between 1937 and 1960
shows that government intervened in negotiations in all but five of
the 16 bargaining opportunities, thereby making the federal government one of the major—if not the principal—source of bargaining
power. While this differs from government's major role in the 1980s
as a protector of markets, it nevertheless represents the historical
dependency of the parties on a strategic actor outside the bargaining
unit.

Our interviews suggest that the producers of flat steel, whether
for automobiles or appliances, have adopted broadly similar labor
relations strategies. All are interested in reduced labor costs but at
the same time they claim to be seeking more harmonious and
cooperative labor relations through a combination of efforts that
include the following, *inter alia*, separate contracts; labor cost
concessions; profit-sharing programs; a commitment to gain-sharing
programs; and efforts at increased communication and information
sharing. Admittedly, we do not know how much variation actually
exists among the companies due to differences in the implementation of these programs. Absent this information, it would appear that
labor relations in the integrated producer segment of the steel
industry is being more heavily influenced by the broad and general

economic conditions of the industry rather than the business necessities of particular product markets.[6]

Have the parties adopted more cooperative and constructive labor relations? Is this a strategic change? Oddly enough, this same question was asked in the early 1960s when the parties agreed to the Human Relations Committee and again in the early 1970s when the union and companies agreed to the Experimental Negotiating Agreement, (ENA) one of the first voluntarily negotiated interest arbitration arrangements for major contract negotiations. ENA was a perfect example of the adaptive response of the parties to their circumstances and needs; when it failed to meet those needs it was abandoned (Stieber 1980, pp. 151-208).

Judging from the most recent innovations, cooperation in the steel industry has a long way to go. While there have been several attempts to develop job-site employee groups (a practice that builds on the industry's history of shop-floor productivity, safety, and problem-solving), the union's willingness to accept profit-sharing and gain-sharing in most of the industry do not as yet indicate that the union has undergone a metamorphosis. Apart from National Steel's special contract, the major producers have agreed to share profits up to the amount of the concessions the unions made in the last round of negotiations. And while agreement exists to give locals the right to accept gain-sharing programs, the steel industry executives we talked with tended to view such programs suspiciously as cost-savings programs and not a new compensation philosophy. Moreover, progress in introducing these plans has been very slow, partly because there is union resistance but also because the employers are not confident they will work.[7]

Two recent examinations of steel industry labor relations from the strategic perspective are worth noting as this point. Kalwa (1985) argues that the history of industrial relations in the steel industry is consistent with the transformation thesis. Due to changes in the business environment, he argues, the locus of industrial relations decision-making moved from the traditional realm of the industrial relations department to a higher, more strategic level, on one hand, and to the workplace on the other. His evidence relating to the role of strategic considerations deals with the more active participation of government, while the development of company-by-company negotiated settlements—that is, the decentralization of bargaining—is identified as evidence of the greater role of workplace issues in industrial relations.

In our opinion, Kalwa (1985) tends to associate structural changes in the locus of decision-making with the emergence of a strategic thrust of bargaining. While the structure of bargaining has decentralized in steel recently, Kalwa (1985) seems unwilling to recognize a history of business decisions motivating labor relations practice in this industry.

Christiansen (1983), in a broader study of the consistency between business and industrial relations strategies, looks at three steel mills as part of a sample of nine companies in three industries. She finds evidence that firms having consistency between their industrial relations and business strategies have improved performance. Industrial relations strategies are operationalized as being centralized or decentralized; and business strategies are defined in terms of whether a firm is seeking to be the low cost producer in an industry or is seeking to compete on the basis of product quality and service. She believes that firms can achieve this consistency by manipulating those practices in purposeful ways.

To a great extent, we agree with her perspective. All of the steel firms seemed, at one level, to have the same general business orientation, so it was logical for them to have the same type of labor relations. But, if we are correct in defining strategy in terms of product markets, one would anticipate significant differences in labor relations practices among these same companies. Also, if her definition of strategy is the correct one, she is still placing too much weight on the ability of the company to control its industrial relations and not enough weight on other factors such as collective bargaining, the union, and government.

Thus, there are at least three different interpretations of the relationship between business strategy and industrial relations practices in the steel industry: Ours, which claims that the two have always been related in this industry; Kalwa's (1985), which notes the recent emergence of this relationship in terms of a changing locus of decision-making; and Christiansen's (1983), which emphasizes the substance of strategy as the motivating force.

The issue for the field is not to reconcile these different views empirically. That would be the types of mistake industrial relations scholars have made before. Rather, the next step must be to generate a more deterministic model of the connection between business strategy and industrial relations.

Summary and Conclusions

KKM have called our attention once again to the role that management business decision-makers play in the industrial relations process. The question is whether this represents a transformation or a continuation of past practice. We have argued that the relationship between business strategy and industrial relations in the steel industry is not inconsistent with the adaptive model interpretation insofar that industrial relations has long been influenced by business decisions, as we have defined them.

Perhaps the real test of the transformation hypothesis in the steel industry is coming shortly. Environmental and strategic changes are beginning to take place that will affect the unionized integrated producers, requiring new business strategies and may produce new patterns of industrial relations. However, as we indicated, several conceptual and methodological problems still need to be solved before any comprehensive test of the theory can be accomplished. Important among these is greater specificity in theory construction to make the strategic change model more of a deterministic model.

Notes

1. We wish to acknowledge the support of the Steel Resource Center at Northwestern University.
2. In this regard, KKM is like other significant works in industrial relations which were very controversial when they first appeared. John Dunlop's *Industrial Relations Systems* (1958) was viewed by some as being too static and taxonomic. The enormously influential book, *A Behavioral Theory of Negotiations* by Walton and McKersie (1965) was reviewed in the *ILR Review* by Herbert Northrup, who said, "A new language justifies itself when it leads to new insights previously unknown, or even if an aesthetic improvement results. Careful reading of this book . . . fails to produce such new insights. Aesthetics are a matter of taste." More recently, Getman, Goldberg, and Herman's (*Union Representation Elections: Law and Reality*, 1976) efforts to use quantitative techniques to study union representation elections under the National Labor Relations Act, a book that literally helped to frame public policy, spawned an entire industry of scholars committed to disproving their results.
3. While there is some temptation to follow KKM's metaphor and to call the adaptive approach the New Deal model, the New Deal hasn't got that much to do with it, other than the fact that collective bargaining received great impetus during that period through legislation and supportive public opinion. A more proper appellation might be the postwar manufacturing model.
4. Research on the adaptive model has primarily been institutional. See, for example, Somers (1980).
5. The idea that a firm could pursue an antiunion policy independent of consideration of its business strategy is analogous to Gary Becker's (1971) analysis of racial discrimination as a consumption good. Unless the business plan and the anti-union strategy are self-reinforcing, firms with a more enlightened attitude may drive the discriminating employer out of a competitive market.
6. It would seem, therefore, that the more tightly and concretely one defines the concept of strategy the more difficult it is to associate specific strategies with specific labor relations policies and practices.

7. Surprisingly, there are still proponents of the industry's heavy reliance on individualized incentives.

References

Barnett, D.F., & Schorsch, L. (1983). *Steel: Upheaval in a Basic Industry.* Cambridge, MA: Ballinger.

Becker, G. (1971). *The Economics of Discrimination,* 2nd ed. Chicago: University of Chicago Press.

Blalock, H.M., Jr. (1964). *Causal Inferences in Nonexperimental Research.* Chapel Hill: University of North Carolina Press.

Christiansen, E.T. (1983). Strategy, structure and labor relations performance. *Human Resource Management, 22* (155-168).

Dunlop, J.T. (1958). *Industrial Relations Systems.* New York: Holt.

Getman, J.G.; Goldberg, S.B.; & Herman, J.B. (1976). *Union Representation Elections: Law and Reality.* New York: Russell Sage Foundation.

Juris, H.A. (1969). Union crises wage decisions. *Industrial Relations, 8,* 247-258.

Kalwa, R.W. (1985). *Collective Bargaining in Basic Steel, 1946-1983.* Dissertation submitted for the Ph.D. at Cornell University.

Kochan, T.A.; Katz, H.C.; & McKersie, R.B. (1986). *The Transformation of American Industrial Relations.* New York: Basic Books.

Lewin, D. (1987). Industrial relations as a strategic variable. *In* M.M. Kleiner, R.N. Block, M. Roomkin, & S.W. Salsburg (eds.), *Human Resources and the Performance of the Firm.* Madison, WI: Industrial Relations Research Association.

Livernash, E.R. (1961). *Collective Bargaining in the Basic Steel Industry: A Study of the Public Interest and the Role of Government.* Washington, DC: U.S. Government Printing Office.

Marcus, P., & Kirsis, K.M. (1987, June 24). *Word Steel Dynamics: Recurring Surprises in the Domestic and International Steel Market.* Presentation to Steel Survival Strategies II Conference, New York City.

Mintzberg, H. (1978). Patterns in strategy formation. *Management Science, 24.*

Northrup, H.R. (1966, April). Review of Walton & McKersie: A behavioral theory of labor negotiations. *Industrial and Labor Relations Review, 19,* 459-460.

Rothman, M. (1988, April 15). *Business Week,* p. 131.

Somers, G.G. (ed.). (1980). *Collective Bargaining: Contemporary American Experience.* Madison, WI: Industrial Relations Research Association.

Stieber, J. (1980). Steel. *In* G.G. Somers (ed.) *Collective Bargaining: Contemporary American Experience.* Madison, WI: Industrial Relations Research Association.

Thurley, K., & Wood, S. (1983). *Industrial Relations and Management Strategy.* Cambridge, MA: Cambridge University Press.

Walton, R.E., & McKersie, B. (1965). *A Behavioral Theory of Labor Negotiations.* New York: McGraw-Hill.

COMMENTS ON ROOMKIN AND JURIS

John Fossum

THIS CONFERENCE PRESENTS AN interesting format for a unique critique of a major work in contemporary industrial relations, *The Transformation of American Industrial Relations,* by Kochan, Katz, and McKersie (KKM, 1986). All of the papers delivered in these sessions focus either on the methods or findings in the KKM work, or use their work as a basis for analyzing current practice in a given industrial sector.

Having earlier reviewed KKM (Fossum, 1988), I have interpreted my role here to include: (1) an extension of that review, (2) a discussion of the use of the KKM framework by Roomkin and Juris (RJ, 1990, chap. 5), and (3) comments on both the use of KKM by RJ and on RJ's findings.

As I stated in my review of KKM in the *Academy of Management Review,* I think its primary values are in its synthesis of information from disparate sources which leads to its resulting model and its stimulation of research (an example of which has just been delivered). Written, as it was, during a period of extreme dislocation for American industry and the labor movement, it will be for future scholars to determine the robustness of its model and conclusions. (It should be noted, however, the KKM recognized a number of possible alternative scenarios resulting form the turmoil).

The determination of which one of these scenarios becomes dominant is probably much less influenceable by organized labor that it has been in the past given the internationalization of the economy and the continued national level organization of the labor movement. On the other hand, the more desperate aspects of economic performance that plagued the first half of the decade seem to have abated and recent economic developments should inspire feelings of déjà vu. Consider, for example, that unemployment has dropped into the low 5 percent range for the first time since the early

1970s; and that most of the new jobs created over the last six months have been in manufacturing and filled by males. Consider also that the recent Chrysler-UAW agreement was certainly a pattern settlement. Consider further, that increased evidence suggests that U.S. manufacturers are increasingly low cost producers as transportation costs are factored into purchase decisions. Consider finally, that as corporate profits have increased, the bargaining power of employers (at least in the short run) has declined and the historical relative wage advantage of unionized workers may again increase.

In their critique and application of KKM, RJ indicate that past industrial relations research appears to have viewed management as passive (or at best, reactive). Clearly, KKM do not, but their strategic change model may cast the union in a corollary role. Might the assignment of management and/or union roles be dependent on the dominant economic climate at the time the process is studied? Other things equal, it's likely that management would have enhanced power to institute employment changes favorable to it during periods of relatively high unemployment and/or low profits, while the union should able to seize the initiative during periods of high profits and high labor demand relative to supply. Given most evidence that negotiated wages lag price changes, it's likely that proaction in bargaining will be with the side that is relatively better off economically.

Managements have used the relative differences in economic performance of their units to break pattern settlements during the 1980s. This is most possible when the employer is involved in disparate industries or has made the decision not to be vertically integrated. Decentralization has enabled certain organizations to perform well economically in the 1980s because it has enabled them to make favorable supplier choices during a period of intense competition. Consider the auto industry again. During the 1970s, Chrysler was seen to be at a relative disadvantage to Ford, and particularly GM, since it made a relatively smaller proportion of its own parts for assembly. In the 1980s, however, Chrysler's profits improved most rapidly because it could extract concessions not only from its employees but its suppliers as well. As capacity utilization increases in the supplier industries, Chrysler may again be at a disadvantage. During these periods, centralization and vertical integration may again become attractive and pattern bargaining will be advantageous to employers to prevent whipsawing by its own supplier plants.

Tactics may be expected to follow a change in strategy. When managers become more responsible for the performance of their units, they can be expected to become more involved in personnel/

industrial relations activities. Flexibility in staffing and compensation become more important as short-run goals are emphasized. The ability for heavy line involvement may decrease during the 1990s as the supply of labor becomes tighter.

The steel industry has suffered greatly in terms of profits and employment during the 1980s. Big Steel has been the victim of an unfavorable foreign exchange environment and dumping by its foreign competitors and the increasing success of low-wage and low-overhead minimills. However, as minimills and foreign producers have expanded, Big Steel's strategy appears to be involved with shifting investment from steel production to other areas. U.S. Steel's purchase of Marathon Oil and Texas Oil and Gas substantially decreases the power of the USW in negotiations since the company no longer needs to depend on steel production for as large a proportion of its revenues and potential profits.

Is there however, an industrial relations strategy? Or is there only a response to a catastrophe? If there are strategies, do they relate to the external and/or internal labor markets? Or is the apparent set of tactics simply a reaction to changes in the product market? Most of what appears in the steel industry simply appears to be a concession-oriented strategy with relatively little changed in the overall practice of industrial relations.

Strategy in industrial relations for employers would appear to require two prongs: a strategy to improve the competitive position of the employer vis-à-vis others in the industry, and a strategy to innovate in employee relations activities. The latter would be expected in situations where the employer desired to remain nonunion. Employees would then decide whether or not to be represented depending on their perceptions of the competition between the employer and the union and their abilities to deliver positive employment outcomes.

References

Fossum, J.A. (1988). The medium creation and the message: Review essay on the transformation of American industrial relations. *Academy of Management Review, 12,* 445-448.

Kochan, T.A.; Katz, H.C.; & McKersie, R.B. (1986). *The Transformation of American Industrial Relations.* New York: Basic Books.

Roomkin, M.J., & Juris, H.A. (1990). Strategy and industrial relations: An examination of the American steel industry. *In* J. Chelius & J. Dworkin (eds.), *Reflections on the Transformation of Industrial Relations.* Metuchen, NJ: IMLR Press.

COMMENTS: REFLECTIONS ON STRATEGY

Joel Cutcher-Gershenfeld

Introduction

At its best, research does more than provide answers—it redefines the questions. Unquestionably, this is the deepest contribution that Kochan, Katz and McKersie have made in their analysis of *The Transformation of American Industrial Relations* (1986). The nature and scope of this contribution becomes evident as critics begin to wrestle with the text.

The purpose of this paper is to examine "Strategy and Industrial Relations: An Examination of the American Steel Industry," by Roomkin and Juris (1990, chap. 5). What Kochan, Katz and McKersie highlight as "strategic choice" becomes the point of departure for Roomkin and Juris to develop a framework for understanding the role of strategy in industrial relations. This framework is illustrated via the case of the U.S. steel industry, which in turn raises core questions regarding just what constitutes a transformation of American industrial relations. I will be examining both the way Roomkin and Juris approach the concept of strategy and the extension of their analysis to the case of the steel industry.

Inevitably, my comments on the work of Roomkin and Juris will be filtered through my own views on the work of Kochan, Katz and McKersie. Thus, after reviewing the Roomkin and Juris paper, I will highlight some of the common threads in that commentary. This will not be a complete review of *The Transformation* text,[1] but it will serve to codify my views of what constitutes a transformation.

Adaptive Systems Versus Strategic Change

At the heart of the Roomkin and Juris paper is a contrast between what they term an adaptive systems view of industrial relations and a strategic change view. Dunlop's focus (1958) on a web of rules reflecting environmental changes is termed the adaptive systems view. Kochan, Katz and McKersie are credited with introducing a strategic change perspective. Before turning to the substance of the comparison (which does raise important questions about the concept of strategy), I would like to comment on the specific terms used by Roomkin and Juris.

Labeling one of the two views as "adaptive" carries the implication that the other is not. Yet, part of the story that Kochan, Katz and McKersie tell does involve adaptation to changing markets and technology (with strategic choice embedded within that). Moreover, the adaptive features of Dunlop's perspective are very much at issue today. My own reading of the Dunlopian framework[2] would suggest a focus on tracing incremental change, which would only be adaptive during periods of relative stability. Roomkin and Juris do pose what I believe is the most important question, which is how to test one theory against another. As a point of departure, however, I would urge a more precise characterization of Dunlop's theory.[3]

In the area of strategy, Roomkin and Juris give a great deal of attention to what that concept means and how a "strategic" perspective might be tested. They draw on a classic distinction, which is between strategy as process and strategy as substance. Roomkin and Juris focus on the substantive approach as used in the field of Business Strategy. Hence, strategy is the selection of markets in which a firm desires to compete and the methods by which it will compete. For testing theories within this context, they conclude, "it is only necessary to worry about whether the industrial relations strategy is appropriate to the markets selected and the competitive advantage exploited in those markets."

While I do think that the link between approaches to industrial relations and a firm's competitive strategy is an important area for inquiry, it poses what I believe is a much narrower question than that posed by Kochan, Katz and McKersie. The question is narrower in two ways. First, the domain of strategic decision making is restricted to that lofty and fairly ambiguous set of interactions from which emerges a firm's overall competitive posture. Roomkin and Juris recognize the ambiguous nature of interactions at this level—indeed that is one of their main points, but this formulation excludes a host of specific strategic resource allocation decisions such as investment in new technology, plant location, employment security guarantees, and profit sharing.

For Kochan, Katz and McKersie the concept of strategic choice involves tracing the industrial relations implications not just of broad competitive strategy, but also of the subsequent resource allocation decisions. In other words, even within a broad competitive strategy, there remains room for quite a bit of strategic choice around resource allocation and these choices matter a lot. In many ways, the approach that Kochan, Katz and McKersie take is rooted in distinctive features of U.S. industrial relations. They are tracing movement beyond mandatory and even permissive subjects of bargaining under the law, which does not require a jump to decision making around broad competitive strategies. It is already quite a dramatic change when strategic resource allocation decisions become part of the domain of industrial relations. It is the increasing salience of this new domain of interaction (along with shifts in workplace relations) that gives rise to the transformation thesis.

Because Roomkin and Juris have defined strategy in a far narrower sense than Kochan, Katz and McKersie, their test of the theory will be incomplete. Still, their approach does serve to challenge and potentially expand the research in the *Transformation* text. That book does not fully embed strategic resource allocation decisions in the broader context of firms' competitive strategies. While tracing such links is far from an exact science, it becomes increasingly important as union leaders and public officials have greater levels of access to corporate boardrooms. The immediate focus of these new players is usually around strategic resource allocation decisions such as plant closings or full employment policies. In the long run, however, they will need guidance on how a firm's pricing strategy or product mix affects them and their constituents and on how to engage these issues. Thus, even though Roomkin and Juris are narrow in restricting their definition of strategy to broad competitive strategies, there is much to be learned about the links between such strategies and industrial relations.

A second way in which the approach of Roomkin and Juris is narrow stems from the way that tracing the impact of industrial relations on competitive strategy gives primacy to management's business goals. There are, of course, multiple stakeholders in an employment relationship. Links between industrial relations and broad competitive strategy are undoubtedly important to workers, unions, communities, state government, and federal government, but they are not the only strategic links that matter. In this sense, the concept of strategic choice not only involves broad competitive strategies and specific resource allocation decisions within firms, but it involves analogous broader and more specific domains of strategic decision making within unions, government and other collectivities. For example, unions face broad decisions regarding what kind of worker they want to represent and then more specific decisions regarding organizing strategies, political action and representational goals. If anything, tracing these broad and more specific strategies in unions is likely to be even more complex and ambiguous than it is in firms, but the issue is no less relevant. I suspect that it is in order to encompass multiple kinds of strategic decisions by multiple collectivities that Kochan, Katz and McKersie employ the term strategic choice. It is less laden with pure business connotations and it is more suggestive of the variation in practice that they seek to understand.

In sum, I would urge a distinction between two domains of strategic decision making within a firm, which are broad competitive strategies and specific strategic resource allocation decisions. Both represent important domains for tracing new patterns in industrial relations. Further, a similar distinction might be extended to the analysis of strategic decision making among other stakeholders to the employment relationship. Finally, it must be noted that the concept of strategic decision making (at either the broad or the resource allocation levels) implies the existence of strategic choice. While a transformation could occur without explicit choice, it is especially interesting to find observable variation that encompasses fundamental changes and that does reflect strategic choice. The importance of these distinctions can be illustrated by examining the way Roomkin and Juris study the U.S. steel industry.

How To Interpret Developments In The U.S. Steel Industry?

When Roomkin and Juris indicated that the U.S. steel industry would be used to test links between industrial relations and strategy, I felt that it would be a good test of the linkage thesis developed in the Kochan, Katz and McKersie text. After all, the steel industry seems to be characterized by a great degree of variation in broad strategy (ranging from minimills to large integrated producers) and in specific resource allocation strategies. This variation could presumably be tied to variation in approaches to industrial relations. Dramatic shifts in the industrial relations arena might then be better understood.

As a first step in their analysis, Roomkin and Juris attempt to pin down the competitive strategies of various firms in the steel industry. This effort suggests just how ambiguous and complex a task it is to identify a firm's broad strategy. Executives and industry experts could identify strategic problems, but not clear strategies. Despite these difficulties, the authors do succeed in distinguishing the small manufacturers operating minimills from the larger integrated manufacturers and, among the integrated manufacturers, they find strong segmentation of firms—each into their own market niche. This sort of understanding of broad competitive strategies is a valuable contribution.

The authors then turn to industrial relations strategies and find that, across the industry, the larger producers have adopted broadly similar labor relations strategies of reducing costs and seeking more cooperative union-management relations. Yet, their field research is only at a preliminary stage. As a result, they admit that they "do not know how much variation actually exists among the companies due to differences in the implementation of these programs [to reduce costs and promote cooperation]." While I am not an expert on industrial relations in the steel industry, it does seem that there is exactly the sort of variation at the company level that would support the Kochan, Katz and McKersie thesis.

As examples of important developments in the steel industry consider that National Steel, LTV, and Wheeling Pittsburgh all reached collective bargaining agreements with the Steelworkers union that featured wage and work rule changes offered in exchange for increased job security and training. This alone carries the potential for a larger union role in the strategic human resource allocation policies of these firms, which would mark a fundamental change in practice. Moreover, the experience contrasts strongly with the negotiations at USX, in which anger over the Marathon Oil purchase and other corporate strategies helped to fuel a 184-day strike. Here is clear evidence for the costs in today's economic climate of inconsistency between a firm's broad competitive strategy and its goals in industrial relations.

Aside from shifts in the substance of bargaining and variation in the bargaining experience, I would urge that within all the firms there is likely to be variation in specific resource allocation policies at the operating level. Further, I would urge that this variation will interrelate with different approaches to industrial relations—leading (in some cases) to a transformation of industrial relations.

A final example to note is the early experience with nonunion minimills and the attempts of some unionized firms to match that competitive strategy. Here, it would be of great interest to examine the degree to which union status and underlying approaches to employment relations complement or undercut a firms ability to serve as a small, flexible producer. Thus, the variation in both broad competitive strategies and specific strategic resource allocation decisions in the steel industry seems, at least at first blush, to be highly interrelated with variation (and possibly transformation) in industrial relations practice.

Roomkin and Juris have not explored these issues, in part, because their research is still at a preliminary stage. But recall that they have defined the research question solely around broad competitive strategies. It remains to be seen if they will take their field work down to the firm and even the operating unit level. In this paper, however, they keep the focus broad.

As such, it is pointed out that the U.S. steel industry has faced dramatic technological and economic change in the past and the resulting broad shifts in competitive strategies have also been tied to industrial relations innovations. As examples they cite the Human Relations Committee of the 1960s and the Experimental Negotiating Agreement of the 1970s. Because these initiatives were abandoned when they failed to meet the parties' needs, Roomkin and Juris conclude that they were adaptive changes, rather than strategic ones.

While I do think it is important to ask whether (and in what ways) today's changes are different from labor-management initiatives of the past, I find the authors' conclusion confusing. Are they suggesting that any response (or at least any short-lived response) to economic change is adaptive and not strategic? Or are they suggesting that there was no choice for the parties in the steel industry in the 1950s and the 1960s—that they were impelled into these new arrangements and then driven from them?

Ultimately, Roomkin and Juris seem to suggest that a test of the relative explanatory power of Dunlop's "adaptive" approach and the strategic choice perspective of Kochan, Katz and McKersie lies in the extent to which competitive strategy and industrial relations practice have always been linked or are just now becoming linked. However, for me—and I believe for Kochan, Katz and McKersie—the issue is not a question of the historic existence of linkage. We would all likely agree that there have always been highly salient linkages in the U.S. steel industry. Rather, the question goes to the nature of the linkage. Where broad competitive strategies change in ways that do not result in long-lasting fundamental change in industrial relations then adaptive and strategic choice theories are indistinguishable. Where, however, sharp changes do occur at various levels of labor-management relations and where there are distinguishable bundles of changes that might be thought of as industrial relations strategies, then it is not clear that an adaptive model can explain the variation.

Although Roomkin and Juris raise important questions for Kochan, Katz and McKersie regarding just what is meant by strategy, the questions are posed too narrowly. As a result, a test of whether there has been a transformation of industrial relations in the U.S. steel industry is incomplete. I agree with the co-authors that coming events in that industry will more sharply distinguish links between competitive strategies and industrial relations practice, but tracing those links will require significant modifications in the analytical lens than is developed by Roomkin and Juris.

Though Roomkin and Juris have not presented a complete framework, they are to be commended for helping to extend and frame the debate around assessing a transformation of American industrial relations. They have forced a more careful look at the concept of strategy. They have also raised pointed questions about how to go about assessing the relative explanatory power of competing theories in our field. Finally, they have begun to pursue a line of research that could serve as a useful point of comparison for two key theoretical perspectives—that of John Dunlop and that of Kochan, Katz and McKersie. I hope my comments are helpful in that enterprise. In my final remarks, I will attempt to pull some common threads from my comments in order to be more precise about what I think of as a way of understanding the concept of a transformation in American industrial relations.

What Is a Transformation in Industrial Relations?

Roomkin and Juris look for a transformation in U.S. industrial relations at the level of firms' broad competitive strategies. Others may focus at what Kochan, Katz and McKersie term the operating or shop floor level and at the collective bargaining or personnel policy level. Generally, a transformation in unionized relations is taken to mean a greater degree of labor-management cooperation tied to an enhanced competitive posture for the firms. I would like to take issue here with that formulation.

There is a long history of labor-management committees and other cooperative initiatives in this country. Generally speaking, they have either withered or only endured as narrow adjuncts to collective bargaining. This was the essence of Northrup and Young's classic (1968) rebuttal of Golden and Parkers' 1955 study of *The Causes of Industrial Peace*. It was also the central thesis advanced by Gomberg (1967) in his analysis of many of the most famous joint study committees that have existed since the turn of the century. Thus the question often posed today is whether innovation in unionized settings today is any different from so many past initiatives.

To an extent, this question motivates current research into the institutionalization or staying power of new developments in labor-management relations. A close look at one such analysis (Kochan & Cutcher-Gershenfeld, 1988) suggests that today's innovations are, in some ways, just as limited and fragile as those of the past, but that they are in other ways qualitatively different. Based on a longitudinal assessment of developments in ten firms with fifteen associated unions, it is clear that union-management initiatives embark on an iterative path marked by a sequence of pivotal events. These events are pivotal in that the new directions in union-management relations are likely to be either substantially extended or undercut at these moments.

For example, many employee involvement initiatives reach a pivotal moment at the point that successful employee problem-solving raises issues that are traditionally seen as collective bargaining or managerial rights issues. To the extent the problem-solving is foreclosed from such issues it is likely to remain narrow and wither. To the extent that the employee involvement effort is allowed to expand, the joint initiative becomes a much more central feature of the relationship. In this sense, a transformation would not likely happen all at once, but rather at some point in the resolution of a sequence of pivotal events.

But the question remains, what has been transformed? The answer to this question, I feel, really marks the point at which there is clear contrast to be drawn between Dunlop's approach and the alternative perspective that Kochan, Katz and McKersie have begun to develop. At the core of Dunlop's analysis is the assumption that rules are the appropriate unit of analysis. In essence, he argues that they serve as an accurate reflection of the interplay of labor, management and government (Dunlop, 1958). Recently, Dunlop has expanded his model to argue that forums are also an appropriate unit of analysis (Dunlop & Saltzer, 1987).

Yet, accepting rules as units of analysis creates a set of theoretic blinders to the ways that rule-making itself may affect the relationship (such as increasing legalization). Similarly, expanding the focus to include joint forums as a unit of analysis may leave the analysis blind to the way that cooperation in a joint forum may foreclose the surfacing of points of contention. While this argument is developed more fully elsewhere (Cutcher-Gershenfeld, 1987), the importance of the work of Kochan, Katz and McKersie is that they look beyond rules and forums (which are lagging and often distorted reflections of labor-management relations). Instead they trace changes in more micro patterns of interaction at multiple levels and are able to identify instances where the norms and assumptions that guide the parties seem to have undergone a fundamental change.

As such, the transformation of a unionized labor-management relationship would not just be the introduction of various vehicles for cooperation, but a fundamental shift away from the centrality of adversarial collective bargaining norms. While this could involve a flip-flop into a total assertion of commonality, the fundamental shift could also be toward what might be called a mixed-motive ideal whereby equal value is placed on both the resolution of conflict and the pursuit of common concerns. In this formulation, we can also trace the case of transformation in a high commitment nonunion firm that emphasizes a common culture. This sort of setting would certainly be transformed if there were a flip-flop in which the high commitment was replaced with open conflict. But the institutionalization of various mechanisms for individual and collective dispute resolution raises the possibility of a transformation toward a mixed-motive ideal, but in a way that is exactly opposite of the route taken by a traditional unionized setting.

Here I am posing three key assumptions that might guide or frame labor-management relations. One is an adversarial or conflict assumption, under which primacy is given to the resolution of disputes and cooperation is viewed as cooptation or a sophisticated ploy. The second is a consensus or cooperation assumption, under which primacy is given to the pursuit of common concerns and conflict is viewed as avoidable or even as pathological. The third is a mixed-motive assumption, under which parties are assumed to come to the relationship with a mixture of common and competing motives. In this third case, equal value is placed on the pursuit of common concerns *and* the resolution of conflict. Transformation, in this context, would be a shift in the underlying frame or assumptions that guide labor-management relations. This would not likely happen all at once and may or may not endure, but it would unquestionably constitute the point of departure for understanding labor-management relations.

While I have noted that the above analysis is more fully developed elsewhere, it is included here to illustrate the ways that the work of Kochan, Katz and McKersie seems to be pointing the way toward new ways of thinking about industrial relations. Their work has led me to think about the underlying assumptions that frame or guide the governance of employment relations. In the process, it has led to a fairly precise and operational definition of a transformation in the governance of employment relations.

Returning to the work of Roomkin and Juris, I would urge them to look beyond collective bargaining outcomes or new joint structures in their efforts to classify industrial relations strategies in the U.S. steel industry. I would have them seek to surface underlying patterns of interaction from which they might be able to identify the operating assumptions that guide or frame a given employment relationship. I suspect they will find some firms and unions that are operating from fairly pure conflict or low trust assumptions. Others will be operating from a variation of this where they have a basic adversarial stance, but hope to maintain some narrow adjunct cooperative activities. Some (probably nonunion operations) will operate from an almost pure consensus assumption in which there is little room for internal dissent. Finally, there may be some cases where parties are forging a new, mixed-motive approach to employment relations. It is these different approaches to the governance of employment relations that they might seek to link to both the broad competitive strategies and more specific resource allocation strategies of companies, unions and government.

In the past, it seems that the integrated manufacturers have been able to maintain their competitive strategies concurrent with a fairly adversarial set of assumptions underlying the governance of employment relations. More recently, it seems that some minimills have been able to maintain their competitive strategies and assert a fairly strong set of consensus assumptions in the governance of employment relations. However, to the extent that either the adversarial or the consensus approaches to governance are found to be incompatible with successful competitive strategies of companies, unions and government, I would argue that the remedy would be nothing short of a transformation in industrial relations.

Notes

1. I will generally refer to the Kochan, Katz and McKersie text, *The Transformation of American Industrial Relations,* as the *Transformation* text or by the authors' names.
2. Which is more fully developed in Cutcher-Gershenfeld, (1987).
3. Also, while worrying about words, I cannot but add a comment on what Roomkin and Juris term as a search for deterministic models. For me, the term "deterministic" is bothersome not because I challenge the importance of a theory being predictive, but because my own research would suggest that the links between patterns of industrial relations and strategy (however defined) are emergent, negotiated, and contingent. It is still possible to trace these links and I know that the concept of deterministic theories is a term of art for certain methodological purpos-

es, but I would caution against deterministic theories that are also mechanistic.

References

Cutcher-Gershenfeld, J. (1987). *The Collective Governance of Industrial Relations.* Unpublished Ph.D. dissertation, Cambridge, MA: MIT.

Dunlop, J.T. (1958). *Industrial Relations Systems.* New York: Holt.

Dunlop, J.T., & Saltzer, M. (1987). *Forums and Governance.* Unpublished paper, Boston: Harvard University.

Golden, C., & Parker, V.D. (1955). *Causes of Industrial Peace Under Collective Bargaining.* New York: The National Planning Association; Harper and Row.

Gomberg, W. (1967). Special study committees. *In* J. Dunlop & N. Chamberlain (eds.), *Frontiers of Collective Bargaining.* New York: Harper and Row.

Kochan, T., & Cutcher-Gershenfeld, J. (1988). *Institutionalizing and Diffusing Innovations in Industrial Relations.* Washington, DC: US Department of Labor.

Kochan, T.; Katz, H.; & McKersie, R. (1986). *The Transformation of American Industrial Relations.* New York: Basic Books.

Northrup, H., & Young, H. (1968, October). The causes of industrial peace revisited. *Industrial and Labor Relations Review, 22*(1).

Roomkin, M., & Juris, H. (1990). Strategy and industrial relations: An examination of the American steel industry. *In* J. Chelius & J. Dworkin (eds.), *Reflections on the Transformation of Industrial Relations.* Metuchen, NJ: IMLR Press.

6. THOUGHTS ON THE TRANSFORMATION OF INDUSTRIAL RELATIONS

Richard B. Peterson

THIS PAPER IS ORGANIZED AROUND five major sections or themes. First, specific points about what is said in the KKM (1986) book are presented. Second, the present state of the American labor movement is summarized in terms of its contributions and problems. Third, a position on why the present system of industrial relations isn't working well is outlined. Next, the Swedish industrial relations system is discussed as a basis for commenting upon some of the present failures of our own system—particularly as it relates to the upholding of individual rights in the workplace. Finally, some thoughts are presented about a future scenario for the American industrial relations system that is more likely to serve the legitimate needs of employers, employees, unions, and the broader society than either the New Deal or present models.

Thomas Kochan, Harry Katz, and Robert McKersie have written an important book in our field. It identifies the shifts that have taken place, and are still taking place, in the American industrial relations system since the 1960s. By the late 1960s most of us thought that the pluralistic models expounded by Sumner Slichter (1960) and John Dunlop (1958) were widely accepted by the private sector labor market parties. There was even a sense on the part of many academics that the likelihood of future changes in private sector collective bargaining were rather remote. Hence, it was not surprising that many industrial relations researchers shifted their attention to the newly emerging system of public sector industrial relations. The 1980s, however, have forced us to re-direct our energies and research interests back to the private sector because of the rapidly changing economic and political scene. Foreign competition, de-regulation, and the shift towards neo-conservatism have raised doubts concerning the long-run viability of the pluralistic model of industrial relations.

Specific Comments on the KKM Book

One finds oneself in somewhat of a quandary. On one hand, recent events have made the teaching of labor relations much more interesting given all of the new developments that have impacted the IR system. Labor relations today does not fully represent the mature process described by many writers in the late 1950s and 1960s. All sorts of issues are being raised during this decade that were given scant attention in the earlier postwar period. This is the solid plus side.

On the other hand, many of the changes have seriously limited the ability of unions, and more importantly employees, to take their rightful role in helping to determine and implement the "web of rules" surrounding the workplace. Unfortunately, the values of pluralism and workplace democracy have at times given way to unilateral changes by management that restrict individual and collective "voice" in the workplace. Thus a number of these comments are not critical of the authors, but of the system being used by some employers at the "leading edge of changes" in the American industrial relations system.

The comments in this section will be brief. Some points are elaborated upon more thoroughly in later sections.

(1)   One thing that distinguishes the present scene from the New Deal model articulated in John Dunlop's (1958) industrial relations system model is the strong non-presence of government, particularly at the federal level, as a major actor on the industrial relations scene. One of the vital roles of government from 1935 to 1975 in the private sector was to provide mechanisms for balancing the power between management and labor. However, during the Reagan Administration, the federal government has largely neglected its role as an active participant in the industrial relations process. By so doing, it has probably aided and abetted that part of the management community who are philosophically opposed to unions or any other collective presence of employees in the workplace. Democracy in the employment relationship is more likely to flourish when there is a relatively equal opportunity for labor and management to be heard. It is essential that government play a balancing role if the rights of both parties are to be realized.

(2)   It would be difficult to dispute the case made by KKM that most of the human resource management innovations in recent

years like job design, gainsharing, quality circles, and pay for knowledge have originated with management rather than unions. Trade union leadership must take some of the blame for this situation since in many cases they have failed to develop new programs that might better respond to a changing labor force in terms of ethnicity, sex, and values. This lack of a proactive strategy by unions has produced a void that some American employers are quite willing to fill.

(3) The authors are correct in stating that for much of the early postwar years, IR research rarely addressed the position of management as a strategist. Part of the reason is that, with the exception of the late 1950s when employers were particularly concerned with the erosion of managerial rights (MacDonald, 1967), management after the mid-1940s was largely in a reactive mode to the bargaining agendas of union leaders and government legislators. This situation is no longer always true. However, we should keep in mind that many employers continue to deal with their unions in a manner more similar to that found in the 1950s and 1960s. Furthermore, one wonders if many of the employers cited by the authors really had a clearly thought out proactive strategy or whether incremental action was taken that appeared to be carefully developed management strategy on the basis of hindsight.

(4) We still know very little about the specific forces that led a number of American firms to shift from a largely arms-length acquiescence of the union presence to union avoidance strategies. While there is general agreement that economic, social, political, and philosophical forces were at work, what was the relative weighting of each factor in the case of a given employer? It appears that different combinations of forces were at work for specific firms and industries.

(5) KKM do a particularly fine job in highlighting the dominant features of the New Deal IR model. I suspect that we would have been more accurate in our predictions for the 1970s and 1980s had some of our research focused on the behavior of employers during the earlier postwar years in thwarting union attempts to organize the salaried work force. It was there that the reluctance of management to accept unionism was most apparent. Would the present scenario have been different if unions and employee associations had been more aggressive in organizing in the white collar staff so as to have a greater impact on taking wages out of competition?

(6) The authors properly identify most of the major dynamics beginning in the 1960s that have led to the problems facing the American labor movement today. The changing economic environment, deep-seated managerial values opposed to unions, and increased opportunities and incentives of employers to avoid unions

lie at the heart of the problem. The question is whether the unions could have done much to minimize the impact of these factors. It seems clear that tough language in the National Labor Relations Act might have prevented some employers from breaking both the letter and spirit of the law. The J.P. Stevens case offers a classic illustration of the irresponsible use of power by an employer to circumvent the letter and spirit of the law regarding union recognition, safety, and non-discrimination. Stiffer penalties in such cases might have acted to deter such behavior.

(7)   Unions, in general, have been successful when it comes to implementing mechanisms for managing conflict and due process as well as providing a set of work rules through bargaining concerning the work organization. On the down side, some of the extensive work rules seriously reduced management's flexibility to operate. Moreover, unions largely abdicated to the human resource management staff their role to influence the motivation of individual employees. This allowed many employers to develop unilaterally designed and implemented programs to address individual, as opposed to collective, concerns which were of growing interest to many younger members of the labor force. Hindsight suggests that many unions have suffered by not being a more active participant in this process.

(8)   Most of us are aware of companies who deliberately established new plants in the South and Southwest with the expressed purpose of reducing the likelihood of those employees choosing union representation. The more important question though is whether these plants provide a superior alternative to unionism *or* primarily benefit management through lower labor costs and greater managerial flexibility. We really don't have data to test whether employees benefited from company relocation to less unionized sections of the country.

(9)   KKM may overstate the case for the effectiveness of the new union substitution or union avoidance strategies and programs. It is not yet convincing that most employers are willing or able unilaterally to manage conflict in the work setting in a way mutually beneficial to management and its employees. The role demands placed on management make it very difficult to satisfy both parties simultaneously if one accepts Jack Barbash's position (1984). It is not easy to satisfy the employer's concern for profitability, efficiency, and flexibility while at the same time satisfying employee concerns for an improved standard of living, fair treatment, and job and employment security. The union movement emerged, in part, because employers found difficulty in satisfying both sets of goals.

As an example on this point, consider a recently completed review of the literature on non-union grievance procedure (Peterson and Lewin, 1988)—a key element in many union substitution programs. We have found that most employers implemented such programs primarily as a means of reducing the attractiveness of unions (Berenbeim, 1980) rather than as an affirmative right of their employees. In addition, the track record shows that most non-union grievance procedures compare unfavorably with unionized grievance systems on the basis of: allowance for resolution by a disinterested third party; free access to expertise; breadth of grievance issues; and extent of use.

Having worked and taught in human resource management for over twenty-five years, one is struck with the faddishness of most employer generated programs. MBO, job design, cafeteria-style compensation, quality circles, and organizational development have come and gone. Employees and unions rarely had much of an active role in either the design or operation of such programs. We have the know-how to do a much better job of managing human resources in a way beneficial to both management and its employees. However, only in the rare case is top management evidencing the commitment necessary to make day-to-day managing of human resources a top priority. Unions, it would seem, have far less to fear from human resource management programs making their presence unnecessary than may be implied by the authors.

(10) KKM are likely correct in their assessment that most employees are primarily concerned with traditional bargaining issues like wages, hours, and working conditions. Workplace and strategic issues gain less of their attention due to the necessity for trade-offs, lack of expertise and monies to address workplace concerns, and lack of training or pertinent information to involve employees in policy-making activities. Furthermore, most employees learn early-on in their career as to the limits employers are willing to go in employee participation.

(11) Perhaps the ultimate failure of many labor-management cooperation programs in the past (for example, Armour Automation Fund, Human Relations Committee in Steel, Kaiser Progress Sharing Plan) can be explained by the basic inconsistency between the three levels of decision-making that KKM present in Chapter 1 of *The Transformation of American Industrial Relations* (1986). It was probably unrealistic to expect meaningful cooperation to emerge given the history of confrontation between many employers and unions (Peterson and Tracy, 1985).

(12) Christiansen (1987) supports KKM's thesis that management officials responsible for handling labor relations have lost some

influence within their own organizations because of their earlier willingness to accommodate to the union.

(13)   KKM convey the impression that the decentralization of bargaining structure and advent of concession bargaining in the early 1980s were consistent with management's proactive strategy. It seems that one could equally argue that the decline of pattern bargaining and employer demands for pay and work rule concessions were primarily predicated on economic realities. The Frank Lorenzo confrontative style at Continental Air Lines was more the exception than the rule.

Finally, if no major developments take place during the remaining years of this century, the following conclusion of KKM is likely:

> It should be clear by now that no single set of choices of patterns of evolution will capture the diversity of American industrial relations in the future any more than a single pattern characterized the past. The U.S. industrial relations system will continue to display considerable diversity across industries, firms, unions, and occupations. Moreover, there is every reason to expect that the future will continue to be characterized not only by the historic dynamic interplay between union and nonunion systems but also by an increasing variety of arrangements governing employment relationships. (p. 250)

The Contributions and Problems of American Unions

During the 1980s American unions and their leaders have not received much in the way of favorable publicity in the press. Rather, it has been more common for their critics to place a major share of the blame for our country's present economic difficulties at the foot of the labor movement. While union leaders must share some of the blame along with management and government, the unions have also contributed to our country's present strength. Few American employees would wish to return to the system governing the workplace that existed prior to the passage of the National Labor Relations Act in 1935.

Contributions

Freeman and Medoff, in their book *What Do Unions Do?* (1984), identify a number of benefits that unions have provided for their members when compared to the nonunion sector. They found that unionized employees on average received about 15-20 percent higher pay than employees not covered by collective bargaining. Furthermore, a fair amount of the variance was the result of wage movements in the 1970s when parts of the organized workforce benefited from the fact that they received cost-of-living adjustments (COLAs) in addition to negotiated pay increases. These differences have narrowed somewhat since 1984 because pay increases in the nonunion sector have consistently exceeded those in the unionized sectors of our economy.

Unions have been even more successful when it comes to the area of fringe benefits. Freeman and Medoff (1984) reported such benefits as being some 20-30 percent higher for unionized workers. Moreover, collective bargaining has provided the initial thrust for the introduction of almost all of the postwar fringe benefits. The one noticeable exception is profit-sharing schemes that were most commonly instigated by the employer. On average, then, the typical employee covered by a collective bargaining agreement is considerably better off in terms of insurance, health care benefits, vacations, holidays, and pension plans than employees working in nonunion employment.

The unionized grievance procedure, even with its imperfections, provides a "voice" (Hirschman, 1970) vehicle that is superior to either most nonunion grievance procedures or the employment-at-will doctrine.

Other benefits that unions bring to their membership include reduced spread or inequality between workers' pay and stronger protection against layoffs through seniority language. In addition, there is some limited evidence that unionization may contribute to making employers more productivity-conscious (Freeman & Medoff, 1984; Abraham & Medoff, 1984)[1]

Problems for Unions (and Pluralism in the Workplace)

One suspects that at the time of the merger of the AFL and CIO in 1955, neither George Meany nor Walter Reuther had any inkling of the negative developments that would take place for the American trade union movement in the ensuing thirty-three years. Then, unions represented approximately 35 percent of the non-agricultural labor force in the United States.

However, by the late 1950s some private sector employers were already taking a "hard-line" approach in bargaining with their unions. These employers made a concerted effort to seize the initiative in bargaining, roll back the size of wage settlements, and abolish or by-pass restrictive work rules and practices (Macdonald, 1967). They were not overly successful.

The rapid growth of public sector unionization in the 1960s kept union leaders from addressing the growing difficulties in organizing the private sector labor force. For example, Shister (1967) made the following point in his article "The Direction of Unionism 1947-67: Thrust or Drift?":

> But short of some serious economic dislocation in the country or a dramatic shift in public policy favoring unionization—both of which seem most unlikely in the foreseeable future—we will not witness any great spurts of growth in these sectors comparable to the major spurts of blue-collar growth in the past (p. 599).

Between 1955 and 1978 labor unions in this country continued to grow in absolute numbers, but they were losing ground in terms of their share of the labor force (Sandver, 1987). Beginning in 1979 we found a drop in absolute numbers as well. By 1982 union membership had dropped to 17.9 percent of the civilian labor force. More modest drops have taken place since then.

American unions have suffered on two fronts during the past 20-25 years. First, it has been much more difficult for them to organize. And second, even when collective bargaining is present, many unions have encountered difficulties. We will treat these areas separately.

Union organizing. The recent literature suggests a number of reasons why unions of late have won less than 50 percent of National Labor Relations Board (NLRB) supervised certification elections. This is down from a range of 60-75 percent in the period from the late 1930s through the early 1950s. The reasons include the following:

1. The vast majority of cases involve an election rather than a stipulation by the parties based on signed authorization cards (Block and Wolkinson, 1986). An election campaign allows the employer to blunt the effect of the union's message.
2. Delays are more likely to be encountered between the time of the petition and the ensuing election due to the role of the appeal courts (Block and Wolkinson, 1986). Such delays usually favor the employer by allowing them more time to respond to the union message.
3. A larger percentage of employers are likely today to employ a union substitution (for example, IBM, Hewlett Packard) or

union suppression (for example, J.P. Stevens) strategy than in the early postwar years.

4. Unions have been largely unsuccessful in organizing bargaining units of over 100-150 employees. Thus, even when they win the election, the net gain in membership is small (Lawler, 1984; Cooke, 1983).

5. There is some indication that some, but not all, employers raise purposeful objections and create delays between the time of the election and the subsequent certifying of the election results. Research has shown the negative effect of such delays on election outcomes (Cooke, 1983).

6. Even when the union is successful in winning the certification election, the union may have difficulty in winning the first contract due to delays, challenges, discrimination, and the refusal of the employer to bargain in good faith (Cooke, 1985).

7. The growth of the labor force during the 1970s and 1980s has been stronger in the South, Southwest, and West than in the Northeast and upper Middle West where unions have had a stronger presence. The so-called Southern effect and the presence of right-to-work laws have made it much more difficult for unions to organize in these labor force growth areas (Cooke, 1983).

8. Employers have recently made use of more management consultants (Lawler, 1984) and aggressive management tactics to reduce the union's chances of winning the election (Dickens, 1983). Research by Seeber and Cooke (1983) shows this particular dampening effect where the management tactics involve illegal behavior. An example is the large growth in the number of unfair labor practice charges filed since 1960.

9. Finally, unions as an institution do not have wide favor in the eyes of the public in the way that they did during the massive organizing drives of the 1930s and 1940s. This is compounded by evidence that unions were devoting a declining percentage of union expenditures for organizing campaigns in the 1970s than before (Voos, 1984).

Existing union entities. Even if the union won the election, and had a longstanding bargaining relationship with the employer, there have been problems.

1. Basic manufacturing industries were particularly hard hit by the economic downturn in the early 1980s. This was one of the strongest union sectors in the economy. For example, Troy and Sheflin (1985) report that union presence in manufactur-

ing dropped from 42.4 percent in 1953 to 26.0 percent in 1984 (pp. 3-15). The percentage drops were even more dramatic in mining and construction.

2. The deregulation of the airlines, trucking, and telecommunications industries beginning in the late 1970s has resulted in losses of jobs, a stronger nonunion workforce, and, in some cases, some loss of union membership (Hendricks, 1986; Northrup, 1983).

3. There was an acceleration of decertification elections over the 1947-1977 period. While the number of employees involved in such elections has been fairly small, the union has lost the election in approximately 75 percent of the cases (Anderson, O'Reilly, & Busman, 1980; Pearce and Peterson, 1987). This trend has continued.

4. The union movement was vociferous in its condemnation of some of President Reagan's appointees to the NLRB in the early 1980s. Some of the subsequent Board decisions represented dramatic turnarounds from long-established positions of the NLRB. One of the fallouts was that many unions withdrew from using the NLRB certification election process in favor of other organizing approaches. Overall, unions became less active in organizing new bargaining units.

5. Concession bargaining became a far more common event in the unionized sector during the early and middle 1980s than was true in nonunion companies. Moreover, companies that were relatively healthy were asking, and in some cases demanding, such wages cuts or the use of two tier pay contracts (Cappelli, 1983). Bargaining power, in most cases, was shifting to the employer for a variety of reasons.

6. Top management was taking some of the initiative for labor relations away from the labor relations and human resources staffs (Kochan, McKersie, and Cappelli, 1984; Christiansen, 1987). Thus, earlier accords and understandings worked out between union and company negotiators were no longer honored by all employers.

7. Evidence shows that some partially unionized employers developed an unstated policy of shifting much of their new investment from already existing union operations to new, nonunion plants (Verma, 1985).

8. Further evidence shows that the union avoidance strategy of some employers during the 1977-1983 period reduced the unionized workforce by almost three times the number reduced by the average firm in their study (Kochan, McKersie, and Chalykoff, 1986).

9. Finally, perhaps most depressing for unions was the fact that in order to hold their own, unions would have had to grow by 1.6 million members in the 1980-1985 period given the rapid growth in the total labor force. Unfortunately, the labor force growth was most rapid during this period in the service economy where union strength was, and is, particularly weak.

Personal Concerns

A primary concern is that the present system of labor law does not allow employees an uncoerced choice of whether they want to be represented or not. First, let us examine the postwar history of industrial relations.

The New Deal system of industrial relations emerged out of the generally recognized fact that the courts, whether by intent or not, were imbalanced in favor of the property rights of the employer. The hard fought organizing battles of the 1930s and 1940s showed that many employers were reluctant to accept the legitimacy of collective "voice" at the workplace. Some of this reluctance was due, no doubt, to a deeply ingrained valued of "rugged individualism" which assumed that employees should not need to look to labor unions or government for help.

During the 1950s and 1960s there was hope that employers and their unions might follow some of the guidelines for industrial peace as advocated by the National Planning Association (Golden & Parker, 1955). However, the more common route was one of accommodation whereby most private sector employers maintained an "arms length" relationship with the unions representing its blue-collar employees. Most employers, however, were clear that they would fight against any attempted spread of the union to the salaried staff. The amount of bargaining power held by the two parties largely determined who would win at the bargaining table. However, during this time it was possible for both sides to benefit given the year-to-year growth in the nation's economic performance and improved standard of living of most of its workers.

In the 1960s and 1970s it was possible for Congress to pass a series of bills providing protection against pay and employment discrimination, safety hazards, and loss of pension plan rights. It was probably illusory to expect that these legal rights would provide the necessary protection for the vast majority of the labor force—particularly in light of the Reagan Administration's distaste for strong government involvement and the growing recognition of the costs of governmental regulation of the economy.

Thus when the serious recession of 1981-82 arrived, neither management nor unions were prepared to deal with the devastating impact of the economic downturn on parts of the manufacturing sector. Most employers and unions had little experience with cooperative programs that might have led to fairer resolution of how the costs might be more equally shared. History showed that most private sector employers were reluctant to ask, or allow, for independent input from the union side. Labor leadership was itself wary of providing input from the union side. Labor leadership was itself wary of providing input because of the fear of cooptation and the lack of access to the firm's financial records.

Thus, employers adversely affected by deregulation, international competition, and governmental fiscal and monetary policy, took positions that ranged from cooperative to "union bashing." Forced pay cuts for the hourly ranks, or two tier contracts, took place alongside executive pay increases, generous stock options, and beneficent "golden parachutes." In the past, layoffs were most often confined to the hourly paid staff. However, office, managerial, and professional staff in some firms found themselves equally vulnerable to temporary and permanent loss of employment. Many employees and managers were viewed primarily as a cost rather than as an asset. Many early retirement options were less than totally voluntary in nature.

It would appear that the present American industrial relations system as well as the non-union option are at odds with the reality of the work situation we find in late twentieth century America. The overwhelming number of the labor force are employees rather than self-employed. The speed of changing economic fortunes and the complexity of modern society make it very difficult for the individual employee to feel a sense of control over his or her future. Most employers are confronted with multiple demands by customers, government, stockholders and employees so that they are unable to truly represent the special interests and concerns of their employees.

Furthermore, the track record of participative management in our country is not terribly impressive. Many of us in academia were probably somewhat naive in expecting that much of the 1960s rhetoric by Argyris, Bennis, and others in favor of employee input would really result in genuine participation in the workplace. When one reads and hears the pronouncements of some corporate executives who are very comfortable with top-down leadership style, it is possible that we may have regressed. It is generally unrealistic to expect that any sense of participation can emerge in all but a handful of firms without some presence of collective voice and expertise. Otherwise, experiments in participation are doomed to be short-lived because they are dependent on the good-will of current management and its continuing support for such a cooperative corporate culture.

If our modern, complex industrial nation no longer fits the ethos of individualism of the frontier (Wallin, 1976), what changes are needed in the American industrial relations system? Since the Swedish industrial relations system better fits the needs of a modern industrial nation than the system covering labor-management relations that we have developed over the years, it will be outlined before presenting suggested changes for America.

The Swedish Industrial Relations Model

During the late 1950s and through most of the 1960s the Swedish model was extolled as the most successful industrial relations system in the free world. Today it shows some of the problems found in a number of other industrialized nations, but by comparison to the United States, it has certain clear advantages. Why?[2]

First, both private sector employers and trade unions are strong—they largely counter-balance each other. The Swedish Employers' Confederations (SAF), with a membership of over 42,000, represents the interests of almost every private-sector employer of any size in the country. The Confederation of Swedish Trade Unions (LO), with some 2.1 million members, covers about 90-95 percent of all blue-collar workers. The white-collar confederation, TCO, represents over 70 percent of that group. Finally, SACO/SR represents primarily those employees with university-level or other advanced education in both the public and private sectors. Overall, approximately 80 percent of the labor force is represented by a trade union organization.

Second, this means that the voice of both employers and employees (through their union) is assured of being heard by governmental officials. In fact, mechanisms are in place to assure that both of these dominant parties in the labor market are given the opportunity to express their views on pending legislation. LO, in particular, has benefited from its close organizational attachment to the Social Democratic Party over the years. That party has ruled Sweden, by itself or by coalition, for all but eight years since the early 1930s.

Third, the government recognizes the importance of Sweden being competitive in world markets so that the Social Democratic Party is not inclined to disregard employer concerns, even if the votes are there to do so. The economic realities of the 1970s and

1980s have tempered any radical re-structuring of the economy that could be detrimental to economic performance.

Fourth, as early as 1906 SAF and LO reached an agreement that employers would accept the right of employees to form trade unions if unions would recognize the principle of broad managerial rights for the employer. This meant that it was unnecessary to develop governmental agencies, like the NLRB in the United States, that would determine what behaviors were allowed or disallowed during the union organizing process. If the union could show that some of the firm's employees wished union representation, that was it.[3]

Animosity between individual employers and trade unions did not vanish with the 1906 accord, but it never took on the level of confrontation that we found in our country from the 1920s through the end of World War II. The Saltsjobaden Agreement of 1938 between SAF and LO laid to rest the issue of the legitimacy of the employees to have a union negotiate with their employer over wages, hours, and working conditions.

From that time onward, the Swedish trade unions did not feel it necessary to negotiate detailed language into company level contracts that would, or could, seriously restrict the employer's ability to manage the enterprise. From 1932 through the early 1980s the parties used centralized "frame agreements" at the confederation level to handle the major issues like pay and some fringe benefits. Subsequent agreements would be reached at the federation (industry) level. Only the larger Swedish firms would engage in formal bargaining culminating in written company-level contracts. Informal accords or understandings were reached by the principal parties over special issues like industrial democracy, safety and health. These accords provided a fair amount of flexibility in how they would be implemented in a given industry or company. More recently, the unions have used legislation to cover some areas or issues where collective bargaining did not bring changes. Presently, with the notable exception of the engineering industry, most members of SAF still prefer centralized negotiations.

Fifth, unions in the private sector, and much of the public sector, are given the right to strike. However, they have exercised this right sparingly since 1950. Recent strike activity has been most evident in the public sector. The right of the employer to lockout its employees has served as a counter-balancing mechanism in terms of bargaining power.

Sixth, the Swedish economy has generally performed well over the past 70 years. Sweden never suffered from the ravages of the worldwide Depression of the 1930s. She also, as a neutral nation in World War II, was able to have a growing economy beginning after

WWII and continuing into the late 1960s. Her people have one of the highest standards of living in the world today. The Swedish unemployment rate has consistently ranged from 1-4% in the postwar period, much lower than that of most other industrialized nations. Inflation and "wage drift" have been problems, but that has been true for most other industrialized countries.

Seventh, Sweden has a tripartite Labor Court that handles important labor relations questions. However, because of the minimal effect of changing politics on the Court decisions, most key principles and guidelines, once established, are likely to remain. The amount of litigation is minimal in comparison to similar activities before the National Labor Relations Board and state and local labor relations agencies in the United States.

Finally, and most importantly, many Swedish employees explain their membership in a trade union as primarily a means of being heard. They often characterize Sweden as a very organized society in which positions and agendas are voiced and implemented through a variety of key organizations. Just as employers have their various trade associations, employees feel the need to have a "voice" mechanism in the sphere affecting their job. The trade unions provide that vehicle. The trade union member may vote for the Conservative, Center or Liberal Party rather than the Social Democrats. The member may be favorably disposed to the position of employers on such issues as the Wage Earner Funds, but this does not negate his or her concern on collective bargaining questions. What does the Swedish experience have to say for American labor relations in the 1980s?

An Agenda for Changes in American Labor Law

If most Swedish citizens feel the need for organizations to provide collective "voice" for their interests in a country of eight million people, isn't the need even greater in a large, heterogeneous, complex industrial nation like the United States with a population of two hundred and thirty-five million? We delude ourselves if we believe that the typical employee in a private sector firm has considerable influence and control over how he or she will be treated in the employment setting. It is also doubtful that we can expect most non-union employers to develop and implement human resource programs that truly meet the needs of all of their employees. Top management is usually confronted with multiple demands from diverse groups like customers, stockholders, government, and employees. Trade unions in this country have typically been the most active party in protecting and enhancing the rights of their members through collective bargaining, grievance administration, and pushing protective labor legislation. Most of us in the nonunion sector have benefited in some way. However, if the trade union movement in this country was to become even weaker than it is today, how would the "voice" of employees be heard?

A democracy requires (1) a genuine concern for the rights of the individual in his or her economic, political, and social situation and (2) that most of these rights of the individual can best be accomplished through interest groups representing separate and overlapping positions. Pluralism is only effective if the contesting parties have an equal opportunity to be heard so that most decisions are made on their merits rather than the dominant power of one side or the other.

KKM, in their closing chapter, identify several scenarios for the future of union-management relations in the United States. Only one of the four scenarios offers a great deal of encouragement for those people who consider a viable labor movement as a cornerstone of democracy. There is no question that unions need to develop new organizing strategies if they are to find more success in attracting new members as well as blunting the impact of recent employer strategies. However, public policy makers need to amend American labor law to provide employees with an uncoerced opportunity to vote for or against union or employee association representation. Chapter 7 of the NLRA (as amended by the Taft-Hartley Act) is very clear on the point that it is the employee, not the employer or union, who makes the choice for or against union representation.

Our familiarity with the Swedish industrial relations system suggests some basic steps that Congress might take to reform our present system so that in the long run individual "voice" in the employment setting can find expression.

First, there are several assumptions underlying the proposed changes in American labor law affecting union recognition:

1. It is difficult for most employers to create a genuine set of human resource management policies and practices and self-police them. This does not negate the possibility that a small minority of firms like IBM and Hewlett-Packard can operate in such a way that the majority of their employees will choose to remain nonunion.

2. Most nonunion American private sector employers develop unilaterally based human resource management policies and practices with a minimum of employee input into the design and implementation of such programs. Such policies and

practices can be subject to change due to new corporate leadership or changing economic circumstances because there is no formal contract that legally obligates the employer to maintain such policies and practices.

3. The vast majority of American firms are not included in that group of companies that are often cited for their innovative human resource management strategies and programs. Rather, most firms use a rather mechanistic approach to dealing with human resources whether it be in the areas of selection, compensation, performance appraisal, or training and management development. Few nonunion grievance procedures meet Epstein's criteria for a viable due process system (1975).

4. The experience of employees and managers in a number of companies during the last two recessions makes evident the fact that almost everyone is an employee. Employee input was rarely used by firms when faced with the need for down-sizing the workforce. Employee "voice" was generally muted except in those cases where the union leadership had some opportunity to voice their ideas and concerns before cutbacks took place.

5. Finally, there is a great deal of evidence that the present system of labor law results in far too much litigation. The result is hard feelings, power politics, shifting and unstable administrative board decisions, and tremendous financial costs to the parties, government, and society.

Let us now look at proposed changes in labor law. The first step would be to change the process to encourage quick resolution of the certification question. In those cases where the NLRB has clearly identified guidelines covering the potential bargaining unit coverage, signed authorization cards would be the preferred method. The employer and union would be given no more than one or two organized opportunities to argue their case before the employees. An NLRB official would be present to determine whether the messages were presented in a way as to protect "laboratory conditions." The union would then be given no more than 30 days to gain the signatures of a majority of employees covered by the potential bargaining unit. If unsuccessful, the contract bar would limit the union from mounting a second organizational drive before 12 months had elapsed. The authorization card would clearly state that the employee wished to be represented by the union and was legally bound to join the union immediately upon certification of the union by the NLRB. The NLRB would determine the validity of the authorization cards. A similar process would apply where two or more unions were contesting for representation rights.

If the union won the certification, but was judged by the NLRB as having used illegal tactics, the certification would be set aside. If the employer did likewise, the NLRB would be allowed to certify the union as it has the power to do at the present time where the employer flagrantly disregards the law. This is an unpopular position, but the rights of the employee to make a non-coerced choice need to be protected from the interests of both the employer and union. The law, at present, does not provide sufficient "teeth" to discourage use of illegal tactics.

Appeals by either the union or employer would be limited. This would reduce the costs to the employee of delays between petition and election as well as between election and ultimate certification/noncertification of the union.

Next, if the union was certified as the bargaining representative, then the parties would attempt to negotiate a first contract. If no contract was reached within six months of certification, we might experiment with the Canadian system whereby the regulatory board can impose a first contract settlement in those cases where one party maintains a non-negotiating position.

These steps to improve the process should, in the long run, provide several benefits. They include the following: reduce the hard feelings often engendered in the union organizing campaign by the heavy-handed methods used by both unions and employers to gain the employees vote; increase the costs to both sides for intentionally violating the spirit and letter of the law; partially reduce the employees' fear of adverse actions like being fired for taking an active position in support of union organizing; cut down considerably on the number of unfair labor practice charges filed in conjunction with union organizing; increase the chances that the union organizing process will not leave such acrimony that any real attempts at labor-management cooperation are dead from the beginning; and finally, provide assurance that where the employees choose representation, they will have a first contract.

Employees would still retain the right to vote against union representation. Decertification would remain a right, but safeguards would be included to assure that the discontent with the union originated with the union members, not with the employer officials.

These proposals are only first steps. We should be encouraging other changes in the law and in the NLRB rule-making process to improve the system. The present system, whether by intention or otherwise, does not provide the necessary safeguards to protect and encourage the rights of the individual employee to choose whether or not to have collective "voice" in the workplace. Nor does it encourage employees as individuals or through their union (employee association) to have much of an independent "voice" in influencing and/or determining the rules of the game. The result is that most employers benefit only partially in terms of gaining the skills, knowledge and commitment of their workforce.

The cost to the American economy of poor utilization of human resources is considerable. I am convinced that the history of personnel management in our country does not offer us the best way of marshalling our nation's human resources. Pluralism, in the long run, is the more desirable choice for employees, managers, and the employer. It also protects employees against arbitrary or ill-considered decisions by employers. The present deck is stacked against the individual having a full opportunity to choose for or against collective representation.

It was 1947 when the last bill was passed covering union organizing and collective bargaining. Surely there is a need to amend the Taft-Hartley Act by now. The Swedish system of labor-management relations provides some lessons for changes in the American system of labor law. Without needed changes in the legal framework, employee "voice" is likely to experience further decline in the work setting. Both American employers and unions will need to be more responsible for providing a constructive employment relationship that increases our competitiveness as a nation.

Notes

1. The one important area where unions can be criticized concerns the negative association of unions and company performance. This is the area where management has been most vocal in its position—particularly in respect to the way bargained work rules limit the flexibility of the employer. Interestingly, some unions voluntarily or under duress have modified or dropped many such restrictive work practices during the 1980s.
2. Most of the information in this section is drawn from Peterson (1987; 1985).
3. Folke Schmidt (1977) provides a detailed assessment of the right of association under Swedish law. The right of association is based on the individual employee rather than the trade union.

References

Abraham, K.G., & Medoff, J.L. (1984). Length of service and layoffs in union and nonunion work groups. *Industrial and Labor Relations Review, 38,* 87-97.

Anderson, J.; O'Reilly III, C.A.; & Busman, G. (1980). Union decertification in the U.S.: 1947-1977. *Industrial Relations, 19*, 100-107.

Barbash, J. (1984). *The Elements of Industrial Relations*. Madison: University of Wisconsin Press.

Berenbeim, R. (1980). *Nonunion Complaint Systems: A Corporate Appraisal*. (Research Report No. 770). New York: The Conference Board.

Block, R.N., & Wolkinson, B.W. (1986). Delay in the union election campaign revisited: A theoretical and empirical analysis. *In* D.B. Lipsky & D. Lewin (eds.), *Advances in Industrial and Labor Relations, 3*, 21-42. Greenwich, CT: JAI Press.

Cappelli, P. (1983). Concession bargaining and the national economy. *Proceedings of the 35th Annual Meeting of the Industrial Relations Research Association* (pp. 362-371). Madison, WI: Industrial Relations Research Association.

Christiansen, E.T. (1987). Challenges in the management of diversified companies: The changing face of corporate labor relations. *Human Resource Management, 26*, 363-384.

Cooke, W.N. (1983). Determinants of the outcomes of union certification elections. *Industrial and Labor Relations Review, 37*, 402-414.

Cooke, W.N. (1985). The failure to negotiate first contracts: Determinants and policy implications. *Industrial and Labor Relations Review, 38*, 163-178.

Dickens, W.T. (1983). The effect of company campaigns on certification elections: Law and reality once again. *Industrial and Labor Relations Review, 37*, 560-575.

Dunlop, J.T. (1958). *Industrial Relations Systems*. New York: Holt.

Epstein, R.L. (1975). The grievance procedure in the non-union setting: Caveat employer. *Employee Relations Law Journal, 1*, 120-127.

Freeman, R.B., & Medoff, J.L. (1984). *What Do Unions Do?* New York: Basic Books.

Golden, C., & Parker, V.D. (1955). *Causes of Industrial Peace Under Collective Bargaining*. New York: The National Planning Association; Harper and Row.

Hendricks, W. (1986). Collective bargaining in regulated industries. *In* D.B. Lipsky & D. Lewin (eds.), *Advances in Industrial and Labor Relations, 3*, 21-42. Greenwich, CT: JAI Press.

Hirschman, A.O. (1970). *Exit, Voice, and Loyalty: Responses to Declines in Firms, Organizations and States*. Cambridge, MA: Harvard University Press.

Kochan, T.A.; Katz, H.C.; & McKersie, R.B. (1986). *The Transformation of American Industrial Relations*. New York: Basic Books.

Kochan, T.A.; McKersie, R.B.; & Cappelli, P. (1984). Strategic choice and industrial relations theory. *Industrial Relations, 23*, 16-39.

Kochan, T.A.; McKersie, R.B.; & Chalykoff, J. (1986). The effects of corporate strategy and workplace innovations on union representation. *Industrial and Labor Relations Review, 39*, 487-501.

Lawler, J.J. (1984). The influence of management consultants on the outcome of union certification elections. *Industrial and Labor Relations Review, 38*, 38-51.

MacDonald, R.M. (1967). Collective bargaining in the postwar period. *Industrial and Labor Relations Review, 20*, 553-577.

Northrup, H. (1983). The new employee relations climate in airlines. *Industrial and Labor Relations Review, 36*, 167-181.

Pearce, T., & Peterson, R.B. (1987). Regionality in NLRB decertification cases. *Journal of Labor Research, 8*, 253-269.

Peterson, R.B. (1985). Swedish collective bargaining in a time of adversity. *In* H. Juris, M. Thompson, & W. Daniels (eds.), *Comparative Labor Movements*. Madison, WI: Industrial Relations Research Association.

Peterson, R.B. (1987). Swedish collective bargaining: A changing scene. *British Journal of Industrial Relations, 25*, 31-48.

Peterson, R.B. & Lewin, D. (1988). *The Non-Union Grievance Procedure*. Working paper.

Peterson, R.B., & Tracy, L. (1985). Problem solving in American collective bargaining: A review and assessment. *In* D. Lipsky & J. Douglas (eds.), *Advances in Industrial and Labor Relations*, (pp. 1-50). Greenwich, CT: JAI Press.

Sandver, M.H. (1987). *Labor Relations: Process and Outcome*. Boston: Little, Brown.

Schmidt, F. (1977). *Law and Industrial Relations in Sweden*. Stockholm: Almquist and Wiksell International.

Seeber, R., & Cooke, W. (1983). The decline of union success in NLRB representation elections. *Industrial Relations, 22*, 34-44.

Shister, J. (1967). The direction of unionism 1947-1967: Thrust or drift? *Industrial and Labor Relations Review, 20*, 578-601.

Slichter, S.; Healy, J.; & Livernash, E.R. (1960). *The Impact of Collective Bargaining on Management*. Washington, DC: Brookings Institution.

Troy, L. & Sheflin, N. (1985). *Union Sourcebook*. West Orange, NJ: Irdis.

Verma, A. (1985). Relative flow of capital to union and nonunion plants within a firm. *Industrial Relations, 24*, 395-405.

Voos, P.B. (1984). Trends in union organizing expenditures, 1953-1977. *Industrial and Labor Relations Review, 38*, 52-63.

Wallin, T. (1976). The international executive's baggage: cultural values of the American frontier. *MSU Business Topics, 24*, 49-58.

COMMENTS ON PETERSON

William Bigoness

IN HIS PAPER "Some Thoughts on the Transformation of Industrial Relations," Professor Peterson (1990, chap. 6) covers a breadth of topics. He examines the current state of industrial relations in the United States, labor law reform, union organizing campaigns, the Swedish industrial relations system, corporate human resource management practices, and an assessment of Kochan, Katz, and McKersie's book, *The Transformation of American Industrial Relations* (1986).

In general, Professor Peterson's review and insights on these diverse topics reflects mainstream thinking of the academic industrial relations community. As a consequence, in more cases than not, I find myself in agreement with both his assessment of current situations and desirable future changes. At the same time, however, there are instances where I find myself at variance with Professor Peterson's assessments and conclusions. To be somewhat provocative, my comments will be limited to four areas where Professor Peterson and I do not quite see eye to eye.

The relationship between employees and employers in the non-union model portrayed by Professor Peterson appears to me to be somewhat inaccurate and overly jaundiced. He views employer and employee interests as largely mutually exclusive. Game theorists' view of the employer and employee relationship as a mixed motive relationship appears to be a more accurate one. To characterize the employer-employee relationship as largely zero sum in nature is surprising, particularly given recent developments including foreign competition and deregulation which have in many instances promoted unprecedented understanding and cooperation between employers and employees.

The commitment of a majority of employers to progressive human resource management practices is regarded by Professor Peterson as, at best, minimal. This assessment is inconsistent with corporate human resource management developments over the past several decades. Finally, while the past decade has hardly been one of great advances for organized labor, contemporary employee-employer relations are hardly comparable to those of the 1920's.

While one may agree with the position that the nonunion employer model is inferior to the pluralistic union-management model, one is hard pressed to deny the enhanced role and priority that human resource management has achieved during the past decade. This phenomenon, contrary to Professor Peterson's implication, transcends far beyond the boundaries of a few select corporations. Despite its methodological flaws, the overwhelming popularity of Peters and Waterman's book, *In Search of Excellence* (1982), is one, among many, indicators of the elevated prominence given human resource management within contemporary organizations.

Paradoxically, many of the same forces which are commonly identified as contributing to the decline of trade unions in the United States including deregulation, foreign competition, and changing labor force demographics have simultaneously propelled employers to place increased emphasis on human resource management policies and practices.

Clearly multiple motives drive employers to develop and implement enlightened human resource practices. Frequently, human resource management programs are motivated by corporate self interest and a desire to remain nonunion. In other instances, more altruistic motives prevail. Regardless of the primary motive, today's employees are the beneficiaries of human resource policies and practices which have, over time, progressively improved. This assessment does not deny the fact that many human resource management policies were instituted in response to legislative initiatives or the fact that millions of American workers continue to be excluded from the benefits of progressive human resource management practices.

Professor Peterson portrays the Swedish industrial relations system as a model which the United States should, to a degree, seek to emulate. Among all members of the European Community the selection of Sweden as an appropriate role model for the United States is a curious choice. One cannot help but wonder whether Sweden is a relevant industrial relations role model for the United States. Sweden is a highly homogenous nation with a population only 3 percent that of the United States. Sweden has the highest degree of unionization in the European Community, and an economic, political, and cultural history vastly different from the United States.

For persons concerned about the current state of United States industrial relations, far more sobering international comparisons could be gained by examining current developments in Denmark, the Netherlands, England, Greece, or Germany. While each of these nations remains significantly more unionized than the United States, over the past decade the relative and absolute strength of the labor movements in each of these countries has markedly declined.

Commonly cited causes for the decline in European trade unions include industrial restructuring, changing composition of the labor force, diminished public support for unions, improved management practices, high unemployment, and a more conservative political environment. With the exception of high unemployment, these explanations are strikingly similar to the explanations offered to explain the decline of United States trade unions.

The third area where I find myself in some disagreement with Professor Peterson concerns the attitude of United States managers toward unions. Following the turbulent union organizing drives of the 1930's and 1940's, Professor Peterson maintains that American management accepted, albeit reluctantly, the principles embodied in the Wagner Act. Allegedly, beginning in the early 1980's, American management reversed its earlier acceptance of unions and initiated a variety of actions designed to weaken trade unions.

My disagreement with this historical perspective is the contention that by and large American management accepted the fundamental principles of trade unionism and collective bargaining. As Professor Peterson acknowledges, while employers were willing to tolerate the unionization of their blue collar employees, as early as the 1950's employers vigorously resisted attempts to organize their white collar employees. Pertinent to this issue are the comments in the early 1970's of Gerald A. Brown, former Chairman of the National Labor Relations Board, at the time of his retirement. He stated that his biggest surprise in executing his responsibilities as Chairman of the NLRB was observing the continued resistance of management to the principles articulated in the National Labor Relations Act.

Unlike Professor Peterson, I question whether American management ever truly accepted the public policy principles stated in the Wagner Act. Four decades of a generally favorable economic, political, legal, and social environment enabled collective bargaining to grow and in many cases prosper, masking the potential consequences of managerial opposition. During the past decade, however, given a changed economic, legal, political, and social environment the detrimental consequences of managerial opposition to collective bargaining have been amply documented.

Finally, a comment concerning the changes in labor law suggested by Professor Peterson. He thoroughly convinced me of the dire state of American trade unions, impressed me with the Swedish industrial relations model, converted me to the superiority of the pluralistic model of industrial relations, and sensitized me to the numerous limitations of existing United States labor law. Accordingly, I was receptive to the necessity for fundamental and sweeping labor law reform. However, I was offered a surprisingly tame set of proposals designed to merely fine tune existing labor law.

In fact, the proposals recommended by Professor Peterson are less sweeping than those proposed a decade ago in the Labor Reform Act. The Labor Reform Act, which was narrowly defeated by a Senate filibuster, was judged by nearly all observers, including the business community, to be moderate. Given the severity of the illness portrayed by Professor Peterson, and his passionate personal conviction in favor of a truly pluralistic model of industrial relations, a stronger medicine than that proposed here seems clearly warranted.

References

Kochan, T.A.; Katz, H.C.; & McKersie, R.B. (1986). *The Transformation of American Industrial Relations*. New York: Basic Books.

Peters, T.J., & Waterman, R.H. (1982). *In Search of Excellence*. New York: Harper and Row.

Peterson, R.B. (1990). Thoughts on the transformation of industrial relations. *In* J. Chelius & J. Dworkin (eds.), *Reflections on the Transformation of Industrial Relations*. Metuchen, NJ: IMLR Press.

7. A VIEW FROM ABROAD

Jacques Rojot

AT THE OUTSET, it should be pointed out that this chapter is basically in agreement with the main set of positions expressed by Kochan, Katz, and McKersie (KKM, 1986), which offers outstanding insights. There are only minor theoretical additions to the model that could be proposed. However, the model was conceived for the United States and because the European environment is different in some aspects, there are also some adjustments that could be suggested to generalize its use. In meshing these two issues together the following points can be advanced.

The Strategic Choice Perspective

First, and it is a very minor point, the authors consistently insist that they place their work into a strategic choice perspective. However, this may mean mostly that they do not adopt a deterministic view. That is, they postulate that the transformation of the U.S. industrial relations system is not preordained by some outside teleological forces such as the class struggle, god's will or the like. But this being said, and one can only agree with them on that point, it seems that much of what is presented could also fit into an environment dominance or population ecology theoretical framework. There is much emphasis on inertial forces, pressures from the environment, and the existence of too many factors to control them effectively. There is implicitly recognition of the role of chance in the occurrence of reactions to these developments. Indeed the fascinating description of how the New Deal model of industrial relations diffused and then becomes limited to certain sectors of the economy while the intermediary and the non-union models appear and grow in other sectors could almost be used as an example of a cycle of evolution by variation-selection-retention in the population of enterprise industrial relations subsystems.

Model Adaptation for Europe

Second, and this is the basic point of this chapter, it seems that the model of a three-tier industrial relations system can be adapted and generalized to better fit European industrial relations systems in general, and the French one in particular. However this is only a minor adaptation. It should be pointed out that the idea of articulating the three levels and of outlining their interrelationship constitutes a conceptual breakthrough. By itself it helps explain many changes.

The KKM model retains three levels. The top tier is labelled strategic decision making, where governmental policies interact with managerial business strategies and union political and economic strategies. The middle tier is referred to as collective bargaining and personnel policy, where labor law interacts with the bargaining strategies of the parties. The workplace and individual level, where individual rights, duties, and day-to-day operations are established, constitutes the final and lowest tier.

This description is particularly apt for the United States, which has some very specific features. There is comparatively little industry-wide bargaining. There is not much statutory labor law applicable to all employees apart from the minimum wage, Fair Labor Standards Act, state regulations, and OSHA. (In comparison with many continental European countries, this represents little regulation). Furthermore, there is little interindustry bargaining or consultation at the national level. Finally, there is not employee representation in work councils or personnel delegates. There is no employee representation at all if there is no union.

On the contrary, many continental European countries feature a broad array of statutory legislation that applies independent of union membership and creates individual rights. These rights are adjudicated by labor courts. There is also a considerable degree of negotiating or consultation at industry and interindustry levels as well as comprehensive systems of employee representation at corporate and plant levels. We are therefore faced in Europe with a more complex situation which implies a need to partially redesign the KKM model.

It seems that the three-tier model, in its present formulation actually meshes two dimensions. One dimension we could call a geographic dimension where the model distinguishes the workplace tier, as distinct from the bargaining unit tier and the national level as the third tier. The second dimension is concerned with the type of interactions of the actors concerned. The model is not so crude as to allocate strategy to the top tier, tactics to the second tier, and implementation to the third tier. Strategic concerns and issues are present at all three levels. However, there are different level strategies for different geographic units: for instance, the local union as opposed to the national union, or the shop stewards as opposed to the business agent. On the employer side at the top level, there are corporate strategies, and below them all the various levels of management down to first line supervision. The emphasis on strategy formulation obviously is stronger at the highest tier while concerns about implementation are more prevalent at the bottom tier. Also, different parts of the activities of the government apply at each level. Although at their own level, all parties have strategic concerns as well as implementation concerns. However, they are formulated at their level within the constraints of other strategic concerns embodied within decisions taken at higher levels.

A most interesting point of the model is to show how those strategies can be formulated independently at each different level as well as how they influence each other. These influences and interactions among what happens at each different tier and how it affects the other tiers is not specific to the United States; it happens in Europe in the same way. However, it might be helpful in order to take into account the specificities of European industrial relations to alter the three tier model in two ways.

Geographic and Interaction Dimensions

It is useful to distinguish explicitly the two dimensions that are set together in the American model and to consider them apart in order to analyze their influence separately and to take better account of their cross effects. On the one hand, we would have the geographical levels, and on the other hand, the nature of the interactions that take place at each level. This would be helpful because many European industrial relations systems can be compared to a set of successive floors. First, there is a statutory law floor with both a normative and a procedural content. The procedural content could be likened to the Wagner Act for instance: it sets the framework for the parties to interact freely but does not impose the result of these interactions. However, the normative content is much more extended than in the United States. It contains minimum wages and health and safety laws but also many other factors such as a minimum overtime rate, holidays and vacations, and acceptable reasons for individual dismissal. The main concerns here are government as an actor, and public policy. Second, there is an interindustry national floor, when, on top of the statutory minimum, additional terms of interest to all the workforce of the country are addressed: it deals with issues such as cost-of-living allowances, training systems, and retirement pay. This floor is the province of government, national unions and the employers' national association. A third additional floor is the industry level where additional benefits are negotiated industry by industry according to each industry's capacity to pay or other characteristics. National unions (called Federations) and the industry employer association are involved here. Possibly this is further extended at the regional or local level within the industry. Additional floors can be drawn at the corporate level (or even the holding company or conglomerate level), plant level, shop level and finally the individual workplace level.

The conceptualization of the different nature of the interactions that take place at each floor is important because what happens at a level severely constrains what the parties can do at the floor below, but does not dictate it. There is a direct influence from the top down by limiting the degrees of freedom available at lower levels. There is also a more subtle influence from the bottom up, but it is more diffuse and its effects take more time to climb up floors. For instance, innovative practices at the shop floor, or at the company level will slowly diffuse at the industry level and may eventually be enacted in statutes. Such was the case for the fourth and then fifth week of yearly vacation in France, or for the assembly line delegates in Italy.

This presupposes, however, that these innovative practices are not banned by decisions taken at a higher level. For instance in Germany, theoretically, negotiations and strikes cannot take place at the work council level. Only consultation is available there. If such activities are banned, but nevertheless fulfill a useful function or answer a need of the parties (such as the innovations in working time in France) they shall exist unofficially until the law is eventually modified and will spread only on a case by case basis.

An Additional Tier

The second modification suggested by the European experience is adding a level to transform it into a four-tier structure. This is appropriate because industry or interindustry negotiations are much more frequent in Europe. This would, therefore, keep the bottom tier of the workplace and organizational/individual relationships. It would also bring no change at the middle tier of collective bargaining and personnel policy, dealing mostly with plant level and corporate level industrial relations. However, the level of the third tier, the one of long term strategy and policy making, would be divided in two parts: corporate level economic and financial strategies of the parties concerning top management and union leadership plus a national industry and interindustry level of concern to employer associations and national union leadership.

Union Access to the Corporate Level

This division calls for a third remark, which anticipates further developments. The three-tier model rightfully brings attention to the need for union leaders to have access to the corporate level when long term economic and financial strategies are elaborated. This is important because of the impact of what happens at that level upon developments at the middle tier.

To date, the United States is still largely the home country of multinationals rather than the host country. Therefore it is a place where headquarters are located, or where foreign subsidiaries are given substantial freedom of action due to the inexperience of many foreign multinationals in operating there. It is also a very large product market by itself. What is necessary for the union is access to the national (U.S.) corporate decision-making center. In European countries, however, where the size of the national product market is smaller and where many subsidiaries of foreign multinationals operate, the situation is different. The decision-making center for economic and financial strategies in many cases is likely to be located outside the national borders, and therefore outside of reach of the union as well as outside of reach of the national government. This of course brings in additional problems. There have been several well documented cases of the national consequences of multinational corporations strategies (Rojot, 1985) (such as the Badger, Viggo, and Ford cases); the OECD's Committee on International Investment and Multinational Enterprises has elaborated and clarified guidelines in several instance on these points. However these guidelines remain voluntary and unions have proven mostly powerless outside their national borders, several instances to the contrary notwithstanding (Rojot, 1978).

European Industrial Relations More Ambiguous

The fourth point of difference one could make between the European situation and the U.S. one is that, in many European countries, the situation is more muddled and not as clear cut as in the USA.

From an analytical point of view, the New Deal industrial relations model presents the benefit of leaving no place for doubt. In its present condition, its main features, which are the bargaining unit and exclusive jurisdiction, make it immediately visible: it exists or it does not exist. There are no halfway situations. As KKM noted, in the 1950's and early 1960's the model had largely diffused outside of the places where it was actually implemented. In order to avoid unionization, non-union employers were often applying union wages or better and had codified elaborated personnel policies. However, after the evolution of the 1960's and the 1970's, the slow retreat of the New Deal model, and the successful emergence of the non-union model, the United States situation now presents the picture of the co-existence of two models at the plant level: fully unionized or non-union. In most continental European countries, and notably in France, the situation is not as clear cut. There are no provisions like the ones which are characteristic of the New Deal model at the middle tier, the level of collective bargaining and personnel policy. There is no exclusive jurisdiction, there is no duty to bargain in good faith, and no bargaining unit. Workers may individually belong or not belong to a union, and several unions can jointly co-exist at the plant level.

In such situations, it is impossible to clearly distinguish a union and a non-union model. The right to join a union belongs to the individual employees who may or may not take advantage of this right. In France, it is correlated with a right not to join. This right is just as strongly protected, which voids all kinds of union security provisions. The employer cannot, under penal sanctions, interfere with that right. He is not, on the other hand, compelled to negotiate in good faith. Under that picture of nominal uniformity for all plants, case by case, one will find very different practical situations. These variations depend on various factors such as managerial policies, history of the plant, personalities of the union leaders, social, and political environment of the workplace. Under the same legal model, one can in the same industry find plants where the union is stronger with more de facto power than in a New Deal type of plant industrial relations system. However, there are also situations where union influence is just as nonexistent as in a non-union American plant. One can also find all kinds of intermediate situations where management-union relationships run the gamut from collusion to open warfare and illegal union bashing.

The consequence of this New Deal arrangement at the bottom tier of the model is narrow job-control unionism. In most of continental Europe and especially in France, but maybe not in the U.K., such a model has seldom been attempted and has almost never been achieved. In Europe, limitations to managerial power do not come from a detailed and precise document such as the collective agreement but are derived from informal relations that depend on the balance of power. Obviously, this balance of power shifts through time and place, depending on many different factors. If managerial rights in France were sustained by the courts and proclaimed by the employer, because of the de facto power balance, in some cases they could be subjected to limits just as strong or stronger than the ones issuing from a collective agreement (Morel, 1981) and identical or more extensive than the ones present in the situation described by Gouldner in the gypsum plant where he found an "indulgency pattern" (Gouldner, 1954). On the other hand, *within the same legal system,* but with a different power balance and managerial policies, managerial rights could be extended to extremes unknown probably even to the American non-union sector with the only limit being the statutory floor of benefits, and no other guarantee of fair or equitable disciplinary process.

Obviously, a variety of actual situations exists within the two extreme cases that define that range. Therefore, it is more difficult, in such a situation, to delineate specific models and to trace their evolution. One must rely less on hard data and more on interpretations and impressions.

U.S. and European Similarities

Within this framework there are nevertheless some marked similarities with essential features basic to the new American model. The most important one is probably the questionable operational value of the "consensus" ideological element of Dunlop's (1958) industrial relations system concept. Indeed, it was proposed (Rojot, 1978, p. 11) when trying to apply the Dunlop system model to Europe to replace the consensus ideology element of the system by a "common interest" element that would allow for a conflict of interest between employers and their organizations and between workers and their organizations. The "common interest" element was derived from Schelling's (1962) analysis of "incomplete antagonism" or "precarious partnership."

In Europe also, or at least in France, management has adapted to unions because it was at the time the most pragmatic accommodation solution. It can be advanced that, maybe with the exception of some Scandinavian countries, most European managers would rather do without unions and the concomitant union power. This stand has practical, theoretical, and ideological reasons. Briefly stated, on theoretical grounds, unions follow a different logic from the one followed by management. They follow a logic of social want or need, and a logic of effort and reward while management tends to follow, and to be rewarded by following, a logic of economic feasibility, cost control, and rational expectations. Also, the extension of union power, by its own internal dynamic, questions management's authority and managerial rights. Ideologically, there is in Europe a tradition of them versus us, which has historical roots (Kassalow, 1969) and which persists for at least some European actors. This does not permeate the attitudes of the American actors to the same extent, notwithstanding the actual facts and similarities in the conditions of employment and subordination in both cases. In an extreme form, the European ideological division is formulated in Marxist terms of class warfare, which precludes any consensus other than the one establishing temporary relative power positions always subject to modification when the balance of power between the working class and the capitalist owners of the means of production and their representatives is altered. Finally, on practical grounds a union is generally an additional problem to the ones a manager has to face at the worksite. Even if he acknowledges that a union might have long term benefits, such as providing a voice unifying separate concerns from employees and communication processes, in the short term, the union is most often an additional irritant to the daily problems such as scheduling, faulty technology, and lagging sales. At a minimum, the union slows things down because its representatives need to be consulted or informed before implementing changes that the worksite manager would like to be instantaneous. At worst, the union can be seen as a stubborn opposition force to any change in existing custom and practice.

This explains the apparent contradiction outlined by KKM (p. 15) when they note that while "leading executives of large corporations . . . [support] the legitimacy and even the desirability of a free labor movement as a part of one democratic society," lower management rungs oppose and even suppress unions in the very same companies. If the ideological class warfare is absent from labor relations, as it is largely in the USA, then top management may consider, on the grounds of principle that unions are desirable. However, divisional or plant managers who have to face the daily irritants that unions cause would rather do without them in *their* operations. It has also been outlined, in France, that besides products or services, corporations produce two other types of output: social practices *and* statements of purpose and policy (Galambaud, 1983). There "products" emanate from different tiers of the organization. The former tends to emerge from the bottom of the organization and the latter are part of the job of public representation and relations from the top. Therefore, inconsistencies between the two are unavoidable. Here also KKM's model is appropriate.

Similar Environmental Forces

There is no doubt that forces in the environment that came to bear on industrial relations systems in Europe are broadly similar to the ones enumerated by KKM. The slowdown of economic growth after the oil shocks of 1973 and 1979, the global competition and the added competition of the newly industrialized countries, the shorter product cycles, and the changes in values and educational level of the work force all are examples that can be mentioned.

New Technology

However, from the observation of some case studies and from a general feeling issuing from informal contacts at various levels of French industry, two factors may be singled out as having a marked influence. These factors also support KKM's analysis of the new and growing importance of the role of managerial policies. First, there is the introduction of new technology at the level of manufacturing. It used to be an iron law of production in manufacturing that the automation of the production process varied with product standardization; in other words, one-of-a-kind specialty sets of machines and skills were used for one-of-a-kind projects, job shops for variable products produced in many categories by small batches, batch production for relatively stable lines of products, assembly lines for highly similar products, and continuous flow processes for bulk products. To sum up, high volume products could be manufactured with high economies of scale because of total standardization, but changes in the production process or the product design were impossible either because of the inflexibility of the manufacturing process or because they were prohibitively expensive. On the contrary, the production process was highly flexible for some products; but the technology did not allow for mass production, and no economies of scale were possible.

New technology reintroduces a large element of flexibility in the production process. For instance, the use of flexible computer controlled manufacturing systems allows for different products to be manufactured on the same line according to on-line programming within the system. For example, different models or sizes of car may be made on the same assembly line together. Data processing allows for "just-in-time" inventory management and cuts delivery times. The cost in flexibility incurred by the gain in productivity inherent to the former means of automatizing production can now be regained to a large extent. Automating the new technologies not only increases productivity, but also achieves the benefits of flexibility. Customization of product and short reaction time in terms of changes in specification and delivery time are not possible.

A central consequence that will have to be taken into account is that these changes imply a different personnel and industrial relations strategy from management's point of view. The introduction of new technology has not always been successful and a key factor seems to be in the implementation of the system. In other words, robots do not (yet) work totally alone, "people make robots work," but people may decide that they do not want the robots to work. The cooperation of employees is essential to the introduction and smooth functioning of new technology. Its potential for benefits are huge, but it also opens up an even larger potential for mishandling because of its complexity, and needs to be serviced.

Besides, new technology creates a new and different type of job that makes job control unionism and Taylorian inspired methods of job definition and description impractical. The content of some of the new jobs (but by no means all of them) has become too complex and imprecise to be described in detail. What is needed is no longer the accurate execution of well-defined tasks by the employee but his voluntary cooperation and his initiative, which can neither be ordered nor bought. But new technologies carry a consequence for managerial styles and also brings a much more participative type of management in the factory and office as well as a concern with QWL (Rojot, 1986b).

Shift to Services

A second factor brings a similar concern and results from the shift within European economies from industry toward services. Now, over 50 percent of the labor force are employed in services and a larger proportion in white collar jobs in all sectors. Those employees are in contact with the public and generally sell a product or a service often with little differentiation (for example, a hotel room in a given category). In this case of undifferentiated products or services, the competitive edge of one firm against the others and the conditions for its success will depend essentially on the attitudes of the employees in contact with the customers. Here, also this attitude can hardly be "bought" or ordered. It requires from the employee a voluntary degree of initiative and goodwill perceptible in his behavior toward the customer. This yields pressures toward QWL and participative management (Rojot, 1987). Nevertheless, it should be pointed out that to my knowledge there is no non-controversial evidence on the economic benefits of QWL.

Wage Restraint

Other features issuing from the pressures in the environment are largely similar to the ones mentioned by KKM. For several years a policy of wage restraints on the part of some employers had efficiently been carried out in order to control costs. This policy was facilitated by a high degree of unemployment (10 percent) and the tacit approval of succeeding governments carrying out the same policy toward civil servants. Due to the fact already underlined that there is no clear cut division between the union and non-union sectors, this wage differential is not as well documented and not as evident. However, it is likely to follow also a line of division between the sector of the economy "protected" from outside competition and that part of the economy "exposed" to foreign competition.

The Rate of Unionization

The decrease in the rate of unionization has even been more marked. Officially set at 20/25 percent in the late 1970s, it is now estimated at between 9 and 12 percent. I believe, however, that we should distinguish rate of unionization and influence of unions. In some European countries the role of unionization did not drop; in fact, it even rose because the availability of some benefits require union membership. I believe, however, that in such countries the *influence* of unions fell, for instance as it can be measured in terms of capacity to call a strike and to obtain concessions. Conversely in France, when the rate of unionization dropped sharply, the union influence (as measured by the votes that the slates of candidates who are presented by the various unions do receive from the electorate to work councils, Labor Courts, Social Security Board) shows that the main unions are still the dominant forces on the part of the employees who vote. However, the very high and increasing abstention rate shows that fewer and fewer employees bother to vote. Another very important factor seems to indicate that in many conflicts unions have lost the leadership and initiative, and are replaced by "committees from the grass roots." Such is the case in Italy. For instance, during last year's subway and railroad strike, employees were led by autonomous "coordination committees" who used union facilities as they saw fit and only under their own terms. A present wave of strikes seems to follow the same pattern.

In a similar way, in some cases emerging competition from the work council appears. By definition, these councils are established at the plant level and to some extent they compete with the union for employee loyalty. They can be used by management on local issues as a tool to obtain a degree of consensus and cooperation in the joint interests of the company and its employees, whatever the union attitude may be.

Just as in the USA, employers in France have taken a much more pro-active role. Sophisticated personnel management techniques tend to make the union appear as foreign to the management-employee relationship at the unit level. Some of this new management of human resources is clearly anti-union, but by no means is all of it. Some is prompted by the need for a more cooperative work force. Employers have become much more sophisticated in the management of human resources. The trend is toward decentralization of personnel management at the unit of production level and individualization of the relationship between manager and employees (Rojot, 1986a).

Conclusion

In conclusion, the transformation of French industrial relations has been more dramatic than in the United States. It can be set in terms of the long-term survival of the French labor movement; of course, French unions are not dead yet. On the one hand, they still represent a sizeable political weight, even if in many cases they are in opposition to the present government. But they represent voters and political machines. On the other hand, they perform several functions, some of which are irreplaceable and will survive in any case, at least into the foreseeable future.

They are institutional partners of government. They represent in many cases and many instances the voice of labor, whether they are sitting as members of a Social and Economic Council, planning commission, regional commission, or training organization board. They are well implemented institutions with a quasi-exclusive right to represent the labor force and workers. This right still rests unchallenged even from the most vocal quarters of management, which is not the case in the U.S. They are involved in co-determination of part of the economy: sitting on the boards of nationalized companies, wage-setting boards, and joint management of Social Security. They are the institutional partners of Employer Organizations, which are much more powerful in many European countries than in the U.S.

Here the KKM several tier model is particularly well adapted to account for what is happening. For the reasons just listed, at the top tiers the unions are not threatened at all. However, at the lowest tier of the plant and company level, outside of the protected sector, serious questions arise as to the future for unions. French unions were always less well established at the plant level than U.S. ones within the New Deal model. At that level what seems threatened is their capacity to play the part of instruments for the membership to influence collectively their immediate environment, to promote the immediate interests and demands of members in front of management in given economic and political circumstances, and therefore their survival and capacity to recoup their losses and attract new members.

Parts of the French labor movement have proposed that in the new circumstances, the traditional rigid, global demands and stands of the labor movement must be replaced by a much more flexible and decentralized set of strategies. It is no longer a question of rigidly opposing all lay-offs or demanding a general across-the-board increase. It is a question of case by case, enterprise by enterprise negotiations about decreases of working hours against a maintained volume of employment, the introduction of new technology against retraining with job relocation, concession bargaining, etc.

Instead of a global negotiating and opposition force, some leaders want the labor movement to become more of a positive force, being involved in the actual administration and monitoring or retraining, labor mobility, use of resources, etc. However it should be noted that these new policies have gained no further influence for the union that has proposed them. It has seen its membership as well as its share of the votes slip just as the others. Also this policy runs into obstacles: the still largely prevalent idea of the role of the French union as one of protest organizations promoting an ideology alternative to capitalism and working for a change of society.

There are strong divisions within the labor movement with some segments strongly clinging to the traditional strategies and considering these new attitudes as mistaken. This creates a risk of misunderstanding the leadership strategies by parts of the membership; as the grass roots revolution against the flexible national agreement of 1984 amply demonstrates.

References

Dunlop, J.T. (1958). *Industrial Relations Systems*. New York: Holt.

Galambaud, A. (1983). *Des Hommes à gérer*. Paris: Entreprise Moderne d'Edition.

Gouldner, A.W. (1954). *Patterns of Industrial Bureaucracy*. New York: Free Press.

Kassalow, E.M. (1969). *Trade Unions and Industrial Relations: An International Comparison*. New York: Random House.

Kochan, T.A.; Katz, H.C.; & McKersie, R.B. (1986). *The Transformation of American Industrial Relations*. New York: Basic Books.

Morel, C. (1981). *La Grève Froide*. Paris: Editions d'Organisation.

Rojot, J. (1978). *International Collective Bargaining: An Analysis and Case Study for Europe*. Deventer, The Netherlands: Kluwer.

Rojot, J. (1985). The 1984 revision of the OECD guidelines for multinational enterprises. *British Journal of Industrial Relations, 23*.

Rojot, J. (1986a). The development of French employees policy towards trade unions. *Labor and Society, 11*, 1-16.

Rojot, J. (1986b). *Employers' Response to Technological Change*. Paper presented at the 7th World Congress of International Industry Relations Association.

Rojot, J. (1987). Accords collectifs et flexibilité de la main d'oeuvre. *Les cahiers de la Fondation Europe et Société*.

Schelling, T.C. (1962). *The Strategy of Conflict*. Oxford: Oxford University Press.

COMMENTS: A COMPARATIVE PERSPECTIVE ON THE STRATEGIC CHOICE FRAMEWORK

Anil Verma

THE STRATEGIC CHOICE FRAMEWORK (SCF), according to its authors Kochan, Katz, & McKersie (1986; hereafter KKM), is an attempt to "add a more dynamic component to industrial relations theory." The Inter-University set of studies in the 1950s, best known through Kerr et al.'s (1964) *Industrialism and Industrial Man,* was conducted at a time when both industrialization and industrial relations in the western world had matured to a level of stability. Thus Dunlop's (1958) systems framework, a key organizing scheme for *Industrialism and Industrial Man,* was well suited to capturing the stable equilibrium state of industrial relations systems in industrialized economies. For this reason, it has also been very influential in molding our conceptualization of industrial relations.

In proposing the SCF, KKM argue that because industrialization itself has undergone fundamental (and unforeseen) changes, the systems view of Dunlop must be augmented if we are to better understand and manage the subsequent evolution of industrial relations systems. Thus, increased global trade and shifting patterns of competitiveness have created a more dynamic environment in which parties to the IR system face numerous "strategic choices." The strategies that each party adopts or fails to adopt will determine the shape and size of the IR system in years to come. The SCF, then, is both an augmentation of and a substantial departure from Dun-

The author wishes to thank Jacques Rojot for his helpful comments. This paper also draws upon presentations made by J. Larrea Gayarre (Spain), H. Hartmann (West Germany), P. Marginson (U.K.), H-G Myrdal (Sweden), R. Peterson (U.S.A.), J. Rojot (France) & M. Thompson (Canada) at a panel on Managerial Strategies in Industrial Relations in the 1980s at the Second European Regional Congress of the International Industrial Relations Association, December 13-17, 1987, Herzlia, Israel.

lop's systems view which does not place nearly the same emphasis on strategic alternatives open to the parties.

Any new paradigm or framework bears the onus of demonstrating that it improves upon previous frameworks in significant ways. A number of papers in this volume and elsewhere have subjected the SCF to these tests. In this paper, I propose to apply the "comparative" test: how well is the SCF suited to understanding and explaining developments abroad? In other words, does the SCF, derived entirely from developments in the U.S., provide any new insights or useful handles on the evolution of other industrial relations systems? For reasons of space and theoretical simplification, my discussion will be confined mostly to the major western European systems with occasional references to Canada and Australia.

This paper is divided into four sections. In the first section, I briefly outline the SCF emphasizing those aspects of the framework that are important in understanding comparative developments. Next, a number of dimensions along which the SCF is to be assessed are outlined. In the third section, the evidence from France, as presented by Jacques Rojot (1990, chap. 7), and other countries is examined along the four dimensions described in the preceding section. Lastly, some conclusions about the efficacy of the SCF in comparative research are drawn.

Strategy, Strategic Choice and the SCF

A number of scholars in this volume and elsewhere have raised concerns about the lack of conceptual clarity in the SCF.[1] Some of these concerns are about the precise meaning of certain terms. For example, both Lewin (1987) and Marginson et al. (1987) have raised concerns about the precise meaning of "strategic" choice or behavior. Other concerns have to do with the predictions that come out of the SCF. Does the applicability of the SCF to other systems imply that all labor movements are to decline like the American one? While this is not an appropriate forum to engage in a full discussion of these concerns, I will briefly outline a view of the SCF that this paper relies on.

The term "strategy" is not used in a consistent fashion in other fields (Rumelt, 1979) and, given academic idiosyncrasies, it is unlikely that industrial relations scholars will do otherwise. Strategy, a term taken from military usage, has a number of connotations. The SCF employs a number of these including the element of choice or discretion. The notion of strategic choice modifies considerably the paradigm of determinism which suggests that firms' choice of strategy is determined by a number of external factors. Strategic choice theorists, on the other hand, believe that firms facing the same external conditions may choose to respond very differently, that is, they have a choice of a particular strategy for adoption from a menu of feasible strategies (Child, 1972; Schreyögg, 1980). Thus, strategic choice is a very specific dimension of the concept of strategy.

Further, the SCF is a specific application that while employing many of the aspects of strategy and strategic choice, goes well beyond the concept of strategy to add a number of features that are specific to industrial relations systems. Briefly, the following three aspects may be seen as being central to the SCF:

1. Industrial relations decisions are made at three levels: business, collective bargaining and the workplace.
2. Effective strategies are those that act in concert at all the three levels.
3. Parties face a number of choices in adopting a suitable strategy.

The more familiar aspects of strategy that the SCF encompasses are those of time, level and significant impact. As in the original meaning, the SCF implies that strategies are concerted series of maneuvers (also called tactics) that generally unfold over a longer period of time, are conducted from a high level within the organization and have considerable impact on the outcomes of interest to the parties. Lastly, I would like to suggest that strategic conduct must be the result of conscious choices. This is at variance with the authors' view in a related paper that these choices can be unconscious (Kochan, McKersie & Cappelli, 1984). If the choices are seen as being conscious, they are more compatible with the other premises of SCF.

Evaluation Criteria

I turn now to explicate the criteria that must be applied to any new paradigm or framework proposed in place of the extant ones. The principle task of a good theory is to explain reality. Often, this premise leads to the prediction requirement: a good theory, if it models the reality well, should be able to make predictions about outcomes under given circumstances. However, other criteria may be added in the social science context to the exacting requirement of predictive power. Specifically, theory may encompass several or all of the following:

1. *Description.* A good framework adequately describes all as-

pects of the phenomenon being observed by organizing the complex reality in a comprehensive but parsimonious format.

2. *Understanding.* A theory may provide a better understanding of the real world even if it does not have predictive power. Such understanding may help diagnose potential problems or identify critical pressure points in the system.

3. *Prediction.* A theory models the real world in all its complexities. The more comprehensive the theory, the more its ability to predict outcomes in given contexts.

In the terms outlined above, the efficacy of the SCF can be found in the extent to which it describes, diagnoses pressure points and identifies future directions in other industrial relations systems. Moreover, it must do so in ways that the other views have been unable to accomplish. This will be the main thrust of my examination in the next section. In this exercise, the framework is used to examine and explore each system autonomously rather than to connect the development in other countries to those in the U.S. For example, looking for signs of union decline in other systems is not a good test of the efficacy of the SCF. The proposed framework suggests a dynamic in which strategic choices made by the parties interact with each other to produce certain outcomes. While management choices may be similar in several countries, union, and government responses are frequently very different in systems where labor is more coopted into the political process relative to the U.S. The SCF may prove to be a very useful handle on other systems (that is, it may adequately describe the developments and provide a good understanding) even if developments in that country are different from those in the U.S. Thus, convergence of other systems with that of the U.S. can not be justified as a key test of the SCF's efficacy.

The Evidence from Abroad

Description

As Rojot's paper has pointed out, the most obvious difficulty in taking the SCF abroad lies in fitting industrial relations activities at the extra-firm level into the three tiers, all of which are found at the firm or establishment level. In this respect, KKM's formulations clearly bear the stamp of American industrial relations circa mid-1980s where much of collective bargaining is very decentralized, union-nonunion distinction is clearly (that is, formally and legally) drawn and neither the government nor the labor movement has carved for itself a major role in industrial relations at the extra-firm level. In contrast, in most of the western European systems, bargaining is centered at the industry level (or higher in some cases such as Sweden and Austria); the union-nonunion distinction is blurred and both the government and the labor movement are heavily involved in bargaining and lobbying at the extra-firm level.

The obvious solution is to provide for a fourth tier in the proposed framework. In order to so augment the framework, however, we must carefully examine the compatibility of the dynamics at this "fourth" tier with the premises of the rest of the framework. First, examples from several countries such as West Germany, France and Australia indicate that the so-called extra-firm, "fourth" tier may constitute a number of sub-levels. For example, in Australia agreements over industrial relations matters can be found at the national level, the state level, the industry level, and some at the multi-employer level. These sub-levels need to be incorporated separately in the framework only if there is reason to believe that each influences the outcomes in significantly different ways. Else, if the dynamic is much the same, these sub-levels can be grouped together into one extra-firm, fourth tier.

Second, it is important to examine the role that strategies at the "fourth" tier may play in relation to those at the other three tiers. The original KKM formulation suggests that when initiatives at the three levels act in concert, they result in greater effectiveness. The evidence from abroad suggests that the same can be said of the initiatives at the "fourth" tier. The French employer association CNPF combined a number of firm-level policies aimed at enhancing flexibility with talks with the government to fund government-supported training (Sellier, 1985). Many analysts agree that such coordinated initiatives have given the CNPF, once a sleepy organization with few executive powers, a leading and dominant role in French industrial relations. In the Australian case, the national accord struck between the Australian Labour Party and the labour movement (the ACTU) was one component of a strategy which was complemented by initiatives at other levels at the industry and state levels. (Dabscheck & Niland, 1985).

Employer Initiatives

The most salient aspect of the French development that the SCF helps put into perspective is the employers' initiative and dominance within the system in the 1980s. Although management has accepted union presence in many situations, they have shown remarkable ingenuity in opposing any increase in union influence. Delamotte (1987) argues that employers have been so successful in taking the initiative that despite pro-labor legislation such as the *lois Auroux,* there have been few labor gains. The 1982 laws were aimed at helping labor by forcing firm-level negotiations on wages and working time. Employers, however, turned this restraint into an advantage by acting concertedly to obtain a number of agreements favorable to their concern for flexibility. This is the type of outcome that the SCF captures best: one in which strategy is so well conceived and executed that it neutralizes the effects of the law.

The labor movement in France, as Rojot points out, faces an uncertain future and the SCF helps explain a number of aspects of this situation. First, unions do not appear to have a strategy at each of the four levels that reinforce each other in achieving labor's objectives. For example, unions seem to have little access to the level at which corporate business decisions are made. Second, at the workplace, they now face more competition from the works committees (Comité d'Entreprise). Moreover, unions have not taken any major initiatives at this level leaving the management free to grab the lead in introducing employee involvement and communication programs. Employers, for their part, have taken full advantage of the situation to implement a dominant ideology of union containment. This policy is best summarized by the saying, "le syndicat a sa place mais à sa place." In other words, unions have a place *in* their place. Thus, unions are tolerated if they continue to play a minor and subservient role.

The story of employer strategies to contain the union are to be found in most countries including West Germany and Canada where the labor movement has not declined much and continues to play a major role through adoption of new initiatives. In West Germany, works councils now do get some information on introduction of new technologies but the employers have so far successfully resisted co-determination on the issue (Weiss, 1987). The employers are fully opposed to any legislative amendment that might grant these rights to the works councils. The unions, on the other hand, are ill-equipped to engage the employer on this issue as their expertise on specific workplace matters is limited. Thus, a proactive employer strategy on this issue is likely to succeed. In Canada, employers have seized the initiative in collective bargaining by making demands of their own for rollbacks in wages and modification of workrules (Thompson & Verma, 1987; Adams, in press). Employer success on rollbacks has clearly been much more limited in Canada than in the U.S. However, the containment of union gains as a result of such employer strategy is unmistakable. Lastly, employers in U.K. have sought to shape unionism by negotiating single union contracts which sometimes ban use of strikes during the term of an agreement (Marginson, 1987). In other firms, employers have become more aggressive and assertive with the union and have limited union influence by dealing more directly with the employees (Goodman, 1987).

The evidence from all these countries (including Spain discussed later) shows that management has generally grabbed the initiative in setting the agenda for the conduct of industrial relations. That employers everywhere have not followed the American example is also clear; however, as suggested earlier, this lack of convergence does not necessarily detract from the power of the SCF to model these developments. The common elements of all these developments become clear when interpreted as strategic choices exercised by each employer group.

Union Response

Despite similar employer approaches, industrial relations outcomes vary across countries. The SCF suggests that where employers have not succeeded in achieving their objectives, we should first look at the effectiveness of their own strategies followed by an examination of the effectiveness of the counter strategies of labor and/or the government. The most instructive case is that of Canada where the legal framework and other institutional arrangements are similar to the U.S. Despite these similarities, however, recent developments in the two countries have been very different. A number of analysts attribute it to the differential strategies pursued by the labor movement in the two countries (for example, Rose & Chaison, 1985). According to this view, Canadian unions have pursued a broader political agenda of influence through the New Democratic Party, a party of the political left (Bruce, 1988). At the bargaining table, they have resisted wage rollbacks but made a number of changes in workrules on a quid pro quo basis (Verma, 1986, 1989a, in press). At the workplace, the strategy has been to strengthen adversarial style (or "arm's-length") dealings with management. This includes opposing employee participation programs on one hand while emphasizing their role in grievance handling on the other hand. Thus, the success of labor's counter strategy lies in coordinating their initiatives at all the three (or four) tiers.

Similar successful counter labor strategies can be seen in West Germany and Sweden. The metalworkers' union in Germany, IG Metall (IGM), launched a major offensive in mid-1984 to obtain a thirty-five-hour work week. The union employed a sophisticated campaign in which a variety of arguments were used with different groups to build support for an otherwise not-so-popular demand (Hartmann & Horstmann, 1987). Thus, information was successfully used by the union as a strategic weapon. Although the union did not achieve the desired thirty-five-hour week, it did succeed in breaching the forty-hour barrier by bringing it down to a 38.5-hour week. In Sweden, the labor movement has skillfully pursued a strategy in which cooperation is sought from the government and management at all the four tiers. Apart from working closely with the Social Democratic Party on legislative reforms, the LO has always extended a cooperative hand to management on issues such as introduction of new technology (Myrdal, 1987). The labor movement has thus coordinated its initiatives at various levels to achieve its goals.

These developments illustrate the net outcomes in situations where a proactive management strategy of union-containment has been offset by a counter union strategy. The SCF provides a framework in which the effectiveness of these strategies can be assessed. Labor has generally been more successful where it has acted concertedly at all the four levels.

Shifts in the Locus of Industrial Relations

A variety of recent studies have commented on the changes in the structure of collective bargaining and industrial relations. General estimates are that there is a wide-spread move towards decentralization in bargaining and decision-making in industrial relations. Although this is true overall, a careful examination at the firm-level reveals a more complicated shift. In many countries including France, Sweden, U.K., Canada, and the U.S. there are attempts to disaggregate bargaining to a level where wages can be related more directly to the relevant product market. This, however, has not meant that all decision-making in industrial relations matters has been decentralized to plant or division levels. In the U.K., U.S. and Canada, corporate offices continue to monitor and coordinate policies (KKM, 1986; Marginson, 1987; Thompson & Verma, 1987). This apparent paradox between trends in decentralization and centralization are difficult to explain in a deterministic framework but easier to understand within the SCF. The SCF views these developments as two components of the same strategy being implemented at two different levels. The seemingly opposite trends are quite unified when seen in terms of their strategic objectives. These are employer driven changes designed to give the firm greater flexibility in charting the course for the business. Decentralization connects the future of each operation to the relevant product markets while centralization helps to integrate industrial relations considerations to corporate planning.

As Myrdal (1987) points out, in Sweden, the employer federation's (SAF) objectives are to preserve the centralized bargaining structure built-up over the years but to allow flexibility at the local level such that "local wage formation" can take place. SAF wants, like any other employer organization would in its place, to preserve the old strengths while building in newer areas. The SCF suggests that the chances of their success depend upon other initiatives they may undertake at other levels to complement these plans. These complementary initiatives may or may not exist or their substance may not be compatible with LO's counter strategy. The SCF can not make a prediction about these outcomes but it does provide a useful framework in which an analysis can be undertaken.

Individualization

An important development in industrialized economies has been a trend towards stronger bilateral links between the employers and employees sometimes referred to as "individualization" of the employment relationship. This is another employer driven strategy that has found much support among the workers. Because it bypasses the union, it may reduce union influence over the rank-and-file. In the U.S., KKM have documented a number of cases where the nonunion employer has used it expressly with the purpose of wooing workers away from unions. But this trend towards individualization can be found in a number of other countries and in most there is not the same intent to dislodge the union in the American fashion. The question then arises of the relevance and purpose of such a policy. This is another development that is better understood within the SCF.

The elements of individualization are programs aimed at employee communication, participation and involvement in job-related activities. The process of communication and involvement does coopt workers to a certain degree (Verma & McKersie, 1987; Lischeron & Wall, 1975) but whether it will drive a wedge between the workers and their unions depends upon other complementary initiatives that labor or management may adopt at other levels (Cutcher-Gershenfeld, Kochan & Verma, in press). Relations with unions and the extent of unionization among other factors may determine the exact thrust of such policies (Kochan, McKersie & Chalykoff, 1986). Union involvement or lack of involvement can also change the dynamic of such policies (Verma, in press). Thus the precise impact of individualization can not be specified unless such initiatives are framed within the larger contest of strategic choices made at other tiers of the framework.

Examples from the U.K. and Canada well illustrate the differential impact that increased employee communication and involvement can play. In the U.K., employers have increasingly moved towards recognition of shop stewards (Brown, 1985) and single-union contracts (Marginson et al. 1987, Marginson, 1987), thus creating a context in which individualization fits with a broadened role for unions at the workplace level. Unlike their U.S. counterparts, the British employers have not seized the opportunity created by the political context of a conservative, hostile-to-labor government to launch a significant move to derecognize unions. Unions in many industries, notably manufacturing, are content to bargain over wages at the local level rather than to wage large-scale battles over management prerogatives and control (Goodman, 1987). In Canada, employer-run employee communication programs have not threatened union rapport with the rank-and-file because labor initiatives at other levels have largely set the context for their relations with their members (Thompson & Verma, 1987).

Industrial Relations Under Rapid Change

In the preceding sections, I have considered examples from economies that have been largely stable in the political arena. To examine the applicability of the SCF to other contexts, it is instructive to consider the case of Spain which has seen rapid political as well as economic changes in recent years. The Spanish case demonstrates that strategic alternatives become even more critical in times of rapid change.[2]

The Spanish employers' federation, the CEOE, was organized in

1977 in the aftermath of the return of the Spanish political system to democracy. The employers faced a difficult task in building working relationships with both labor and government. Many in the labor movement saw employers as collaborators or agents of dictatorial interests. Though Franco had pursued pro-capital policies, his government did not take much advice from the employers. Now employers were saddled with credit for policies they had little to do with. Neither did the CEOE fare much better initially with the government of the right or left. The center-right government of the UCD was considered pro-market but it developed large policy differences with the CEOE. Towards the end of the UCD term, the CEOE was opposing a large number of UCD policies. Then came the socialist government with whom the CEOE had a number of fundamental differences at the beginning.

Recognizing the difficult task ahead, the CEOE formulated a strategy that was to undertake initiatives at different levels outlined in the SCF. As early as 1979, it engaged in three-way talks with the government and labor to arrive at a broad understanding on wage negotiations, now known as the Moncloa Agreements. Further, despite early differences they have actively collaborated with the socialist government on enacting labor legislation. For example, the CEOE supported the industry reconstruction and restructuring bill in 1984. They also supported legislative reform in areas such as education, university restructuring and investments in research and development. Such a strategy of dialogue and collaboration has brought many dividends. The CEOE persuaded the socialist government to make changes that permit employers to hire workers on temporary or limited contracts.

These "fourth" tier initiatives were complemented with negotiations with the socialist labor federation, the UGT, to arrive at guidelines which are applied to specific negotiations. There are many contentious issues on which the parties do not agree from time to time. But both sides find each other "usually open to dialogue." The CEOE accepts the reality of unions although they, like other employers, would prefer weak or no unions. Currently, unions are plagued by their own crisis of falling interest among rank-and-file and, hence, do not pose a formidable challenge to the employers.

In summary, the CEOE acted in a concerted manner by coordinating their policies at a number of levels. They have taken the initiative in achieving a relationship with the government and the unions that has strengthened their position and protected their interests. Though it is hard to assess the extent to which they have succeeded in their objective, it can be safely said that the CEOE's accomplishments would have been considered ambitious in 1977, the year of their birth. This case shows that strategic options are even more numerous in times of rapid change and the SCF helps us to sort through them at four levels and to assess their effectiveness by examining the extent to which choices at one level are linked to choices at other levels.

Summary and Conclusion

This paper has tried to interpret the SCF in light of the generic usage of the term strategy. Strategic behavior or action in the SCF is interpreted as a policy or initiative that unfolds at all the four tiers of industrial relations decision-making in a coordinated manner. These policies are chosen from a menu of options and, thus, parties have discretion in choosing the desired policy independent of the market or technological conditions facing them.

In examining developments from abroad, the SCF appears, with the addition of a fourth tier, to provide a good description of the systems examined. Beyond description, it provides a good understanding of the events that have been unfolding in recent years. It also provides for a strong diagnostic tool that can be used to identify pressure points in the system and potential directions for parties' strategic choices. The SCF does not directly help predict outcomes; rather, it generates a testable hypothesis on the effectiveness of strategic choices. It proposes that in order to be effective, parties must act in a coordinated way at all the levels of industrial relations decision-making.

The evidence from abroad provides a number of illustrations of strategic decision-making and of the conditions under which they become effective. The case for Spain suggests that the greater the change in other parts of the environment (in this case, political), the greater are the opportunities for parties to act strategically. The discussion in this paper shows that the SCF is a powerful tool for analyzing and understanding industrial relations developments elsewhere. It also makes for a useful diagnostic tool for troubleshooting and identifying new directions for policy making. The bottom line, however, is that the SCF is only a *framework* and not a full-fledged theory. It can not, therefore, predict the exact outcomes. It is a significant advance, though, on previous frameworks because it formalizes the role of choice or discretion in industrial relations decision-making.

Notes

1. It is not unusual for some confusion to arise around newly proposed paradigms especially in the social sciences. Such confusion, however, leads to debate which is a potent tool for further creation of knowledge.
2. The following discussion is derived largely from Larrea Gayarre (1987).

References

Adams, R.J. (in press). North American industrial relations: Divergent trends in Canada and the United States. *International Labor Review.*
Brown, W. (1985). The effect of recent changes in the world economy on British Industrial Relations. *In* H. Juris, M. Thompson, & W. Daniels (eds.), *Industrial Relations in a Decade of Economic Change.* Madison, WI: Industrial Relations Research Association.
Bruce, P. (1988, February). *Political Parties and the Evolution of Labor Law in the United States and Canada: 1930-85.* Paper presented to the Third Berkeley Conference on Industrial Relations.
Child, J. (1972). Organisational structure, environment & performance: The role of a strategic choice. *Sociology, 6*(1).
Cutcher-Gershenfeld, J.; Kochan, T.A.; & Verma, A. (in press). Recent developments in U.S. employee involvement initiatives: Erosion or diffusion. *Advances in Industrial and Labor Relations, 5.*
Dabscheck, B., & Niland, J. (1985). Australian industrial relations and the shift to centralism. *In* H. Juris, M. Thompson, & W. Daniels (eds.), *Industrial Relations in a Decade of Economic Change.* Madison, WI: Industrial Relations Research Association.
Delamotte, Y. (1987). La loi et la negotiation collective en France: Reflexion sur l'experience 1981-1985. *Relations Industrielles, 42*(1), 92-109.
Dunlop, J.T. (1958). *Industrial Relations Systems.* New York: Holt.
Goodman, J.F.B. (1987, December). *Recession and Revival?* Paper presented to the Second European Regional Congress, International Industrial Relations Association, Herzlia, Israel.
Hartmann, H., & Horstmann, J. (1987, November). A trade union information strategy: The case of the German metal workers union. *British Journal of Industrial Relations, 25,* 371-388.
Kerr, C.; Dunlop, J.T.; Harbison, F.H.; & Myers, C.C. (1964). *Industrialism & Industrial Man.* New York: Oxford University Press.
Kochan, T.A.; McKersie, R.B.; & Cappelli, P. (1984). Strategic choice and Industrial Relations Theory. *Industrial Relations, 23*(1), 16-39.
Kochan, T.A.; McKersie, R.B.; & Chalykoff, J. (1986, July). The effects of corporate strategy and workplace innovations on union representation. *Industrial and Labor Relations Review, 39,* 487-501.
Kochan, T.A.; Katz, H.C.; & McKersie, R.B. (1986). *The Transformation of American Industrial Relations.* New York: Basic Books.

Larrea Gayarre, J. (1987, December). *Managerial Strategies and Political Class in the Spain of 1980's.* Paper presented to the Second European Regional Congress, International Industrial Relations Association, Herzlia, Israel.

Lewin, D. (1987). Industrial relations as a strategic variable. *In* M.M. Kleiner, R.N. Block, M. Roomkin, & S.W. Salsburg (eds.), *Human Resources and the Performance of the Firm.* Madison, WI: Industrial Relations Research Association.

Lischeron, J.A., & Wall, T.D. (1975). Employee participation—An experimental field study. *Human Relations, 28,* 863-884.

Marginson, P. (1987, December). *Managerial Strategies and Industrial Relations: Recent developments in the U.K.* Paper presented to the Second European Regional Congress, International Industrial Relations Association, Herzlia, Israel.

Marginson, P. (1988, August-September). *Multidivisional Structure and Corporate Control.* Paper presented to the 15th EARIE Annual Conference, Rotterdam, The Netherlands.

Marginson, P.; Edwards, P.K.; Purcell, J.; and Sisson, K. (1987). *Managing Industrial Relations: What Do Corporate Head Offices Really Do?* Working paper. Industrial Relations Research Unit, University of Warwick.

Myrdal, H.G. (1987, December). *Employer Strategies and Industrial Relations in the 1980's: The Swedish Case.* Paper presented to the Second European Regional Congress, International Industrial Relations Association, Herzlia, Israel.

Rojot, J. (1990). A view from abroad. *In* J. Chelius & J. Dworkin (eds.), *Reflections on the Transformation of Industrial Relations.* Metuchen, NJ: IMLR Press.

Rose, J.B., & Chaison, G.N. (1985). The state of the unions: United States and Canada. *Journal of Labor Research, 6,* 97-111.

Rumelt, R.P. (1979). Evaluation of strategy: Theory and models. *In* D.E. Schendel & C.W. Hofer (eds.), *Strategic Management: A New View of Business Policy and Planning.* Boston: Little, Brown.

Schreyögg, G. (1980). Contingency and choice in organisation theory. *Organisation Studies.*

Sellier, F. (1985). Economic change and industrial relations in France. *In* H. Juris, M. Thompson & W. Daniels (eds.), *Industrial Relations in a Decade of Economic Change.* Madison, WI: Industrial Relations Research Association.

Thompson, E., & Verma, A. (1987, December). *Managerial Strategies in Industrial Relations in the 1980's: The Canadian Experience.* Paper presented to the Second European Regional Congress, International Industrial Relations Association, Herzlia, Israel.

Verma, A. (1986). Changing workrules in collective bargaining: The British Columbia experience. *In* E. Thompson (ed.), *Is There a New Canadian Industrial Relations?* Proceedings of the 23rd Annual Meetings of the Canadian Industrial Relations Association.

Verma, A. (in press). Joint participation programs: Self-help or suicide for labor? *Industrial Relations.*

Verma, A., & McKersie, R.B. (1987, July). Employee involvement: The implications on noninvolvement by unions. *Industrial and Labor Relations Review, 40,* 556-568.

Weiss, M. (1987, December). *Works Council's Influence on the Introduction and Implementation of New Technologies.* Paper presented to the Second European Regional Congress, International Industrial Relations Association, Herzlia, Israel.

8. A REACTION TO THE DEBATE

Harry C. Katz, Thomas A. Kochan, and Robert B. McKersie

Introduction

We appreciate this opportunity to respond to the many thoughtful papers presented at this conference and the engaging discussions that followed presentation of the papers. In response to the central issues in dispute we offer this paper. In the first section we address four issues that surfaced repeatedly in the comments made of our book (Kochan, Katz & McKersie, 1986). The four issues are: defining more clearly what is and is not a transformation of American industrial relations; the role of strategic choice versus environmental factors in shaping the course of American industrial relations; the nature, viability and fairness of nonunion personnel systems; and the international applicability of our arguments.

Since much has happened in American industrial relations since the writing and publication of the *Transformation of American Industrial Relations* it is appropriate to also ask how well the book holds up in explaining those developments. In the second section of this paper we offer our thoughts on that question.

What is a "Transformation" in Industrial Relations?

A number of commentators suggested that our book misinterprets (or mislabels) the continuing evolution of American industrial relations as a "transformation." For example, Roomkin and Juris (1990, chap. 5) argue in their paper that concession bargaining, the decline in union membership, and other industrial relations developments in the 1980s should be seen as *adaptive* change rather than transformative change. Block (1990, chap. 2) also argues that events in the 1980s were an *evolutionary* extension of earlier trends, a trend itself best understood as employer dominance in collective bargaining.

One of our answers to this criticism is to return to the arguments offered in our book. The book offers a three tiered framework to understand industrial relations developments. We agree that, taken alone, changes in any single feature within one of the tiers (for example, concession bargaining, growth of worker participation, or the shift in power within management from industrial relations staff to line managers) would not constitute a transformation. Instead, we claim that industrial relations in the 1980s involved a shift in the locus of activity to the strategic and workplace levels of the system and away from the traditional collective bargaining level. In our view it is the *systematic* nature of the changes occurring in the American industrial relations system that distinguish recent events as a transformation. We see changes occurring at all three levels of the industrial relations system. In particular, the shift in activity so heavily to the strategic and workplace levels and the movement away from the traditional "New Deal" system in the activity that remained at the collective bargaining level led us to use the label of transformation.

Another way to address the issue of defining what is and is not a transformation is to analyze a question asked by Jim Chelius during the conference. Chelius asked us to specify what kinds of evidence would refute our theory. We can think of three.

Our book argues that the traditional New Deal industrial relations system is ill equipped to respond to the competitive challenges confronting the American economy and the strategic initiatives of employers. We then go on to recommend various changes in public policy that could help to reorient industrial relations practices to bring them in better alignment with economic challenges. Contradicting evidence would show that the New Deal bargaining system returned *without major* changes in either public policy or union strategies *and* the operation of this traditional system was producing economic outcomes that met competitive pressures. We might add that since publication of the book we have not seen widespread evidence of a return to traditional collective bargaining practices, an issue we return to in more depth later in this paper.

Our claims also would be contradicted if in the future there was a steady growth in union membership that had not been prodded by major alterations in public policies and union organizing and representational strategies. Such a recovery in union strength would call into question our assertions regarding how deeply the sophisticated nonunion and other employer strategies have undermined the appeal of the traditional bargaining and representational policies used in the New Deal system.

Our book includes a number of what could be called smaller hypotheses and predictions. Contrary developments in this third set of hypotheses would also raise doubts about the accuracy of our theoretical approach.

One of these "smaller" hypotheses derives from the material presented in Chapters 6 and 7 in the *Transformation* where we claim that a narrow form of quality of work life (QWL) program could not produce sustainable improvements in economic performance. Our views were based in part on a number of cases where successful QWL programs broadened to include more substantial alterations in work and industrial relations practices. If subsequent research were to document cases of narrow QWL, such as programs amounting to only quality circles, that had sustained positive impact on firm economic performance then our analysis would be in doubt.

One of the important hypotheses implied by the occurrence of concessions is the extent to which recent wage determination has produced outcomes that differ from past wage behavior. One way to test this is to model the wage setting process and see if equations that predict wage determination in earlier periods in the U.S. can accurately predict wage outcomes in the 1980s. In Chapter 5 we report some of our own findings on this matter. The analysis we conducted with Wayne Vrooman (and research by Daniel Mitchell, 1985) suggests that simple wage models including independent variables such as the inflation and unemployment rate can well predict wages in the 1960s and 1970s but these models substantially overpredict wage levels in the 1980s. Much more research needs to be done on this question, research that will require analysis of wage data for a number of years (in the late 1980s and beyond.). If later research were to show a return to wage equations similar in form to those for the '60s and '70s, this would shed doubt on our claims regarding the structural nature of changes underway at the collective bargaining level in the U.S.

Our field research identified a number of unionized workplaces that have been experimenting with what we refer to as a new industrial relations system. The new system involves: team systems of work organization, contingent compensation, employment security, and enhanced worker and union participation in business and strategic decision making. Our research suggests that this new system has generated favorable economic performance relative to nonunion alternatives in some cases. We were not (and still are not) convinced that this new industrial relations system will spread naturally across the economy. Our final chapter discussed the many public, union, and management policies needed to encourage such a development. Yet, if subsequent research were to show that this new industrial relations system was neither sustainable nor productive then we would have to rethink our claims.

Strategic Choice versus Environmental Determinism

Some of our critics claim that we rely on the poorly defined notion of strategic choice to explain events that were in fact determined by environmental factors. Lewin (1987) makes this point in a paper in a recent IRRA research volume and this line of criticism was offered in the Block and Roomkin-Juris papers and repeated frequently at the conference. We do believe that choices made by management, labor and the government have strongly influenced post-World War II developments in the American industrial relations system and will continue to do so in the future. In the *Transformation* we use Peter Cappelli's research in the airlines industry to illustrate how corporate business strategies can shape industrial relations strategies. We also describe how the business strategies of the Schneider Trucking Company influenced industrial relations developments.

More recent events in industrial relations continue to show the important choices confronting the parties and the role played by business and industrial relations strategic decisions. For example. contrary to the arguments of Roomkin-Juris, we believe that bargaining across the steel companies in 1986 and 1987 (in the aftermath of the abandonment of a master steel agreement) provides a rich illustration of diverse strategies and choices on the part of labor and management.[1]

Our critics claim that we have not outlined fully how business strategy matters of the various strategic options available to each party. They also find our evidence regarding the independent impacts of strategy to be weak. We agree with this part of the criticism and believe there is much room for further research on these matters. Our critics also claim that environmental factors were a causal influence upon many of the developments we discuss. Again, we agree. When we say that strategies matter we do not mean that environmental factors thereby play no or only an insignificant role. But it is one thing to ask for a clearer or more complete account of how strategic choice matters and another to claim that a *deterministic* model can explain outcomes.

Take the dispute concerning the role of labor law. Block argues that economic pressures and the nature and implementation of American labor law contributed to the weakening of union bargaining power. We certainly agree. Our differences here concern whether the law or other environmental factors fully determined the course of events. We claim that there is an important explanatory role played by strategic actions and choices. In particular, we claim that managements' initiative in developing a sophisticated nonunion personnel system and in using a variety of investment and locational decisions reveal the discretion that remains even in the face of environmental factors. Indeed, it is often the case that the business decisions that are taken because of competitive pressures, for example, opening a new plant or introducing advanced technology, provide management with the opportunity to pursue new industrial relations and human resource strategies.

We agree with Begin's (1990, chapter 3) point that there are many similarities between our account and contingency theory. Yet, we believe that contingency theory (like some economic models) is too deterministic. A strict application of contingency theory leaves too little room for the historical and institutional factors and the strategic choices that have shaped American industrial relations.

While there is some semantic confusion in this debate and there is certainly room to argue about the relative causal contributions of various factors, there also is an extremely important issue at stake. We see our views regarding the role of choice as an extension of the position held by earlier institutional economists. Our position is closely related to that espoused by Ross (1948) in his debate with Dunlop (1944) and the position taken by Lester (1946) in his debate with Machlup (1946). As a result, we are rather surprised by the criticisms from our industrial relations colleagues who seem to be taking a position more frequently espoused by neo-classical economists. We believe there is much room to refine notions concerning where and how business and labor strategies matter, but we think it would be a gross error for researchers to claim that a deterministic model can be constructed that eliminates an important role for strategies and choice.

In his paper Block is as concerned with the normative consequences of the decline in union power as he is with identifying the causes of that decline. In his passionate statement as part of the final panel of the conference, John Delaney joined Block by arguing that it was time for IR researchers to abandon their purely academic focus and present a more forceful defense of the positive roles played by unions in democratic society. We also worry that the decline in union membership may be bringing the country to the point at which unions no longer are an effective interest group in American society. We do worry about the loss in diversity this would imply for American politics and we wonder whether the further weakening of unions will lead employers away from progressive personnel policies. At the same time we do not regret our choice of a "positive" (analytical) approach to issues in our effort to understand events and the implication of various alternative policy choices. We prefer to separate the presentation of our research findings from the expression of our normative beliefs.[2] We do have views regarding the normative issues involved and the policy implications that derive from those views, but we prefer to express those views through other forums.[3]

The discussion of strategic choice at the conference raised the question of whether unions really have (or ever had) a strategy. Someone phrased the issue nicely by asking if the union strategy box in our three tiered framework was an empty cell. We do not think so. We focus in the book on managerial strategies because is was management that exercised the initiative throughout the 1970s and 1980s. We argue that these managerial initiatives set the stage for the dramatic changes in collective bargaining that followed in the 1980s. But unions had strategies in the past and have them now. As we mention in the book, we believe that one of the reasons why business unionism and the New Deal system came to dominate the American collective bargaining scene was because most unions and workers preferred those systems.

Another illustration of union strategy is provided in the active debates unions have been engaged in recently concerning corporate reorganizations and the actions that at times have followed those debates. We discuss some of those initiatives below. For now our point is that unions strategies exist although they often have been overshadowed by management's actions.

The Nature, Sustainability, and Fairness of Nonunion Industrial Relations Systems

In the conference we debated whether in the *Transformation* we exaggerated the extent to which a set of sophisticated human resource management (HRM) personnel policies have spread in the U.S. Some did not quarrel with our assessment of the use of those policies but rather argued that we were too complimentary regarding the policies. We stand by our claim that the sophisticated HRM personnel policies represent a very different industrial relations system as compared to traditional "paternalistic" or "bureaucratic" nonunion systems.[4] In fact, it is the nature and appeal of these HRM policies that has created so much of the organizing difficulties confronted by unions. Further evidence on this score has been provided by the fact that unions have had only modest success in recent organizing campaigns even when those campaigns have followed layoffs or plant closing. We interpret these difficulties as testament to our claim that unions will have to make substantial changes in their organizing and representational strategies in order to organize the sophisticated HRM employer.

We see the emergence of this alternative nonunion system as one of the key developments contributing to the transformative nature of recent American industrial relations. At the same time, we agree that a full account of the evolution of the various nonunion personnel policies and an accurate assessment of their implications is one of the major research agendas in the field of industrial relations. Important new work has been completed on these issues by Osterman (1988) and Jacoby (1988), but much more research is needed. We agree fully with Strauss (1990, chap. 4) that it would be an enormous mistake on the part of industrial relations scholars to cede consideration of nonunion systems to those in other research disciplines.

International Applicability

We are particularly encouraged by questions raised at this conference regarding the international applicability of *Transformation*. We have a number of thoughts concerning potential future research in this area and along with the nonunion sector view international industrial relations issues as the major underresearched topic of the day. International comparisons provide an opportunity to test the roles played by institutions and strategy by looking across countries (or industries) facing similar economic pressures. Recent commonalities in economic pressures across countries have made such tests potentially fruitful.

Will the three tiered framework offered in our book and our other hypotheses be useful in explaining international developments? Our preliminary analysis of events in Europe suggests that the framework does hold, yet clearly this is a question that requires much more detailed comparative research. We expect that such analysis might well require the sort of amendments to our framework suggested by Rojot (1990, chap. 7) in his conference paper. For example, we agree with Rojot that when applied to the analysis of European developments the three tiered framework would have to be modified to account for the greater reliance on national and multi-industry bargaining and more extensive governmental regulation of *substantive* employment conditions.

Peterson (1990, chap. 6) reminds us how much stronger unions are in Sweden and lauds the virtues of that country's industrial relations system. We certainly agree that the stronger presence of unions in Sweden when compared to the U.S. has altered the course of Swedish industrial relations. At the same time, we are not as convinced that the changes we describe in American industrial relations are as foreign to Swedish experience as Peterson appears to be claiming. Our reading of the evidence suggests, for example, that a shift in industrial relations activity to the strategic and workplace levels is occurring in Sweden and in a manner not very different from events in the U.S. In particular, on the shop floor in Sweden, it appears that unions are struggling to find their place in the midst of experiments to institute team systems of work and new channels of communication and participation in a manner remarkably similar to American unions.

In many ways we are struck by the extent to which European industrial relations is being transformed along similar lines to changes underway in the U.S., even though most European unions entered the 1980s with a larger fraction of the workforce organized and with greater substantive involvement by the government in the determination of employment conditions. As we now set out to pursue comparative research we are searching for the source of that similarity as well as for the influences national institutions exert as sources of diversity.

Updating the Story

Most of the writing of the *Transformation* was completed by the spring of 1986 and much has happened in American industrial relations since then. Have subsequent events contradicted the predictions presented in the book or suggested weaknesses in our arguments?

We remain convinced of the usefulness of the framework presented in the book and would argue that recent events provide further substantiation to our claims. We find continuing evidence that the locus of activity in American industrial relations has shifted to the strategic and workplace levels. For example, in the airline industry at a number of carriers including Eastern (now Texas Air), Pan Am and United, unions are trying to affect corporate financial affairs by searching for "white knights" to finance restructuring. Financial machinations on Wall Street represent a glamorous and well publicized forum for union strategic involvement, but our discussions with various unions and firms lead us to believe that many other unions are now continuously confronted by and involved in similar strategic issues in less obvious ways. The extensive corporate re-structuring and attendant changes in production sourcing have forced unions to be concerned with strategic issues.

Block suggests that recent events show a return to more conven-tional collective bargaining and suggests that similarities in the 1987 agreements at Ford, General Motors and Chrysler typify the return to pattern bargaining and more generally, to traditional collective bargaining. We disagree. The company agreements among the Big Three and the UAW in 1987 did include a similar wage settlement and in some other ways exhibit greater pattern following as com-pared to auto bargaining in the early and mid 1980s. Yet we believe collective bargaining in the auto industry continued (and continues) to manifest the breakdown of the New Deal collective bargaining system as described in chapters 5, 6 and 7 of the *Transformation.* Note, for example, although the wage settlement was similar across the Big Three, auto worker earnings varied substantially as a product of the diverse payouts in the profit sharing plans of the three companies. More generally, auto bargaining revealed a continuing emphasis on strategic and workplace issues. On the shop floor there is extensive experimentation with a new industrial relations system that includes the features we described. This restructuring is accom-panied by enormous debate between and within the ranks of labor and management due in part to the depth of the changes underway and the parties' doubts regarding where they fit in any new system. Our work as instructors in a training program at General Motors where these events and debates are openly discussed convinces us that there is little sign of a return to traditional collective bargaining in the auto industry. Our knowledge of events in other industries suggests the same conclusion.

The terms and scope of the debate underway within unions is interesting in its own right and provides further evidence that the union strategic cell in our three tier framework is not an empty one. Unions are struggling to define whether and how they should fit in the new system of industrial relations and on what terms they should accept participation in such a system. The debates in the auto industry mentioned above are but one illustration of these discussions.

There are also interesting and important debates underway within the ranks of national trade union leadership. National unions, just as their local unions, are reassessing their representation and organiz-ing strategies given the managerial initiatives that prevail. In particu-lar, national unions appear to be searching for a way to encourage an institutionalized forum for their involvement in and regulation of work teams and participatory processes. Some of the recent discus-sion seems to be asking whether there is an American form of works councils and codetermination that might be feasible and attractive. We have participated in some of these discussions and it is clear that the issues are complex and there are no easy solutions to recommend. It is especially difficult to think of codetermination possibilities that should be recommended given the legitimate doubts union leaders have regarding management's willingness to share information and authority.

National union leaders also appear to be reassessing the political agenda of unions given the changes underway in collective bargaining and the world economy. Traditional policy approaches, while still appealing to some, do not appear to confront economic changes and are not attractive to the increasingly diverse American workforce.

Unions are searching for a way to link their appeal to the many unsettled employee "rights" issues that derive from the diverse interests of the workforce. While unions have seen little recent organizing success, even in the face of the dislocations confronted by the workforce, it does appear that employees are not satisfied with the status quo, either by the protections currently provided by public policy or the assurances offered by employers. We and many others have been struck by the fact that 80 percent of the population expressed support for federal legislation requiring prenotification in advance of plant closings and major layoffs (Yang, 1988). The workforce also appears to have unsatisfied demands concerning issues such as pay equity, career development, day care and maternity leave. We believe there could be a role for unions as the organizer and voice of these various rights issues. The challenge for unions is to reassert their place in these rights appeals and link the rights issues to the still important pay and employment security concerns felt by the workforce.

The vacillation and debate that appears within the ranks of trade unions is paralleled by the variety of strategic responses in managements' ranks to economic pressures. The employers' dilemma is much as we described it in the book. American management continues to be torn between, on the one hand, business strategies that compete on the basis of low costs and the minimization of labor input, and on the other hand, product and technological strategies focused around innovative capabilities, high skill content, and a commitment to human resource development. In the last three years we have seen some firms pursue the first option through aggressive downsizing and increased outsourcing with little concern for the effects these actions have on employee motivation. Meanwhile, other firms have reorganized to confront competitive pressures but have done so while addressing employee career development and redeployment.

One criticism others have made of our work that did not surface at the conference is that our book has little to say about the role of the "state" (public policy) in realizing a transformation to a new industrial relations system. This is a fair criticism. One reason we gave so little emphasis to the role of the government was that we interpreted events of the early 1980s as very much of a "pre-public policy" period of experimentation of the part of labor and management without an active government role.

Much of our research since the publication of the book has focused more directly on the role of government policy in diffusing and institutionalizing innovations in industrial relations. This work has convinced us that broad diffusion and institutionalization of a new industrial relations system will indeed require an active government policy—one that endorses the new model and treats it as a necessary micro-foundation for macro economic and social policies.

A debate over the relevance of industrial relations practice is now beginning to be joined. The anticipation of a new administration in Washington in 1989 has spurred discussion of the relationship between labor and human resource policies and macro economic and social policies designed to revitalize the economy. Our position in these debates is that the transformed industrial relations system we described in the book provides a more suitable micro foundation for the economy and workforce of the future than either the traditional New Deal system or the cautious experimentation with a new system now underway.

The decision by some future political administration to adopt an activist labor policy supporting the diffusion of a new model of industrial relations, however, would constitute a strategic choice as important as any of the transformative events discussed in our book. There is no guarantee that such a choice will be made and current trends make if difficult to predict future government policies. Perhaps this further validates the importance of including room for such strategic choices in models of industrial relations.

While the union, employer, and government strategies that will shape the future are not yet clear, it is clear that actions both above and below the traditional level of collective bargaining continue to reshape American industrial relations. We look forward to further debates concerning these developments.

Notes

1. See Kochan and Katz (1988, p. 386-387) for discussion of developments among the integrated steel producers and Arthur (1987) for a description of the varied IR strategies among minimills.
2. We might add that we have been criticized elsewhere for having a pro-union bias in the book.
3. Although it was not a relevant constraint we are not so sure that the three of us have the same normative views and prescriptions.
4. See Kochan and Katz (1988, p. 373-376) for a more complete discussion of the various patterns of industrial relations policies.

References

Arthur, J. (1987). *Industrial Relations Practices in Steel Minimills in the United States.* Unpublished M.S. thesis. Ithaca, NY: Cornell University.

Begin, J. (1990). An organizational systems approach to the transformation of industrial relations. *In* J. Chelius & J. Dworkin (eds.), *Reflections on the Transformation of Industrial Relations.* Metuchen, NJ: IMLR Press.

Block, R.N. (1990). American industrial relations in the 1980's: Transformation or evolution? *In* J. Chelius & J. Dworkin (eds.). *Reflections on the Transformation of Industrial Relations.* Metuchen, NJ: IMLR Press.

Dunlop, J.T. (1944). *Wage Determination Under Trade Unions.* New York: Macmillan.

Jacoby, S.M. (1988, April). *Reckoning with Company Unions: The Case of Thompson Products, 1934-1964.* Paper presented to the conference on: Historical Perspectives on American Labor: An Interdisciplinary Approach. NYSSILR, Cornell University.

Kochan, T.A., & Katz, H.C. (1988). *Collective Bargaining and Industrial Relations.* 2nd ed. Homewood, IL: Irwin.

Kochan, T.A.; Katz, H.C.; & McKersie, R.B. (1986). *The Transformation of American Industrial Relations.* New York: Basic Books.

Lester, A. (1946, March). Shortcomings of marginal analysis for wage-employment problems. *American Economic Review, 36,* 63-82.

Lewin, D. (1987). Industrial relations as a strategic variable. *In* M.M. Kleiner, R.N. Block, M. Roomkin, & S.W. Salsburg (eds.), *Human Resources and the Performance of the Firm.* Madison, WI: Industrial Relations Research Association.

Machlup, R. (1946, September). Marginal analysis and economic research. *American Economic Review, 36,* 519-554.

Mitchell, J.B. (1985). Shifting norms in wage determination. *Brookings Papers on Economic Activity, 2,* 575-609.

Osterman, P. (1988). *Employment Policy and Internal Labor Markets.* Oxford: Oxford University Press.

Peterson, R.B. (1990). Thoughts on the transformation of industrial relations. *In* J. Chelius & J. Dworkin (eds.), *Reflections on the Transformation of Industrial Relations.* Metuchen, NJ: IMLR Press.

Rojot, J. (1990). A view from abroad. *In* J. Chelius & J. Dworkin (eds.), *Reflections on the Transformation of Industrial Relations.* Metuchen, NJ: IMLR Press.

Roomkin, M. & Juris, H. (1990). Strategy and industrial relations: An examination of the American steel industry. *In* J. Chelius & J. Dworkin (eds.), *Reflections on the Transformation of Industrial Relations.* Metuchen, NJ: IMLR Press.

Ross, A.M. (1948). *Trade Union Wage Policy.* Berkeley: University of California Press.

Strauss, G. (1990). Toward the study of human resources policy. *In* J. Chelius & J. Dworkin (eds.), *Reflections on the Transformation of Industrial Relations.* Metuchen, NJ: IMLR Press.

Yang, J.E. (1988, July 7). Bill on plant closings and layoffs clears senate in new effort on trade matters. *Wall Street Journal,* p. 50.

9. ANALYZING THE TRANSFORMATION: A RESEARCH PERSPECTIVE

David Lewin

To PROVIDE AN OVERVIEW let alone an integration of a set of papers that are themselves devoted to an overview and perhaps an integration of the thesis that U.S. industrial relations (IR) have recently been transformed is, to say the least, a formidable task. Indeed, it is probably an impossible task and, even if it were to be accomplished, would probably not be very satisfactory for the reader. Instead and in an attempt at parsimony, this paper will identify and elaborate certain research themes which emerged from the Purdue conference on which this volume is based and which are germane to assessing available evidence about the IR transformation thesis.

One way of testing the transformation thesis is to analyze the IR policies and practices of firms within a particular industry and to attempt, ex-post facto, to understand the differences in these policies and practices among firms. In this type of research, the (industry) environment is, in effect, held constant, and analysis of the variation in firms' IR policies and practices may help to shed light on the nature of their anticipation of responses to this environment.

This is apparently what Myron Roomkin and Hervey Juris (R-J) (1990, chap. 5) seek to do as they focus on business strategy and IR policy and practice in the U.S. steel industry. One contribution of R-J's work is to identify three distinct environmental contexts or stages of the U.S. steel industry: a classic oligopoly in the pre-1970 period; a subsequent period of declining market demand and emergent overcapacity, roughly 1970-1985; and a post-1985 period of rising profits and undercapacity associated with "successful" import restrictions. If individual steel companies responded differently to one or another of these environmental phases, then evidence could be adduced in favor of a strategic IR thesis—and perhaps even of an IR transformation thesis.

The problem presented by this analysis, however, is that there is little evidence to demonstrate differential responses among U.S. steel producers in any stage of the industry's changing environment (though, as R-J note, "information of the specific ways in which firms are reacting to these realities is very hard to come by"). In an oligopolistic stage, perhaps differential firm responses should not be expected. But in more competitive stages, and whether the industry is in an expansion or a recession, such differential responses might well be expected. Yet, apart from identifying firm size as a determinant of differential responses to the changing economic environment of the steel industry (whereby smaller firms are more likely than larger firms to become mini-mills), R-J produce no evidence to show that there are other interfirm differences in responses to changing economic circumstances, let alone that there are different strategies of response. This is an especially important point given that the IR transformation thesis rests so heavily on the notion of business strategy as the guiding force behind IR policy and practice.[1]

Professor John Fossum (1990), in his comments on the R-J paper, in effect supports this point. He asks whether steel firms have had an industrial relations strategy or "only a response to a catastrophe?" In the absence of evidence to support the concept of a strategic response—and Fossum's comments show that no such evidence is produced by R-J—it is just as [or more] plausible to conclude that steel producers have by and large responded to catastrophe, not planned strategically or preparedly to deal with new economic conditions. Furthermore and expanding on Professor Fossum's comments, the fact that management is now the dominant "actor" in steel industry labor relations whereas the union was the dominant actor in earlier eras does not mean that the union (but not management) acted strategically then or that management (but not the union) is acting strategically today. To substantiate such a claim requires a more precise definition of strategy and more refined empirical evidence than is provided by R-J.

Joel Cutcher-Gershenfeld's (JCG) (1990) comments are broadranging and often provocative, but are more centrally directed toward the transformation thesis propounded by Thomas Kochan, Harry Katz, and Robert B. McKersie (KKM) (1986) than to the steel industry analysis provided by R-J. Nevertheless, JCG does point out that R-J equate a transformation of unionized industrial relations with "a greater degree of labor-management cooperation tied to an enhanced competitive posture for the firms," and he then proceeds to take issue with this position.

However, JCG's issue-taking consists of the proposition that unionized labor relations may take an adversarial form, a cooperative form, or a mixed motive form wherein the parties can pursue a combination of competing and common agendas. This is a sound proposition, but the larger point for industrial relations researchers is that R-J, KKM and others have not as yet provided systematic evidence about the determinants of these different patterns of unionized labor relations or about the effects of these different patterns on businesses' competitive position. This is probably too much to expect from one intraindustry study of the type conducted by R-J. In fact, an important research lesson to be drawn from R-J's paper and from the discussants' comments is that sets of intraindustry and interindustry studies are required in order to sort out better the IR responses of firms' to changing economic and other environmental forces.

Richard Block's paper (1990, chap. 2) is perhaps the clearest and most pointed of any in this volume. He states that "the industrial relations practices that have developed over the last ten years and that have been identified by KKM as a transformation in industrial relations are primarily a result of the evolution of the industrial relations system that was established in 1935 and the adaption of this system to a change from sheltered product markets to competitive product markets."

Now this point has been made (though perhaps less cogently) by others, including, for example, John Dunlop whose own theorizing about industrial relations has often been contrasted with that offered by KKM.[2] But what distinguishes Block's conclusion from those of others is his careful and thorough review of the evidence presented by KKM, and his demonstration that this evidence is not sufficient to support the transformation thesis.

Indeed, one can easily go further. The ostensible evidence of an IR transformation presented by KKM is also fully consistent with the rational expectations school of economics, and with the notion, embedded in microeconomic theory, that increasing product market competition is associated with reduced managerial discretion and control in directing the enterprise. This evidence is also consistent with the concept of appeasing behavior, rather than optimizing behavior, on the part of business managers. And, if managers appease, then perhaps their devotion to business strategy formulation and implementation is considerably less than KKM would have it. Furthermore, recent changes in financial, information and telecommunications markets clearly have increased the short-term financial performance orientation of business managers, and this is more consistent with short-term reactive managerial behavior than with long-term strategy formulation-implementation behavior. A financial economics perspective on the IR transformation thesis also emphasizes the need for large scale samples and data sets to test concepts of business strategy, as opposed to collections of case studies at the workplace, business unit, or corporation levels of enterprise.

Professor Block also observes that KKM advocate a broadened role for labor-management cooperation and employee participation in decision making as appropriate responses to increasing economic competition across industries. But Block also raises the key question of whether or not workers' jobs and economic interests should depend on managers' judgments—preferences for or against worker participation in decision making; and, Block says "no," they shouldn't. Instead, he says, labor unions should be institutionalized as an essential actor in a pluralistic industrial relations system. Critics of this position might contend that unions are already institutionalized on the U.S. scene, but Block really means more than this, to wit, "we must develop a legal system in which the union and the employer have equal status in addressing issues that are critical to both of them."

What happens, however, if through legal means employers are able to develop effective substitutes for unions or to prevail over unions in union representation elections? KKM identify such behavior as part of the IR strategy of certain (many?) businesses; and even if one does not embrace KKM's notion that such actions are strategically driven or that they constitute a transformation of U.S. industrial relations, the prevalence of such actions cannot be denied. Hence, Block's well-taken criticisms of the transformation thesis are nevertheless colored, and perhaps devalued, by his forthright normative position that unions must be strengthened by changes in public policy.

James Martin (1990) by and large agrees with Block's interpretation of developments in U.S. industrial relations—and, therefore, also differs in some respects with Professors Kochan, Katz, and McKersie. Put differently, Martin supports the notion of evolutionary rather than transformed industrial relations. However, he also believes that Block's analysis would be strengthened by devoting more attention to the nonunion sector, which as he observes "currently appears to be strongly affecting the nonunion sector." The importance of this observation may lie in its implicit questionings of KKM's assertion that a shift in managerial values has recently occurred such that opposition to labor unions has become more acceptable and more prevalent than before. Yet as KKM and Martin note, such opposition has long existed in the U.S. (and more strongly than elsewhere), but changing economic forces have made it easier for managers to act on this opposition in the contemporary period. If economic forces are a key determinant in this respect, then changes in such forces would seem to support Block—and Martin's—contention that U.S. industrial relations reflect an evolution for more than a transformation.

To test the changing values thesis, IR researchers might well conduct cross-sectional and longitudinal studies of the value orientations of U.S. managers and union officials. Moreover, such research could be guided by some of the recent scholarly work on constituency management, which suggest that unionized employees are but one among several constituencies that business managers must contend with—and perhaps "strategize" about.[3]

Professor Richard Peterson (1990, chap. 6) covers a good deal of ground in his paper, and goes well beyond a critique of the IR transformation thesis. Like Block, he is especially concerned about the declining viability of labor unions in the U.S., but unlike Block he offers several specific proposals for strengthening organized labor; these will be further discussed below.

What is perhaps most interesting about Peterson's proposals are that they derive largely from an analysis of the Swedish system of industrial relations. That analysis shows that Swedish workers are substantially organized, with an overall unionization note of about 80 percent; employers and unions are well represented in and closely involved with government officials; the Swedish government is concerned with being competitive in world markets so that it does not disregard employers' interests in favor of unionists' interests; Sweden does not have an NLRB-type regulatory agency, apparently because Swedish employers voluntarily recognize labor unions if their employees demonstrate an interest in union representation; private and most public sector unions have the right to strike and employers have strong lockout rights, but these rights are rarely invoked; the Swedish economy has a generally strong record during the 20th century; Sweden maintains a Labor Court to resolve serious labor issues, but it is only infrequently used and litigation is sparse relative to that in the U.S.; and, finally, Swedish employees appear to regard their unions largely as a mechanism by which to be heard—to exercise voice—rather than to bargain hard (and adversarily) over terms and conditions of employment.

Proceeding from this analysis of Swedish industrial relations, Peterson turns his attention to labor law reform in the U.S.—reform which he advocates "so that in the long run individual 'voice' in the employment relationship can find expression." The first such reform is to permit the NLRB to certify a union as the bargaining representative of employees where the majority of employees in the (ostensible) bargaining unit have (legally) signed authorization cards indicating that they wish to be represented by the union in question.

The second reform would come into play when a union was certified as the employees' bargaining representative under either the present election procedure or the aforementioned authorization card procedure. It would empower the NLRB to impose a first contract settlement in cases where the parties had negotiated unsuccessfully for a minimum of six months following certification of the union. Peterson notes that this second reform (indeed, both reforms) would parallel Canada's regulation of private sector labor relations, but he does not actually analyze or provide data about the Canadian experience in this regard.

Peterson says that these labor law reforms flow directly from the assessment of U.S. industrial relations contained in KKM's work; however, there is reason to question this point. Consider that KKM also examine certain human resource management policies and practices of U.S. businesses, and much of that examination strongly suggests that these policies and practices are motivated by employers' desire to avoid or rid themselves of labor unions. And, though there is evidence showing that some human resource policies and practices of U.S. firms do not enhance and may even reduce individual employee voice in the employment relationship,[4] there is other evidence that employees themselves favor such policies and practices, that is, that they favor individual voice over unionization or collective voice.[5] Further, under the form of representative government which prevails in the U.S., employers, like other interest groups, are free to "organize" for the purpose of opposing labor law reform or other measure which they believe will enhance union power—and they have done so! Peterson does not examine whether a shift in relative interest group power has occurred such that the probability of his proposed reforms being enacted is any greater today than it was in the late 1970s when several (more sweeping) labor law reform measures proposed to the U.S. Congress were rejected.[6]

Indeed, in his comments on the Peterson paper, William Bigoness (1990) expresses surprise at the modesty of the labor law reforms proposed by Professor Peterson. Bigoness observes that if the case for reform is as strong as Peterson (and presumably KKM) make it out to be, then broader and more fundamental reforms appear to be required. In fact, says Bigoness, U.S. employers never really embraced the principles embodied in the Wagner Act, the most fundamental of which was the institutionalized acceptance of unionism.[7] Peterson, in contrast, believes that employers did adopt these principles, and it is this view which may help to explain the "modest" reforms of U.S. labor laws which he advocates.

Professor Bigoness also disagrees with the Peterson analysis in two other respects. First, he says, Sweden may not be an especially propitious choice for making labor relations comparisons with the U.S. because Sweden is a small, homogeneous nation with a very high unionization rate and a much different cultural, political, and economic history from that of the U.S. Second, and perhaps more important, Peterson's notion that U.S. employers' commitment to "progressive" human resource management policies and practices is minimal does not square with a variety of evidence and observations, according to Bigoness. In addition, he says, Peterson seems to view employer and employee interests as being mutually exclusive, whereas Bigoness contends that a game theoretic—mixed motive view of these interests "appears to be a more accurate one."

From a research perspective, Bigoness' mixed motive perspective of the employment relationship could well be tested empirically by, for example, assessing the extent of dual loyalty—loyalty to the employer and loyalty to the union—among samples of unionized workers, and by comparing organizational loyalty measures across samples of unionized and nonunion workers.[8]

As to the human resource management policies and practices of U.S. employers, "progressive" or otherwise, these could well be examined in terms of their contribution (or lack of it) to the economic performance of U.S. businesses. The relevant research question in this regard is "do certain human resource management policies and practices truly provide U.S. businesses with a competitive edge?" Fortunately, some large scale work on this question is now underway, and offers the potential for providing the first systematic evidence about an issue which has heretofore been examined largely on a case study or anecdotal basis.[9]

Finally, Professor Bigoness' comments on the Peterson paper, and, of course, the Peterson paper itself, underscore the importance for industrial relations scholars of venturing onto the international scene to conduct relevant comparative research. By relevant is meant research which clearly identifies an issue, problem, or set of them—for example, labor-management cooperation, workplace due process, employee training and development, group incentives and employee profit-sharing schemes, bargaining structure—and which uses data from several country samples to identify the determinants and consequences of the industrial relation/human resource management policies and practices that are used to address the particular issue or problem being investigated. What is probably not appropriate here is another piece of research that compares two or three countries in terms of their overall industrial relations systems.[10] This type of study lacks the parsimony which both Peterson and Bigoness imply is required if comparative IR/HR studies are to contribute meaningfully to the field.

Jacques Rojot (1990, chap. 7) takes a small step in this direction by addressing in his paper the question of how well KKM's model for the analysis of U.S. industrial relations fits European industrial relations. Of course there is no one type of industrial relations in Europe because there are many countries in the region and because the particular economic, political, and cultural characteristics of each country affect and shape its industrial relations. Rojot in effect recognizes this even though he draws largely on the French experience to "test" the applicability of the KKM model beyond U.S. borders.

Professor Rojot provides some useful counterweights to KKM's notion of three-tiered industrial relations in the firm. For example, Rojot notes that the concept of an industrial relations decision flow form the corporate (top) level through the industrial relations policy (middle) level to the workplace (bottom) level is a relatively more complex, interactive process in European enterprises. To illustrate, in addition to a top-down strategy—policy influence on workplace industrial relations, there is often a reverse flow that is initiated by innovative practices on the shop floor. Sometimes these innovations permeate or are diffused to the external environment and may eventually be enacted into law. This occurred in the case of the fourth and fifth week of annual vacation in France, and in the case of provisions for assembly line delegates in Italy.

Rojot also proposes that KKM's model be expanded to incorporate a fourth level, namely, national intraindustry and interindustry associations of employers and unions. Such national associations are virtually unknown in the U.S., but are common in European nations. One reason for this, suggested by Rojot, is that in Europe product markets typically encompass several countries whereas the U.S. constitutes "a very large product market by itself." Another, related reason is that in Europe much more than in the U.S. the locus of decision making for economic and financial strategies is outside of the national borders of a particular country. Thus, employers band together on an intraindustry and even an interindustry basis to represent and protect their interests; correspondingly, union leaders do the same. These structures are often intimately involved with multinational corporations whereas such interactions are far less common in the U.S.—or at least it would seem so since this level of industrial relations activity is absent from KKM's model.

But perhaps the most important point made by Rojot is that the

major distinction between a union and a nonunion model of industrial relations is far less tenable for Europe than it (apparently) is for
the U.S. In European countries, for example, there are statutory
provisions governing national bargaining, work councils, employee
delegates, the resolution of bargaining disputes (via Labor Courts),
national health insurance, conditions of employee discharge, infor-
mation-sharing with employees, and many other "terms and conditions" of employment which, in the U.S., are the subjects of
collective bargaining (via explicit contracts) or of individual bargaining (via implicit contracts). Yet, in European countries, one does not
find U.S.-type requirements for exclusive union representation or
for the parties to bargain in good faith. In fact, in these countries
workers may individually belong or not belong to a union even when
a union is present (that is, there are no U.S.-type union "security
arrangements" in Europe), and several unions can co-exist at the
workplace (plant) level. Therefore, according to Rojot, the concept
of separate union and nonunion models of employee relations
breaks down when one focuses on the European scene.

Taken together, Rojot's observations imply some major limitations on KKM's model—that is, one may question whether theirs is
a truly generalizable model—yet Rojot also claims that this model
fits "perfectly adequately the European situation." Well, this just
can't be; either the model fits European industrial relations well or it
doesn't, but it can't do both! Nevertheless, recognition of this
contradiction is useful for identifying certain industrial relations
research issues.

First, because so much of Rojot's "evidence" is drawn from
France, the same problem of two country comparisons noted in
regard to the Peterson paper emerges here. Therefore, it is necessary to examine certain industrial relations policies and practices in
several European (and other) countries to learn whether Rojot's
criticisms of the KKM model can be generalized or whether that
model does provide a widely generalizable framework of analysis.
Second, it appears that unionization rates are declining throughout
Europe. Therefore, researchers would do well not only to examine
the reasons for this and to compare them with factors that have been
identified as contributing to the decline of U.S. unionism, but to go
further and assess whether the notion of separate unionized and
nonunion sectors is becoming more applicable to European industrial relations. If it is, then the model offered by KKM may indeed turn
out to fit the European scene "perfectly adequately." Third, and as
was true of the Sweden-U.S. comparisons made by Professor
Peterson, more systematic evidence than is provided by Professor
Rojot for France is required in order to validate empirically the

KKM model (or other models) outside of the U.S. context. This is true—or required—whether one is comparing France alone with the U.S. or several countries with the U.S. in terms of industrial relations policy and practice.

George Strauss (1990, chap. 4) attempts the most formidable task of any of the authors of papers included in this collection, namely, to reorient the study of industrial relations. In particular, Strauss argues forcefully that industrial relations as a field of study should strengthen its concern with macro-human resource management and management policy issues. Put differently, industrial relations scholars, says Strauss, must be prepared to consider "unionism without unions," and to "pay more attention to managers, professionals, and unorganized white-collar workers, particularly as the distinctions among occupations decline in a computer age." Ideally, observes Strauss, the "traditional" IR curriculum will become an IR-HR (or HR-IR) curriculum and will encompass the perspectives of organizational behavior, (the new) labor economics, and perhaps a bit of traditional "personnel."

Well, Professor Strauss has clearly thrown down the gauntlet, but the reader may well ask, What steering mechanism has he provided to guide students (and IR faculty) through the thicket of a revamped industrial relations field? Strauss provides two such mechanisms, though to be accurate he describes these not as integrating frameworks or models but as "a sampler of important macro-HRM issues that are of critical importance today for management and *should* receive the attention of IR academicians" (emphasis in original); these are "employment systems" and "justice systems."

Under employment systems, Strauss identifies four types: unstructured, craft or occupation, the traditional internal labor market, and high commitment HR policies. Strauss concentrates, indeed strongly advocates, the last of the systems, the characteristics of which (say Strauss) include broad job classifications, substantial opportunities for worker participation, lifetime or lifetime-like employment, and emphasis on skill and attitude training, and new forms of compensation, including profit-sharing and pay-for-knowledge.[11]

The concept of a justice system is more diffuse than that of an employment system, at least as presented by Professor Strauss, but seems to encompass job rights and privacy; fringe benefits, such as sick leave, pensions, and medical care; and procedural justice, which refers to one or another internal mechanism by which employees can exercise voice, and also to external dispute resolution mechanisms, such as arbitration and the courts. Strauss properly notes that all of these justice system issues have been widely debated in legislative forums (though rarely subjected to legislative action), and that they are rife with public policy implications. Put differently, these justice system issues do appear to be (in Strauss' terminology) macro-HRM issues.

The fundamental limitation of Strauss' two-pronged systems approach to HR/IR is that neither provides an integrating mechanism for study, practice, or research in this field—or at least they don't in Professor Strauss' formulation of them. This is because employment systems, especially high commitment work systems, and procedural justice systems are not really systems at all. Instead, they are collections of issues or problems which, while well worth studying and teaching, in no way provide an integrating framework for IR, HR, or IR/HR. However, one difference between the high commitment work system and the procedural justice system described by Strauss is that the former apparently stems from the analysis of nonunion employers' human resource policies and practices conducted by KKM. But even if KKM do provide the intellectual superstructure for high commitment-type work systems—and this also may be questioned—Strauss seems to go considerably further in strongly advocating such systems, both in practice and as the lynchpin for IR/HR studies. Implicit in this position, too, is an acceptance of the strategic choice foundation of the industrial relations transformation thesis forwarded by KKM—despite the fact that several of the authors represented in this volume have fundamentally questioned this strategic choice foundation of the perspective.

Jack Fiorito (1990) echoes these criticisms, noting, for example, that Professor Strauss' "employment systems and justice notions might be useful pedagogical devices, but they do not add up to an integrating framework." However, Professor Fiorito's main concern is not with Professor Strauss' search for an IR/HR integrating framework; rather, it is with KKM's transformation thesis and with these authors' apparent rejection of the industrial relations systems framework associated with the work of John Dunlop (1958). Thus, says Fiorito, "in their haste to identify some of the dramatic changes in IR of recent years, KKM and associates have at times confused IR changes with the question of the IR systems framework's continued relevance."

Professor Fiorito is careful to point out that Dunlop's industrial relations systems framework has often been oversimplified ("bastardized," says Fiorito) so as to limit it to three actors, namely, management, unions, and government, who interact to "produce" a web of rules.[12] The real IR system, notes Fiorito, is considerably broader than this and, among other things, can be interpreted to include a fourth actor, that is, employees; to not require formal organizations to represent employees; and to imply an active, not passive, role for management. Further, says Fiorito, this systems view is "hardly deterministic," as some scholars have claimed. Consequently, Fiorito concludes that while neither Professor Strauss nor KKM have offered a new integrating framework for the study of industrial relations, "the often maligned IR systems framework, properly specified, holds more promise in this regard." But if this is so, and Fiorito makes a strong case that is so, then one may question the "value added" by KKM in their strategic choice driven conception of an IR transformation model.

The research implications of the Strauss-Fiorito "debate" are several. First, scholars should define more precisely what they mean by high commitment work systems, and then test for the determinants and consequences of such systems. The same should be done for other "systems," if possible, such as the traditional internal labor market, craft or occupation, and unstructured types. If any of these employment systems cannot be more precisely defined or operationalized, they should be abandoned for analytical and pedagogical purposes.

Second, procedural justice systems should also be assessed on a comparative basis so that the field of industrial relations has something empirical to say about the relative consequences of unionized grievance procedures, nonunion grievance procedures, arbitration "settlements," ombudsman procedures, mediation, court decisions, etc.[13] Further, IR scholars appear to be well equipped to conduct the type of research which will help to determine which employment-related or procedural justice issues should be subjected to government policy, for example, fringe benefit retention and privacy rights, and which issues should be determined by private parties, individual or collective, for example, job security, job assignment, the effects of business restructuring, and third party dispute settlement procedures.

Third, there is no apparent reason why both research topics identified above cannot be studied on an international or comparative basis. Indeed, one of the lessons of the Peterson and Rojot papers (and of the respective discussants' comments) is that comparative IR research should be issue rather than country focused. High commitment and other type employment systems, on the one hand, and justice systems, on the other hand, are two specific topics that seem to lend themselves to focused theoretical and empirical research on a comparative multicountry basis. It is even possible that such research would help to stimulate the otherwise dormant supply of new comparative IR scholars—scholars for whom there is apparently an excess demand in the academic labor market.

James Begin's (1990, chap. 3) paper is itself and in part an attempt to integrate the various perspectives and critiques offered by the authors of other papers in this volume; consequently, it will receive relatively limited comment here. Professor Begin uses Henry Mintzberg's well-known work on business strategy and organizational behavior to develop a fourfold typology of employment relations systems (ERSs); these are simple ERS, machine ERS, professional ERS, and adhocratic ERS. These configurations, says Begin, are defined in terms of the environmental and organizational influences that drive the ERS authority distribution, which itself encompasses the sources of authority within an ERS, including the role of employees in decision making with or without unions.

Now the reader will recognize this as a contingency model of the type which is common to the organizational behavior area, but relatively rare in the industrial relations area. Nevertheless and somewhat surprisingly, Begin says that "the KKM model is basically a contingency model"; if this is so, then Dunlop's industrial relations systems model appears to be a contingency model, and so, too, do some of the models proffered by other industrial relations researchers.[14]

In light of this observation, one may ask "what is a contingency model and what are its limits?" This question is posed to underscore the point that if "everything" is contingent, no patterns of behavior will be evident; everything will be ad hoc and, thus, unexplainable from a theoretical perspective. Clearly this is not what Begin has in mind, and the notion of developing industrial relations contingency theory is at the least intriguing and at the most paradigm-inspiring. But, Begin also says that his model differs from those of all other researchers, including KKM, in that it "introduces organizational level variables [which] these authors tend to treat as black boxes."

This statement simply does not square with the detailed institutional modeling of Dunlop (1958) and, even more, Neil Chamberlain (1951); it also overlooks the explicit treatment of the black box issue contained in KKM. Therefore, it is difficult to accept the assertion that Begin alone among industrial relations researchers has paid attention to, if not fully opened, the black box of organizational behavior in relation to IR. What is perhaps more compelling is Professor Begin's observation that KKM have largely confined their transformation analysis to "old manufacturing companies"—companies whose transformation paths accord well with the predictions of organization theory. In other words, these companies' ERSs have come to look more like the adhocratic type and less like the machine type.

Thus, the key research question implied by Professor Begin's paper is something like the following: "What are the determinants of ERSs, and do different ERS patterns emerge in response to these determinants?" If this question can in fact be answered, then Begin's fourfold typology may become a centerpiece of modern industrial relations theory. If the question can't be answered, that is, if the null hypothesis cannot be rejected at acceptable confidence levels, then this organizational behavior-driven industrial relations typology will risk falling by the wayside. This is a large risk—but then Professor Begin has thrown down his own gauntlet and challenged the field of industrial relations to, in effect, prove him wrong. Such venturesomeness is rare in IR, and Professor Begin is to be commended for it.

Conclusion

It is not necessary to comment here about KKM's reaction to the debate about their work; these authors' "retrospective" stands on its own. What can be said by way of conclusion is that this volume and the Purdue conference on which it is based clearly show that intellectual ferment is the order of the day in industrial relations. This is a positive sign because it indicates that IR is alive and well, not a dormant field of study, and that (perhaps confirming Professor Strauss) the supply of industrial relations scholarship is not simply a function of the rate of employee unionization in the society. This is an important (and comforting) thought even if this volume and the Purdue conference on which it is based have not fully identified a superordinate model for the study, practice, and teaching of industrial relations/human resource management.

Notes

1. See Lewin (1987b) for elaboration of this point.
2. See Dunlop (1958) and Block, Kleiner, Roomkin and Salsburg (1987).
3. See Shriver and Kuhn (1989).
4. See Lewin (1987a) and Lewin and Peterson (1988).
5. See Kochan (1979).
6. See Weiler (1983).
7. For additional support of this view, see Jacoby (1985).
8. See Barling and Fullagar (1987) and Barling and Fullagar (forthcoming).
9. See Delaney, Lewin and Ichniowski (forthcoming) and Ichniowski, Delaney and Lewin (forthcoming).
10. However, it should be noted that some prior attempts at larger scale comparative IR research have had little or no impact on the field. See,

for example, Kerr, Dunlop, Harbison and Myers (1960) and Cochrane (1979).

11. Note that profit sharing and pay for knowledge appear to be contradictory in that one reflects the criterion of pay for output, the other the criterion of pay for input. Contradictions such as this call into question the analytical meaning of "high commitment work systems"—and perhaps also the fervor of those who advocate such systems.

12. Fiorito is also careful to note that KKM (1986) do not engage in such oversimplification—in fact, they also criticize this tendency among some scholars.

13. See, for example, Lewin and Peterson (1988), Lewin (1987a), Ichniowski and Lewin (1988), and Sheppard (1984).

14. For example, Chamberlain (1951).

References

Barling, J., & Fullagar, C. (1987). Toward a model of union commitment. *In* D. Lewin, B. Lipsky & D. Sockell (eds.), *Advances in Industrial and Labor Relations, 4.* Greenwich, CT: JAI Press.

Barling, J., & Fullagar, C. (in press). Dual and unilateral commitment: An examination of causes and consequences. *Proceedings of the Forty-First Annual Meeting of the Industrial Relations Research Association.* Madison, WI: Industrial Relations Research Association.

Begin, J. (1990). An organizational systems approach to the transformation of industrial relations. *In* J. Chelius & J. Dworkin (eds.), *Reflections on the Transformation of Industrial Relations.* Metuchen, NJ: IMLR Press.

Bigoness, W. (1990). Comments on Peterson. *In* J. Chelius & J. Dworkin (eds.), *Reflections on the Transformation of Industrial Relations.* Metuchen, NJ: IMLR Press.

Block, R.N. (1990). American industrial relations in the 1980's: Transformation or evolution? *In* J. Chelius & J. Dworkin (eds.), *Reflections on the Transformation of Industrial Relations.* Metuchen, NJ: IMLR Press.

Block, R.N.; Kleiner, M.M.; Roomkin, M.; & Salsburg, S.W. (1987). Industrial relations and the performance of the firm: An overview. *In* M. Kleiner, R.N. Block, M. Roomkin, & S. Salsburg (eds.), *Human Resources and the Performance of the Firm.* (pp. 319-343). Madison, WI: Industrial Relations Research Association.

Chamberlain, N.W. (1951). *Collective Bargaining.* 1st ed. New York: Mc-Graw-Hill.

Cochrane, J.L. (1979). *Industrialism and Industrial Man in Retrospect.* New York: Ford Foundation.

Cutcher-Gershenfeld, J. (1990). Reflections on strategy. *In* J. Chelius & J. Dworkin (eds.), *Reflections on the Transformation of Industrial Relations.* Metuchen, NJ: IMLR Press.

Delaney, J.T.; Lewin, D.; & Ichniowski, C. (in press). *Human Resource Policies and Practices in American Firms.* Washington, DC: U.S. Department of Labor, Labor-Management Services Administration.

Dunlop, J.T. (1958). *Industrial Relations Systems.* New York: Holt.

Fiorito, J. (1990). The wider bounds of IR systems. *In* J. Chelius & J. Dworkin (eds.), *Reflections on the Transformation of Industrial Relations.* Metuchen, NJ: IMLR Press.

Fossum, J.A. (1990). Comments on Roomkin and Juris. *In* J. Chelius & J. Dworkin (eds.), *Reflections on the Transformation of Industrial Relations.* Metuchen, NJ: IMLR Press.

Ichniowski, C.; Delaney, J.T.; & Lewin, D. (in press). The new human resource management in U.S. workplaces: Is it really new and is it only nonunion? *Relations Industrielles/Industrial Relations, 44*(1).

Ichniowski, C., & Lewin, D. (1988). Characteristics of grievance procedures: Evidence from nonunion, union and double-breasted businesses. *Proceedings of the 40th Annual Meeting, Industrial Relations Research Association.* (pp. 415-424). Madison, WI: Industrial Relations Research Association.

Jacoby, S.A. (1985). *Employing Bureaucracy: Management, Unions and the Transformation of Work in American Industry, 1910-1945.* New York: Columbia University Press.

Kerr, C.; Dunlop, J.T.; Harbison, F.; & Myers, C.A. (1960). *Industrialism and Industrial Man.* Cambridge, MA: Harvard University Press.

Kochan, T.A. (1979, April). How American workers view labor unions. *Monthly Labor Review, 102*(4), 23-31.

Kochan, T.A.; Katz, H.C.; & McKersie, R.B. (1986). *The Transformation of American Industrial Relations.* New York: Basic Books.

Lewin, D. (1987a). Dispute resolution in the nonunion firm: A theoretical and empirical analysis. *Journal of Conflict Resolution, 31,* 465-502.

Lewin, D. (1987b). Industrial relations as a strategic variable. *In* M.M. Kleiner, R.N. Block, M. Roomkin, & S.W. Salsburg (eds.), *Human Resources and the Performance of the Firm.* (pp. 1-41). Madison, WI: Industrial Relations Research Association.

Lewin, D., & Peterson, R.B. (1988). *The Modern Grievance Procedure in the United States.* New York: Quorum.

Martin, J. (1990). Comments on Block's analysis. *In* J. Chelius & J. Dworkin (eds.), *Reflections on the Transformation of Industrial Relations.* Metuchen, NJ: IMLR Press.

Peterson, R.B. (1990). Thoughts on the transformation of industrial relations. *In* J. Chelius & J. Dworkin (eds.), *Reflections on the Transformation of Industrial Relations.* Metuchen, NJ: IMLR Press.

Rojot, J. (1990). A view from abroad. *In* J. Chelius & J. Dworkin (eds.), *Reflections on the Transformation of Industrial Relations.* Metuchen, NJ: IMLR Press.

Roomkin, M., & Juris, H. (1990). Strategy and industrial relations: An examination of the American steel industry. *In* J. Chelius & J. Dworkin (eds.), *Reflections on the Transformation of Industrial Relations.* Metuchen, NJ: IMLR Press.

Sheppard, B. (1984). Third party conflict intervention: A procedural framework. *In* B.M. Staw & L.L. Cummings (eds.), *Research in Organizational Behavior, 6.* Greenwich, CT: JAI Press.

Shriver, D.W., & Kuhn, J.W. (1989). *Beyond Success: A Business Ethic for the 90s* (unpublished manuscript, Columbia University).

Strauss, G. (1990). Toward the study of human resources policy. *In* J. Chelius & J. Dworkin (eds.), *Reflections on the Transformation of Industrial Relations*. Metuchen, NJ: IMLR Press.

Weiler, P. (1983, June). Promises to keep: Securing workers' rights to selforganization under the NLRA. *Harvard Law Review, 96,* 1769-1827.

INDEX